FIRST FACTS
of
AMERICAN LABOR

FIRST FACTS
of
AMERICAN LABOR

A Comprehensive Collection of Labor Firsts
in the United States Arranged by Subject

Fully Indexed

Philip S. Foner

HM
HOLMES & MEIER
New York   London

First published in the United States of America 1984 by
Holmes & Meier Publishers, Inc.
30 Irving Place
New York, N.Y. 10003

Great Britain:
Holmes & Meier Publishers, Ltd.
131 Trafalgar Road
Greenwich, London SE10 9TX

Book design by Rose Jacobowitz

Library of Congress Cataloging in Publication Data
Main entry under title:

First facts of American labor.

  Includes index.
  1. Labor and laboring classes — United States — History
—Dictionaries.   I. Foner, Philip Sheldon, 1910–
HD8066.F55   1983   331'.0973   81-7074
                                                  AACR2

ISBN 0-8419-0742-0

Manufactured in the United States of America

To my brother Henry

Contents

Preface,   ix
First Facts of American Labor,   3
Index,   217

Preface

In February 1883, the Hartford *Post* featured a letter from Boston under the heading "The First Strike," in which the writer noted: "The first strike among our working people, I think, was at Dover, N.H., in 1827 or 1828." He went on to point out that it occurred at the mills of the Cocheco works when the "factory girls" walked out in protest against fines imposed because of lateness. "The mills were idle," he observed. "Every operative was out, leaving the overseers to run them alone. They met at some convenient square, and, forming a procession, with a band, and bearing the American flag, they paraded the town, under a leader whom I very well knew a year later, and a stalwart manly guard of one for their protection. The corporation came down at once, the offensive rules were withdrawn for the time, and everything went on harmoniously."

It is fortunate that the writer added "I think" to his characterization of this walkout as the "first strike," for it was not, although it may have been the first time that a male guard protected female strikers. Nevertheless, the story aroused a great deal of interest and was widely reprinted. *The New York Times* featured it in its February 6, 1883, issue.

The article is quoted here to illustrate how difficult it is to determine the "first" in any category of American labor. Labor events were poorly chronicled in so many cities and towns that it is impossible to date the formation of unions, the calling of strikes, and other labor activities in these communities, especially for periods from which few labor papers survived. Nevertheless, there is substantial evidence in multivolume labor histories, in histories of specific unions, in biographies and autobiographies of labor leaders, and in monographs on specific strikes and political movements by labor groups. The press of the large cities provided ample coverage of labor news and is an important source, along with the many labor papers that are available either in their original form or on microfilm. All in all, there is enough information to permit a collection of this nature to be compiled. Of course, further research into published and unpublished sources may disclose additional "firsts" or correct some that are included here. But then, apart from a thirty-page pamphlet (*Labor Firsts in America*), published by the U.S. Department of Labor, the present volume itself is a "first" of its type.

While the subject arrangement may appear, at first glance, to eliminate some "firsts," the comprehensive index I have prepared will enable the reader to locate them conveniently. In order to avoid repetition of "the first," I have at times merely listed the event.

In preparing this work, I have had the cooperation of the staffs of the State Historical Society of Wisconsin, the Labadie Library of the University of Michigan, the Tamiment Institute Library of New York University, the Library of Congress, the New York Public Library, and the libraries of Columbia University, Harvard University, and Lincoln University in Pennsylvania.

Philip S. Foner
Emeritus Professor of History
Lincoln University, Pennsylvania
Visiting Professor of Economics
Haverford College, Pennsylvania

FIRST FACTS
of
AMERICAN LABOR

Academy Award Winner

1976 — Barbara Kopple's *Harlan County, USA* was the first prounion film to win the Academy Award for best documentary. The film depicted the thirteen-month strike of the United Mine Workers at the Duke Power Company's Brookside Mine in Harlan, Kentucky, which ended in a union victory, and showed how indispensable the support and activities of the miners' wives and daughters were to that victory.

1980 — For the first time, an actress won the Academy Award for portraying a union organizer. Sally Field's role in *Norma Rae* was based on the experience of Crystal Lee Jordan, who in 1974 helped organize a union at the Roanoke Rapids, North Carolina, plant of J. P. Stevens, a leading textile manufacturer. After attending a union meeting in a black church where she was one of ten whites among seventy blacks, Crystal Lee Jordan was informed that she was dismissed and that the police were on the way. She returned to her work table, and in a scene made famous in the film *Norma Rae,* "pulled out a sheet of cardboard, and with her black marker lettered on it, 'UNION.' She climbed on her table and slowly began to turn, holding the sign high so the side hemmers, terry hemmers, terry cutters and packers could see what she had written. . . ." Later that night, she was taken to jail and booked on a disorderly conduct charge.

Accidents

January 10, 1860 — In the collapse of the Pemberton Mill in Lawrence, Massachusetts, 77 workers were killed and 134 injured, 14 of whom died afterward. This was the first major industrial accident in the United States.

1869 — The first major tragic mine explosion occurred at Avondale (Luzerne County), Pennsylvania, resulting in the deaths of 109 miners.

1886 — The first law requiring the reporting of industrial accidents was passed in Massachusetts.

1907 — The first public exhibit dedicated to industrial safety appeared at the American Museum of Safety, which had been established in New York City by the American Institute of Social Sciences.

December 1907 —The largest coal mine disaster in American history took place when 361 miners died in an explosion in the Monongah No. 6 and No. 8 mines of the Fairmount Coal Company in Monongah, West Virginia.

1907–1908 —The first survey of industrial accidents in the steel industry, the Pittsburgh Survey by Crystal Eastman, was conducted. It recorded the killing and maiming of hundreds of laborers on the job over a period of one year. Many of these accidents, she found, were not caused by worker negligence.

March 25, 1911 —The Triangle Waist Company fire, the first major accident in the women's garment industry, took place in a building at the corner of Washington Place and Greene Street in Manhattan, New York City. The fire caused the deaths of 145 women workers employed at a ladies' garment industry sweatshop typical of the period.

June 23, 1977 —The first woman shipbuilder was killed. Janet Sloan, a twenty-two-year-old welder, fell to her death in the hull of an uncompleted oil tanker at Sun Shipbuilding and Dry Dock Company in Chester, Pennsylvania. Three days previously, OSHA (Occupational Safety and Health Administration) had cited the company for numerous safety violations.

October 2, 1979 —Thirty-five-year-old Marilyn J. McCusker became the first woman to be killed while working in a U.S. mine. Mrs. McCusker was a general laborer assigned to work as a roof bolter at the Rushton Mining Company's deep mine near Osceola Mills, Pennsylvania. She was running a bolting machine when the roof caved in.

Actors

1951 —John Davis Lodge became the first actor to be elected governor of a state. Lodge, who had been a Hollywood screen actor, was elected governor of Connecticut and served from 1951 to 1955, after which he spent six years as ambassador to Spain.

November 1980 —The first actor to become president of the United States, Ronald Reagan, a former Hollywood actor and president of the Screen Actors Guild, was elected president on the Republican ticket, defeating Jimmy Carter, the Democratic incumbent.

May 1, 1981 —Aliens and residents began paying the same dues to Actors Equity—a minimum of $52 and a maximum of $2,052 a year. The action by the union equalizing dues followed a decision by the U.S. Court of Appeals in March 1981 confirming an order that Actors Equity discontinue its two-tiered policy requiring foreign actors to pay higher dues than American actors.

Advertising

June 2, 1786 — The first advertisement inserted by workers on strike appeared in the weekly *Pennsylvania Mercury and Universal Advertiser* of Philadelphia on June 2, 1786, followed by the signatures of twenty-six journeymen printers. The advertisement announced that "In consequence of an attempt having been made by some of our employers to reduce our wages to thirty-five shillings per week. RESOLVED, That we will not engage to work at any Printing-Office in this city or county, under the sum of Six Dollars per week. RESOLVED, That we will support such of our Brethen as shall be out of employment on account of their refusing to work for less than Six Dollars per week." This was not only the first authentic strike in the United States, but probably the first provision for strike benefits in America. It ended in victory for the workers.

May 1977 — For the first time, a union congratulated itself in a public advertisement on the nature of an agreement. The United Steel Workers of America spent more than $100,000 for full-page newspaper ads in about sixty-five steel-mill localities describing a new steel-labor contract as "unprecedented," "impressive," and "dramatic." According to the *Wall Street Journal* of May 17, 1977: "The union says the ads are an effort to improve communications with members."

Agricultural Workers

1903 — The first union of agricultural workers, the Sugar Beet and Farm Laborers' Union of Oxnard, California, was formed by Mexican and Japanese workers. The AFL (American Federation of Labor) refused to grant the union a charter because of its Japanese membership.

August 3, 1913 — The first great strike of agricultural workers took place at Durst Ranch in Wheatland, California. Led by the IWW, the workers presented ten demands to the ranch owners, among them: improved working conditions, including the furnishing of drinking water in the fields twice a day; improved sanitary conditions in the camps, especially separate toilets for men and women; a flat rate of $1.25 per hundred hops picked; and reinstatement of the "high pole men." The last demand sprang from Durst's elimination of the men who detached the hop vines from the highest wires for the women and children, making it easier for them to reach the high-growing hops. "Blackie" Ford and Herman D. Suhr, the strike leaders, were indicted on a murder charge, convicted, and sentenced to life imprisonment in Folsom Penitentiary.

August 1, 1914 — The first statewide strike to obtain release of labor prisoners, the Hop Pickers General Strike in California, was called by the Hop Pickers General Strike Committee of the IWW (Industrial Workers of the World), and endorsed by the AFL

Councils in California. Its object was to obtain the release of Ford and Suhr, who had been imprisoned after the Wheatland strike of the year before. Even though the strike was effective, California Governor Hiram Johnson refused to pardon Ford and Suhr, and the men remained in prison for several more years — Ford until September 11, 1925, and Suhr until October 26, 1926.

April 21, 1915 — The first convention of the famous IWW Agricultural Workers Organization 400 was organized at a conference of IWW locals near the grain belt in Kansas City. It demanded $3 a day for no more than ten hours' work for farm workers and it developed a complete "job delegate" system.

1927 — The first significant collective action of Mexican-American workers was inspired by several Mexican mutual-aid societies in Los Angeles.

March 23, 1928 — The Confederation of Mexican Labor Unions (Confederación de Uniones de Obreros Mexicanos) was officially organized and adopted a constitution.

April 1928 — The Imperial Valley Workers' Union (La Unión de Trabajadores del Valle Imperial) was formed by mutual-aid societies in El Centro and Brawley, California. In May 1928, the union issued a set of demands to the cantaloupe growers, including a raise in wages from 13½ cents to 15 cents per crate for cantaloupe picking, free picking sacks, ice for drinking water, lumber for sheds and outhouses, and employer responsibility for accident indemnity. A strike broke out, which was put down by arresting workers for vagrancy. However, the union won some concessions.

1930 — The Alabama Sharecroppers Union was organized in Tallapoosa, Alabama. It enlisted about five thousand members around a program calling for extensive federal relief for the unemployed, redistribution of land, and total racial equality. It was organized by the Communists and centered in Birmingham, Alabama.

August 4, 1933 — The first strike of California pear pickers took place in Santa Clara County. The strikers won a substantial wage increase.

September 7, 1933 — The first strike by cranberry pickers took place in the bogs of Cape Cod. The strikers formed the Cranberry Pickers Union, but their strike was unsuccessful.

October 1933 — The first strike against the cotton growers in California was led by the Cannery and Agricultural Workers Industrial Union (formerly the Agricultural Workers' Industrial League). The union demanded pay of $1 per hundredweight, abolition of labor contractors, and union hiring without discrimination. The strike involved up to eighteen thousand workers — Mexicans, blacks, and Anglos—and the picket lines stretched for 114 miles up and down the valley. On October 12, two strikers were killed and several wounded by gunfire from the ranchers. The strike ended with the union reluctantly accepting a fact-finding committee's recommendation of a 75-cents-per-hundredweight scale, compared with the 42 cents before the strike.

July 1934—The first local of the Southern Tenant Farmers' Union, an interracial organization of sharecroppers, was organized in Arkansas by members of the Socialist party.

1935—In their first strike, the Southern Tenant Farmers' Union demanded an increase in cotton-picking wages from the prevailing 30–35 cents to 65 cents per hundredweight. The strike was so comprehensive that an investigation by an Arkansas deputy labor commissioner found only five people working in three counties. The strike was settled with a compromise on the wage increases. The victory expanded STFU membership to thirty-five thousand, and locals were organized in neighboring states, especially Oklahoma.

July 1937—The first union to unite agricultural, cannery, and other related workers, the United Cannery, Agricultural, Packing, and Allied Workers, CIO (Congress of Industrial Organizations), was formed, with Donald Henderson as its president.

January 1939—The first sit-down strike by sharecroppers took place in Missouri. Hundreds of sharecroppers, mostly black, camped along the highways in what was known as the "Bootheel" area of Missouri—the seven counties in the southeastern part of the state. They struck for decent wages and working conditions for cotton sharecroppers, who were being displaced by their landlords without any consideration for their welfare. The strike was led by a black sharecropper and preacher, Reverend Owen H. Whitfield, who was the organizer and head of the Missouri Council of the United Cannery, Agricultural, Packing, and Allied Workers of America (UCAPAWA), CIO, with which the Southern Tenant Farmers' Union had briefly affiliated. By "sitting down" by the roadsides in the heart of winter, the men, women, and children finally brought their conditions and struggles to the attention of the nation.

September 30, 1962—The National Farm Workers Association was formed at a convention called by Cesar Chavez in an abandoned theater in Fresno, California. It adopted a plan for the organization of agricultural workers individually because it had no hope of negotiating contracts until it became strong enough to conduct a successful strike. The Spanish song that emerged from this meeting went, in part:

> In the year '62
> With effort and uncertainty
> There began a campaign
> For the campesino.

Cesar Chavez started it
He became a volunteer
And went forth as a pilgrim
To fulfill his destiny.

September 1965 —Members of the Agricultural Workers Organizing Committee, AFL-CIO, launched a strike in California's Coachella Valley to raise the wages of Chicano grape pickers from $1.20 to $1.40 an hour. As the strike spread, the National Farm Workers Association, led by Cesar Chavez, voted for the same demands, and both organizations joined forces in the first major struggle of "La Causa."

Easter Sunday 1966 —This date marked the end of the first mass parade of agricultural workers. After walking three hundred miles over twenty-five days, ten thousand workers and sympathizers gathered in front of the state capitol in Sacramento, California, to present their cause.

April 1966 —The National Farm Workers Association succeeded in negotiating its first contract. Schenley signed a contract recognizing the union, agreeing to the union hiring hall, and granting an immediate increase of 35 cents an hour and a checkoff for the Credit Union.

July 29, 1970 —The first collective union agreement in the history of American agriculture was signed by the United Farm Workers Organizing Committee, headed by Cesar Chavez, with the owners of twenty-six big

vineyards in Delano, California. The contract, which ended a five-year struggle, provided for wage increases and improved working conditions.

February 1972 —The United Farm Workers Organizing Committee was chartered by the AFL-CIO and became the United Farm Workers, a full-fledged union, headed by Cesar Chavez.

Airline Flight Attendants

December 1944 —Ada J. Brown, a stewardess employed by United Airlines, organized the first successful union for flight attendants at United Airlines.

1946 —For the first time a union of flight attendants was recognized in contracts signed by United Airlines.

Airline Pilots

January 1930 —The first charter to unionize aviators and airline pilots was issued by the AFL to an Aviators' and Pilots' Union in Muskogee, Oklahoma.

February 11, 1932 —The first strike in the history of American airline transportation began when pilots at Century Air Lines walked out after the company demanded that they sign a "yellow dog" contract and accept a drastic wage cut. The twenty-three pilots affected were members of the newly organized International Air Line Pilots' Association, which was affiliated with the AFL.

Air Traffic Controllers

August 1981 — In the first strike ever called by air traffic controllers, members of PATCO (Professional Air Traffic Controllers Organization) struck for higher wages, shorter hours, better retirement provisions, and relief from intolerable tension on the job. The response from the federal government, initiated by President Ronald Reagan, was a series of actions designed to destroy the union completely and irrevocably by removing its legal right to represent federal employees.

In a 1970 labor dispute, the controllers' union had staged a "sick-out," after which it was temporarily barred from bargaining on behalf of federal employees. William J. Usery, Jr., then assistant secretary of labor with authority over federal employees' unions, found that a permanent ban on the union would be an unwarranted deprivation of the controllers' right to representation by a union of their choice. No such principle influenced the conservative Reagan administration. Using the excuse that no one had the right to strike against the government, Reagan had 17,500 striking PATCO members fired and the union decertified, bringing about its destruction.

Amalgamations and Mergers

1876 — The first amalgamation of three separate craft organizations in the iron and steel industry was effected. The Amalgamated Association of Iron and Steel Workers was comprised of the United Sons of Vulcan (puddlers), Associated Brotherhood of Iron and Steel Heaters (roughers, rollers, and catchers), and Iron and Steel Roll Hands. The association had three thousand members, 85 percent of whom were puddlers.

1881 — A union of cloak makers joined a newly organized group of dressmakers in New York City and they allied themselves with the Knights of Labor.

1885 — The first call for joint activity by railroad workers through a federation of the railroad brotherhoods was issued by Eugene V. Debs in the *Locomotive Firemen's Magazine.*

June 1889 — The first federation of railroad unions, the United Order of Railway Employees, united four brotherhoods. Frank P. Sargent was president of the new federation and Eugene V. Debs was secretary; both men came out of the Brotherhood of Locomotive Firemen. The United Order of Railway Employees lasted until 1891.

April 1891 — The United Garment Workers of America (UGW) was founded in New York by forty-seven cutters and tailors from the five largest clothing manufacturing centers. It affiliated with the AFL that same year. The UGW's aim was to abolish the sweatshop system and halt the flow of unlimited immigration through adoption of a literacy test.

January 1901 — The first common body of waterfront trades was formed in San Francisco. It was called the City Front Federation.

August 1901 — The first organization that united unions in the meat-packing industry was the Chicago Packing Trades Council. It combined twenty different locals.

April 1908 — The first system federation of railroad shop crafts was established on the Southern Railroad.

June 20, 1911 — The first system federation of railroad crafts was formed on the Harriman railroad lines. The board of forty-eight consisted of one representative from each of the six crafts on the eight Harriman lines.

April 15, 1912 — The first federation of railroad employees was formed by two hundred delegates from roads west and south of Chicago at a convention held in Kansas City.

1914 — The Amalgamated Clothing Workers of America was formed by tailors and related workers on men's clothing in opposition to the rigid policies of the conservative United Garment Workers. At first, the group operated as a dissenting branch of the UGW, but when the AFL refused to acknowledge the union, it was renamed the Amalgamated Clothing Workers of America. In early 1915, Amalgamated wrested control of the New York unions from the UGW.

September 1915 — The first united movement of all four railroad brotherhoods was inaugurated when seven hundred delegates at a conference of the four brotherhoods on railroads of the southeastern territory reached agreement on a joint demand for the eight-hour day and a wage increase.

April 15, 1935 — The first federation of maritime unions was effected at a conference in Seattle called by Harry Bridges. Delegates from all the maritime unions established the Maritime Federation of the Pacific, but internal conflicts led to its early demise.

February 22–23, 1936 — Electrical and radio workers' unions (representing federal AFL unions and independent unions) were amalgamated into one industrial union whose goal was to organize all workers in the electrical and radio industry. In March 1936, the amalgamated groups constituted themselves the United Electrical and Radio Workers of America.

February 1955 — The International Fur and Leather Workers Union, an independent union that had been expelled from the CIO for alleged communist domination, merged with the Amalgamated Meat Cutters and Butcher Workmen of North America of the AFL.

December 1955 — In a historic merger, the American Federation of Labor and the Congress of Industrial Organizations became the American Federation of

Labor and Congress of Industrial Organizations (AFL-CIO), headed by George Meany.

July 1, 1967 — The International Union of Mine, Mill, and Smelter Workers, another independent union that had been expelled from the CIO for alleged Communist domination, merged with the United Steel Workers of America of the AFL-CIO.

June 1968 — The merger of the United Packinghouse Workers of America and the Amalgamated Meat Cutters and Butcher Workmen of North America brought together in one union all the organized meat-packing workers in the United States and Canada.

1969 — The largest industry merger in labor history took place when five railroad unions — the locomotive firemen, trainmen, conductors, brakemen, and switchmen — merged to form the United Transportation Union.

June 3, 1976 — At a joint convention, the Amalgamated Clothing Workers of America and the Textile Workers Union of America merged to form the Amalgamated Clothing and Textile Workers Union. The new union had 450,000 members, 325,000 from the ACWA and 125,000 from the TWUA. One of its first actions was to launch a massive boycott campaign against the antiunion J.P. Stevens and Company in the South.

American Plan

June 1921 — The first action by the Merchants and Manufacturers (M & M) Association of Los Angeles in the American Plan open-shop drive was to establish the "Labor Temple," a free hiring hall for nonunion workers. Registrants were required to sign the following statement: "I pledge myself to conform to the American Plan of Open Shop."

American Revolution

1765 — Working men, mechanics, and artisans formed the Sons of Liberty to carry on organized opposition to continued British rule.

March 5, 1770 — The first workers to lose their lives in the struggle against the British — Crispus Attucks, a black seaman who had escaped from slavery; Samuel Gray, a ropewalk worker; James Caldwell, a young seaman; Patrick Carr, an artisan; and Sam Maverick, a joiner's apprentice — were killed in the "Boston Massacre" by British Redcoats as part of the struggle of Colonial labor against the competition of off-duty British soldiers. The five were buried in a common grave.

1772 — The Patriotic Society was formed to preserve the rights of mechanics, as well as "our just Rights and Privileges to us and our Posterity against every attempt to violate . . . the same, either here or on the other side of the Atlantic." Two years later, the society became the Mechanics' Association of Philadelphia.

Anti-Chinese

August 1877 —The first anti-Chinese trade union, the Workingmen's Trade and Labor Union of San Francisco, was organized by Denis Kearney.

October 5, 1877 —The first anti-Chinese political party, the Workingmen's Party of California, was formed, with Denis Kearney as president.

1882 —The first Chinese Exclusion Act was passed by Congress. It prohibited the entrance of Chinese into the United States for ten years.

1901 —*Some Reasons for Chinese Exclusion: Meat vs. Rice, American Manhood Against Coolieism, Which Shall Survive?* by Samuel Gompers and Herman Gutstadt was the first AFL attack on the Chinese to be published.

Anticommunism

June 23, 1947 —Congress passed the Taft-Hartley Act over President Truman's veto. Under the act, for the first time in American history, every union official of a national or international union that desired to use the services of the National Labor Relations Board had to file an affidavit assuring the govern-ment that he was not affiliated with communism or the Communist party.

October 1949 —The CIO convention voted to expel unions it considered "Communist-dominated." On this basis, eleven unions were cast out of the CIO: the United Electrical, Radio, and Machine Workers of America; International Fur and Leather Workers Union; Mine, Mill and Smelter Workers Union; International Longshoremen's and Warehousemen's Union; United Farm Equipment Workers; Food, Tobacco, and Agricultural Workers; United Office and Professional Workers; United Public Workers; American Communications Association; National Union of Marine Cooks and Stewards; and International Fishermen and Allied Workers. Thus over a million workers were expelled from the CIO.

December 1949 —The International Confederation of Free Trade Unions was formed. It was largely the product of the AFL and CIO's determination to unite all noncommunist labor federations in the world.

Anti-Imperialism

July 15, 1898 —George E. McNeill was the first labor leader to participate in the Anti-Imperialist League. He announced his support of the league at an anti-imperialist meeting in Boston.

November 1898 —Samuel Gompers, the president of the AFL, became the first national labor official to be elected vice president of the American Anti-Imperialist League.

Antistrike Laws

1863 —The first laws providing for fines and imprisonment for strikers who prevented other persons from working were passed by Illinois and Minnesota.

June 23, 1947 —The Taft-Hartley Act reinstated injunctions, gave the courts the power to inflict fines for alleged violations, outlawed mass picketing, and established a sixty-day cooling-off period during which strikes could not be called.

Antitrust Act

March 25, 1893 —The Sherman Anti-Trust Act was applied to labor unions for the first time in a suit instituted by New Orleans employers in the federal Circuit Court against forty-four union leaders, black and white, who were involved in the New Orleans general strike. The union leaders were charged with violating the Sherman Act by entering into a conspiracy to restrain trade. They were found guilty by Judge Billings, but the conviction was eventually quashed.

Anti-war

July 1846 —The first labor organization to pledge never to enlist in the army or navy or to support any war, the League of Universal Brotherhood, was established by Elihu Burritt, the "learned blacksmith."

June 10, 1847 —The first condemnation of the Mexican War by labor was contained in a resolution adopted by the Second Industrial Congress.

March 19, 1899 —The first proposal for a general strike by labor to prevent war was made by Samuel Gompers at a meeting in Boston's Tremont Temple sponsored by the city's trade unions. "If international peace cannot be secured by the intelligence of those in authority," Gompers said, "then I look forward to the time when the workers will settle the question by refusing to handle materials that are to be used to destroy their fellow men." Gompers was accused of "treason" in the proimperialist press for this statement.

February 4, 1917 —A proposal for a nationwide strike if the United States should declare war and enter World War I on the side of the Allied powers was made by James H. Maurer, the socialist president of the Pennsylvania Federation of Labor, at a mass meeting in Philadelphia.

February 25, 1965 — The first union protest against the war in Vietnam was lodged by Local 1199, Drug and Hospital Workers Union, in telegrams to President Lyndon B. Johnson and the two senators from New York State — Jacob K. Javits and Robert F. Kennedy. The union urged, in the name of its twenty-five thousand members, an "all-out effort to negotiate a peaceful settlement in Vietnam."

April 1965 — The International Longshoremen's and Warehousemen's Union became the first national labor organization to oppose the war in Vietnam. Its convention called for an end to United States intervention in Vietnam.

May 28, 1965 — Delegates at the Fifth Annual Convention of the Negro American Labor Council adopted a "World Peace" resolution submitted by President A. Philip Randolph. It included an appeal that the war "be stopped in Vietnam and a negotiated peace be initiated" by the nations involved.

November 11–12, 1967 — The first national labor meeting against the war in Vietnam took place when over five hundred labor officials from the AFL-CIO and independent unions met in Chicago at the Labor Leadership Assembly for Peace. They adopted a statement of policy calling for "an immediate and unconditional end to the bombing of North Vietnam," together with "a clear

and unambiguous statement" by the U.S. government of its "intention to negotiate a settlement of the war with the parties directly involved in the conflict, including the National Liberation Front in South Vietnam."

May 6, 1970 — In his last public statement, issued four days before he was killed in an airplane crash near Pellston, Michigan, Walter Reuther attacked President Nixon for widening the war in Southeast Asia by invading Cambodia.

June 23–24, 1972 — The founding Conference of Labor for Peace was held in St. Louis, Missouri, following the return of a labor delegation (David Livingston, Clifton Caldwell, and Harold Gibbons) from a peace visit to Hanoi in North Vietnam. Acting Chairman Emil Mazey, secretary-treasurer of the UAW (United Auto Workers), read a statement of policy to the conference, which adopted it unanimously. The statement read, in part:

> We, 985 representatives of organized labor, who count in our ranks millions of members, have been brought together . . . out of our common concern and a sense of frustration and anger over the failure of our government to end the war in Vietnam. . . .
> We are . . . resolved that the voice of American labor, which has been raised in every struggle for justice and decency in our nation's history, shall not remain silent during this critical period. As men and women of labor,

who treasure our country's heritage and future, we proclaim our responsibility to harness every effort to end the Vietnam war NOW.

Apprentices

1847 —The first union to limit the number of apprentices was the Baltimore Typographical Society. It set a limit of one apprentice to three journeymen.

May 1850 —The first union to establish rules for the regulation of apprentices, the New York Hat Finishers' Protective Society, drew up a list of regulated items that included the number of years apprentices must serve, their wages, and acceptable working conditions.

1872 —The first employee-training course for apprentices in a private firm was set up by Hoe and Company, a printing establishment.

Arbitration and Mediation

(*Arbitration* is usually applied to the plan whereby the settlement of differences or disputes between workers and employers is referred to an "impartial" agency, public or private, with powers to conduct an independent investigation of the matter and to hand down a "neutral" decision or award. Arbitration may be either voluntary or compulsory. The award may or may not be binding on the contending parties, according to the terms under which the dispute was submitted to arbitration.

Mediation refers to the intervention of some "outside" impartial person or body, with a view to promoting the settlement of a dispute by mutual agreement between the contending parties. In arbitration, on the other hand, the dispute is taken out of the control of the contending parties and settled by a third party, who acts as a judge on the merits of the case.)

1865 —The first contract providing for arbitration was negotiated by the Pittsburgh iron puddlers, who belonged to the Sons of Vulcan.

1871 —The first scholarly espousal of arbitration was incorporated in a paper read by Eckley B. Coxes to the Philadelphia Social Science Association. Coxes defined "conciliation" as the entrance of nonparticipants into negotiations to assist disputing parties, and "arbitration" as a technique whereby an arbitrator or judge, would make decisions on the matter in dispute.

1871 —For the first time, a union agreed to submit its dispute with an employer to a judge. The Workingmen's Benevolent Association submitted its disputes with the Anthracite Board of Trade to Judge William Ewell.

1872 —The first union to institute a constitutional requirement for arbitration before a strike could be approved was the International Molders' Union. It amended its constitution to provide for the banning of strikes whenever the dispute had not first been referred to an "arbitration committee" consisting of two union and two employer representatives, with a fifth individual of "good character." Only if arbitration failed would a strike be sanctioned by the International.

1878 —The first law authorizing a state to participate in the settlement of labor disputes was passed in Maryland.

1883 —The first state law authorizing voluntary arbitration was enacted in Pennsylvania.

1886 —The first permanent boards of arbitration were established in Massachusetts and New York. These boards were influenced by the studies of Carroll D. Wright.

1888 —The first U.S. president to call for arbitration was Grover Cleveland, who asked Congress to "engraft" on the Bureau of Labor a commission to prevent major strikes.

1888 —The first arbitration law, the Arbitration Act of 1888, was passed. It covered only railroad workers and provided for voluntary arbitration by a presidentially appointed three-man board. The commissioner of labor served as the chairman *ex officio*.

1895 —U.S. Commissioner of Labor Carroll D. Wright headed a group that reported on the Pullman Strike. One of the group's recommendations provided the basis for the Erdman Act of 1898, under which the commissioner of labor and the chairman of the Interstate Commerce Commission were to try to mediate railroad disputes. This was the first effort by the federal government to provide mediation in such disputes.

1898 —The Erdman Act was passed. This was the first law authorizing government mediation in labor disputes involving interstate commerce.

October 23, 1902 —The 163-day anthracite coal strike ended on this date, with both sides agreeing to abide by the findings of the Anthracite Coal Strike Commission. The commissioners met for nearly three months before awarding the mine workers a 10 percent wage increase instead of the 20 percent they had asked for, and a nine-hour day instead of the eight-hour day they had demanded (ten hours was then the standard workday). Although the operators refused to recognize the United Mine Workers Union, a six-man arbitration board (three to be selected by employers and three by workers) was created to settle disputes that could not be adjusted between the workers and the mine officials. This was the first successful attempt by the federal government to end a major strike by arbitration.

January 14, 1911 —The first agreement in the men's clothing industry providing for the settlement of grievances by an arbitrtion board with equal participation by the employer and the union was concluded between Hart, Schaffner, and Marx and the United Garment Workers. The company established the first labor complaint department, putting Professor Earl Dean Howard of Northwestern University in charge.

October 1911 —The first joint effort by governors of several states to mediate a strike came during strikes against the Illinois Central and the Harriman lines shop federation. The governors' effort failed.

January 1912 —Arbitration was used to settle the first concerted demand made by engineers on fifty-two eastern railroads. The engineers won a slight pay increase.

1913 —The first conciliation service for disputes other than on railroads was set up by the same act that created the Department of Labor. The act authorized the secretary of labor "to act as mediator and to appoint commissioners of conciliation in labor disputes whenever in his judgment the interests of industrial peace may require it to be done. . . ."

June 2, 1913 —The U.S. Department of Labor mediated a strike settlement for the first time. On May 24, 1913, Glossbrenner Wallace William Hanger, chief statistician of the Bureau of Labor

Statistics, had been assigned by Secretary of Labor William B. Wilson to mediate the dispute between the Railway Clerks and the New York, New Haven, and Hartford Railroad. He successfully settled the dispute through mediation.

January 27, 1920 —The first strike against compulsory arbitration took place when four hundred Kansas miners walked off their jobs to protest the first compulsory arbitration law passed by any state in the United States. The strike lasted one day and was unsuccessful.

February 28, 1920 —The first legislation establishing Railroad Labor Boards provided that all controversies between workers and employers in the railroad industry should, if possible, be decided by the parties concerned, acting through Joint Adjustment Boards.

1922 —The first arbitration association, the American Society of Arbitration, Inc., was formed in New York City.

August 5, 1933 —The first National Labor Board was established under the National Industrial Recovery Act. It consisted of seven members; Senator Robert F. Wagner was its first chairman. The board's purpose was to mediate disputes or controversies between employers and workers. It only lasted until July 9, 1934.

June 21, 1934 —The first National Mediation Board replaced the U.S.

Board of Mediation provided for in the Railway Labor Act of May 20, 1926. The new board was created by an amendment to the Railway Labor Act in order to "avoid any interruption to commerce or to the operation of any carrier engaged therein . . . to provide for the prompt and orderly settlement of all disputes concerning rates of pay, rules, or working conditions." Its first chairman was Dr. William Leiserson.

December 1975 — The first decision marking the end of the "reserve clause" in baseball was handed down. The clause bound every player irrevocably to the club holding his contract, thereby fixing his place of employment and ensuring that his salary would ultimately be determined by the whim of the team owner. A three-man arbitration panel ruled that two players — Andy Messersmith of the Los Angeles Dodgers and Dave McNally of the Montreal Expos — were released from their team affiliations because they had played out their existing contracts, plus an additional year, and were therefore free agents, entitled to sign up with whatever club they wished at any pay they could command.

Automation

July 1957 — The first agreement to prevent job loss due to automation was won when 157 employees of the Maccabees insurance firm, members of Local 157 of the Insurance Workers of America, obtained the following commitment from their employer: "That during the term of this agreement there will be no layoffs or loss of pay resulting to the present employees as the result of changes in methods of operation [automation]."

Baseball

November 1889 —The first public objection by baseball players to the reserve clause came in a manifesto entitled "To the Public," in which the players declared: "Reservation became for them [the baseball magnates] another name for property rights in the player. By a combination among themselves, stronger than the strongest trust, they were able to enforce the most arbitrary measure, and the player had either to submit or get out of the profession in which he had spent years in attaining a proficiency. Even the disbandment and retirement of a club did not free the players from the octopus clutch, for they then were peddled to the highest bidder."

November 1889 —Baseball players announced they intended to form their own league for the 1890 season. The Brotherhood League set up player control of all matters affecting players. Three-year contracts at raised salaries were agreed upon after negotiations based on players' records. Salaries could be raised, but not lowered, during the three years of the contract. Any player who had a chance to better himself by moving from one team to another had the right to do so. Franchises were granted to Buffalo, Chicago, Brooklyn, New York, Cleveland, Boston, Philadelphia, and Pittsburgh under the management of the baseball stars of the day. Eighty percent of the National League players of 1889 went over to the Brotherhood League for the 1890 season. Even so, the league lasted only that one season.

Battle

November 29, 1874 —The first mass battle between strikers and scabs took place along the Youghiogheny River in Elizabeth Township, Pennsylvania. In the "Battle of Buena Vista," twelve workers, mainly strikebreakers, were killed and thirty were wounded. The miners at the Armstrong Works had walked out for a four-cent raise in daily wages. The strike was settled when an arbitrator awarded the strikers a raise of two cents per day.

Benevolent Societies

1662 —The first benevolent society was established by porters in New York City. Members' dues went to aid the ill.

Bill of Rights

1959 —The first bill of rights for union members was included in the Landrum-Griffin Act, passed by Congress after the McClellan Committee exposed corruption in several unions. This law assured union members freedom of speech and assembly and also required unions to file financial statements and have their officers and staff bonded.

Blacklists

March 1836 —In the first blacklist, master tailors of New York announced that they would "not receive into their employ any man who is a member of the 'Union Trade Society of Journeymen Tailors in the City of New York.'"

Black Workers

1526 —The first revolt of black slaves within the present borders of the United States took place near the mouth of the Pedee River in what is now South Carolina.

1619 —The first blacks were sold into indentured servitude in Jamestown, Virginia.

1640 —The first sentence of servitude for life was imposed on John Punch, a black servant who ran away from his master in Virginia. Two white servants who also ran away from their masters were only required to serve four additional years. The decision paved the way for the legal establishment of chattel slavery for Negroes.

April 7, 1712 —The first bona fide slave revolt in Colonial America took place in New York when twenty-two black and two Indian slaves rose up in revolt, killed nine whites, and wounded five or six others. The slave rebels were outnumbered by militia and their revolt was crushed, after which the rebellious slaves were sentenced to death. Six, including a pregnant woman, were reprieved by Governor Hunter; the others were executed. Governor Hunter wrote: "Some were burnt, others hanged, one broke on the wheel, and one hung alive in chains in the town, so there has been the most exemplary punishment inflicted that could be possibly thought of. . . ."

October 29, 1763 —The first combination of black workers was formed by chimney sweepers in Charleston, South Carolina, who refused to work unless their price scale was met. This was not a strike against employers, but a protest against prices set by the city.

July 1850 —The first organization of black workers, the American League of Colored Laborers, was organized in New York City, with Frederick Douglass as its first vice president. The league's purpose was to provide training and other opportunities for blacks.

February 1853 — In the first strike by black workers in the nineteenth century, Negro waiters of New York City compelled employers to raise their wages to $16 a month, while white waiters continued to receive $12.

March 30, 1853 — In the first invitation issued by a union of white workers to black workers to address it, the newly organized Waiters' Protective Union of New York City asked black waiters to explain how they had managed to raise their wages to $16 a month. However, the Waiters' Protective Union did not allow black waiters to join it.

July 1858 — For the first time, black workers organized to defend themselves against efforts by white workers to drive them out of their trade. The result was the Association of Black Caulkers of Baltimore.

July 1862 — The first organization of seamen, the American Seamen's Protective Association, was organized in New York City for the protection of black seamen by William P. Powell, a black leader.

1865 — The first white union to admit black workers was the Carpenters and Joiners Union No. 1 of Boston.

February 12, 1866 — The first black cooperative, the Chesapeake Marine Railway and Dry Dock Company, was founded by black ship caulkers of Baltimore, with Isaac Myers as president.

June 18, 1866 — In the first collective action taken by black women workers, colored washerwomen of Jackson, Mississippi, sent a petition to the mayor setting forth their price list and announcing that "any one belonging to the class of washerwomen, violating this, shall be liable to a fine *regulated by the class.*"

September 1866 — The first bona fide black trade union, the Colored Caulkers' Trade Union Society of Baltimore, was founded. Isaac Myers was the union's first president.

July 1867 — The first labor appeal to white workers to organize and unite with black workers came in the *Address to the Workingmen of the United States,* drawn up by a committee appointed by the 1866 convention of the National Labor Union. It was actually the work of Andrew C. Cameron, editor of the *Workingman's Advocate* of Chicago, and read in part: "The interests of the labor cause demand that all workingmen be included within its ranks, without regard to race or nationality; and . . . the interests of the workingmen of America especially require that the formation of . . . labor organizations should be encouraged among the colored race and that they be invited to cooperate with us in the general labor undertaking."

1867 — The first union of black long-shoremen was founded: the Longshoremen's Protective Union of Charleston, South Carolina.

1868 — The first union of black hod carriers was formed: the Hod Carriers' and Laborers' Association of Philadelphia.

1868 — The first union of black brickmakers was created: the Colored Brickmakers' Association of Philadelphia.

August 19, 1869 — For the first time, a national gathering of white workers advocated the creation of a black labor union and authorized the admission of blacks to its annual meeting. This was done at a meeting held by the National Labor Union. Nine delegates from black trade unions, headed by Isaac Myers, president of the Colored Caulkers' Trade Union Society of Baltimore, attended the NLU meeting.

December 6, 1869 — The first national organization of black workers, the Colored National Labor Union, organized by 214 delegates from eighteen states, met in Washington, D.C. Isaac Myers was elected president.

1870 — The first union of black teachers, the Colored Teachers' Co-operative Association of Cincinnati, was formed. Its president, Peter H. Clark, was the union's delegate to the 1870 convention of the National Labor Union.

April 26, 1879 — The first strike at a summer resort occurred when the Colored Waiters' Protective Union called its members out to protest wages at hotels at the principal watering places and seaside resorts in Saratoga, Sharon Springs, and Newport.

March 1880 — The first strike of black workers on Louisiana sugar plantations took place. The general strike in St. John Parish was for wages of $1 a day for laborers. State troops crushed the strike.

November 15, 1881 — The first black delegate to attend an AFL convention was Peter Grandeson of Pittsburgh.

July 8, 1886 — In the first strike by black members of the Knights of Labor, the blacks, numbering more than one thousand, struck Arkansas plantations for better conditions and won.

October 1886 — The first American labor organization with a substantial black membership was the Knights of Labor. In October 1886, when the union's membership exceeded 750,000, it was estimated that no fewer than 60,000 of the members were black.

October 1886 — For the first time at a national labor convention, white delegates defied the color line in the South. At the Richmond convention of the Knights of Labor, New York and other state delegates declined to stay at hotels that refused to accommodate black delegates, and insisted on accompanying these delegates, especially Frank J. Ferrell, vice president of the Knights of Labor, to Richmond theaters and sitting with them, in spite of the ban against integrated audiences. Ferrell introduced Grand Master Workman Terence V. Powderly to the convention while Virginia Governor Fitzhugh Lee was seated on the same platform.

November 1, 1887 — In the first mass strike of black workers, ten thousand Negro Knights of Labor, members of District Assembly 194, struck the sugar plantations of four parishes in Louisiana. Their demands were: wages of $1.25 a day without board, or $1 a day with board; 60 cents for six hours' "watch" at night; day wages to be paid every two weeks, and "watch" wages every week; and payment of wages in money. The strikers were evicted from the homes rented to them by the planters, and the strike was broken when the militia murdered twenty strikers, including George and Henry Cox, the strike leaders.

1890 — For the first time, the AFL refused to charter a national union because its constitution limited membership to whites. The AFL rejected the National Association of Machinists' application for charter.

1890 — The first black vice president of the United Mine Workers, Richard L. Davis was elected to the union's General Executive Board. The union was an amalgamation of the National Trades Assembly 135 of the Knights of Labor and the National Progressive Union.

July 9, 1891 — The first black commissioned as a general organizer by the AFL was George L. Norton, secretary of the Marine Firemen's Union No. 5464 of St. Louis.

September 9, 1891 — The first strike by black cotton pickers, for $1 a day in Georgia and Arkansas, was lost.

November 1892 — The first interracial general strike in American history occurred when 25,000 black and white workers in New Orleans joined in a general strike for union recognition, the closed shop, shorter hours, and higher wages. Forty-nine unions were involved.

1895 — The first national union readmitted to the AFL after being excluded because of a color bar in its constitution was the International Association of Machinists. It transferred the ban from its constitution to its ritual.

1899 — The first national union to be admitted to the AFL with a ban against Negroes in its constitution was the Order of Railroad Telegraphers.

December 1900 — For the first time, the AFL officially sanctioned a Jim Crow policy of organization. Article 12, Section 6, of the AFL Constitution, revised at the 1900 convention, read: "Separate charters may be issued to central labor unions, local unions or federated labor unions, composed exclusively of colored workers where in the judgment of the Executive Council it appears advisable."

1902 — The first investigation of black membership in trade unions, the Atlanta University study conducted under the supervision of Dr. W.E.B. DuBois, disclosed that forty-three national unions, including the railroad brotherhoods, did not have a single black member.

July 1905 — The first union that made the organization of black workers a key issue and that never formed a segregated local was founded — the Industrial Workers of the World (IWW).

October 24, 1907 — For the first time, blacks were nominated, along with whites, to an arbitration committee set up to settle a strike. The blacks represented the screwmen of New Orleans. When city officials, including the mayor, appealed to the New Orleans Central Labor Union to remove the blacks from the committee, the appeal was rejected and the blacks served.

June 11, 1911 — The first union to unite black and white timber workers in the Deep South, the Brotherhood of Timber Workers, was established at a convention in Alexandria, Louisiana. However, the black workers were organized into separate locals. When the Brotherhood of Timber Workers sought

to affiliate with the IWW in 1912, the IWW insisted that it abandon its segregated local system.

1913 — The Marine Transport Workers Local 3, IWW, of Philadelphia became the first union with rotating black and white chairmen.

1913 — The first union of black workers in the railway mail service (they had been excluded by the AFL's Railway Mail Association) was the National Alliance of Postal Employees.

1915 — The first organization to attempt to organize all black railway workers, regardless of craft or skill, into one union was the Railway Men's Benevolent Association.

1915 — The first "Great Migration" of black workers from the South to the North took place this year. There was a shortage of labor in northern industry because immigration from European nations engaged in World War I had been halted. Industry therefore was forced to recruit southern blacks to fill jobs — other than as strikebreakers — for the first time. Thousands of blacks took part in this Great Migration to the industrial plants in Chicago, Detroit, Pittsburgh, and other cities.

July 2, 1917 — The first anti-Negro riot during the Great Migration occurred in East St. Louis, Illinois, after the Central Trades and Labor Union, a federation of AFL craft unions, demanded that the city halt the influx of blacks. The riot lasted two days and twenty-eight blacks and eighty-five whites lost their lives.

July 1917 — The Colored Employees of America, organized in New York City, represented the first attempt in the twentieth century to form a national federation of black workers.

August 17, 1918 — On this date, the first black leader was sentenced to prison during World War I for violating the Espionage Act. Ben Fletcher, leader of the IWW, received ten years in prison and a fine of $10,000.

February 1919 — The National Association for the Promotion of Labor Unionism Among Negroes, the first organization dedicated specifically to spreading the message of trade unionism among black workers, was founded by A. Philip Randolph and Chandler Owen, editors of the black socialist monthly, *The Messenger*; Reverend George Frazier Miller, a black socialist of Brooklyn, New York, and such white socialists as Morris Hillquit, Joseph Schlossberg of the Amalgamated Clothing Workers, and Charles W. Ervin, editor of the daily socialist newspaper, *The New York Call*.

April 1919 — The first convention of the National Brotherhood of America was organized by black unions.

August 25, 1925 — At a meeting in Harlem, New York City, the Brotherhood of Sleeping Car Porters was launched. The union announced that the porters would not settle for less than (1) recognition of the Brotherhood; (2) an increase in wages to $150 a month, with the abolition of tipping; (3) a forty-hour week and relief from unreasonable "doubling out"; and (4) pay for preparation time.

October 1925 — The founding meeting of the American Negro Labor Congress, the first Communist party organization to mobilize black industrial workers in the fight against discrimination in industry and the trade unions, was attended by thirty-two delegates. The national organizer of the Congress was Lovett Fort-Whitman of Chicago.

December 1926 — The Brotherhood of Sleeping Car Porters affiliated for the first time with the AFL. Thirteen divisions affiliated as federal unions.

1929 — The first national convention of the Brotherhood of Sleeping Car Porters was held. It adopted a constitution and elected its first president — A. Philip Randolph.

December 1932 — A. Philip Randolph introduced the "Randolph Resolution" at an AFL convention for the first time. The resolution called for the abolition of segregated federal unions for black workers, and the appointment of black organizers to recruit black workers into the AFL. It was rejected.

July 1935 — The Negro Labor Committee was formed by Frank Crosswaith in New York City to organize black workers in industries under contract with the AFL.

February 14, 1936 — The National Negro Congress held its first convention, at which 817 delegates, representing 585 organizations with an estimated combined membership of 1.2 million, founded a new, militant organization of blacks with A. Philip Randolph as president. Its mission was to "seek to broaden and intensify the movement to draw Negro workers into labor organizations and break down the color bar in the trade unions that now have it."

August 3, 1936 — The AFL granted an international charter to the Brotherhood of Sleeping Car Porters. It was the first time the union operated as an international union in the AFL, instead of as a federal labor union.

May 1937 — At the first strike of black women in tobacco plants, four hundred women struck against the I.N. Vaughn Company of Richmond, Virginia. They were aided by the Southern Negro Youth Congress and won recognition of their independent union, along with a wage increase and a forty-hour work week. Other independent unions of black tobacco workers were founded and affiliated with the CIO.

August 25, 1937 — The Pullman Company signed its first contract with the Brotherhood of Sleeping Car Porters. This was the first contract between a union of black workers and a major American corporation. It called for union representation, job security, a reduction in the work month from 400 to 240 hours, and a wage increase totaling $1.25 million.

February 10, 1941 — The first agreement between the southeastern railroad carriers and the Brotherhood of Locomotive Firemen was reached, with the aid of the National Mediation Board. It paved the way for the elimination of black firemen under the so-called Washington Agreement, which provided that "nonpromotable" firemen should not exceed 50 percent in every class of the service. A specific clause in the agreement read: "It is understood that promotable firemen or helpers on other than steam power are those in line for promotion, under the present rules and practices to the position of locomotive engineers." Since Negroes were completely barred from such promotion, the process of eliminating black firemen from the roads began in earnest the moment the agreement was signed. By April 1941, the Brotherhood had replaced all Negro firemen.

June 24, 1941 — The first March on Washington for Jobs and an End to Discrimination against Negroes was called off by A. Philip Randolph in exchange for an executive order by President Franklin D. Roosevelt banning discrimination in defense industries.

June 25, 1941 —President Franklin D. Roosevelt issued the first executive order asserting that it is the "policy of the United States that there shall be no discrimination in the employment of workers in defense industry or Government because of race, creed, color, or national origin." The order established the Fair Employment Practices Committee (FEPC).

July 19, 1941 —The first FEPC board was appointed. Its chairman was Mark Ethridge, publisher of the *Louisville Courier*.

June 21, 1943 —At a race riot in Detroit, Michigan, black workers were beaten by white men. Federal troops were sent in to put down the riot. Between June 1940 and June 1943, fifty thousand blacks had migrated to Detroit in search of defense work. Problems soon arose over their living facilities, and on February 28, 1942, whites rioted against blacks who attempted to move into the Sojourner Truth Houses, a federally subsidized housing project. From that time on, race relations in Detroit had deteriorated and the outbreak of June 21 came as no surprise.

July 1943 —The first epidemic of "hate strikes" against the employment of black

workers took place at the Bethlehem shipyards in Sparrows Point, Maryland. All three CIO unions involved—the steel, electrical, and shipbuilding workers—acted to enforce a non-discriminatory policy, and the strikes were called off.

October 1943 —For the first time, a book on labor history was cited during a debate at an AFL convention. A. Philip Randolph, at the 1943 AFL convention, referred to Herbert Northrup's *Organized Labor and the Negro* to prove his contention that racial discrimination against Negro workers was still widespread in AFL unions. Northrup's study noted that thirty international and national unions excluded black workers by constitutional provision, union ritual, or tacit consent, or by arranging "representation" in segregated unions that had only auxiliary status. Randolph condemned auxiliary unions as equivalent to "colonies of colored people in the empire systems" and described their members as groups of "economic, political, and social serfs" who possessed "none of the rights that the white population in the mother country enjoy, except the right to be taxed." Like the colonists, Randolph noted, these workers were used as cannon fodder "in defense of their oppressors when wars break out."

April 24, 1944 —The first contract between the R.J. Reynolds Tobacco Company of Winston-Salem, North Carolina, and Local 22, Food, Tobacco,

Agricultural and Allied Workers (CIO), was signed. Local 22 had fifteen thousand workers, most of whom were black.

August 3, 1944 — The worst "hate strike" of World War II, a wildcat strike staged by white streetcar workers in Philadelphia who were members of the Philadelphia Transportation Company Employees Union, a company union, protested the assignment of eight black porters to jobs as motormen. For six days, the city was without public transportation. The strike ended only after President Roosevelt issued an order placing the company under army control and sent in five thousand troops to restore normal operations.

December 1944 — For the first time, the U.S. Supreme Court ruled that a craft union had the duty to defend the interests of all its members, regardless of race or color. The case involved Bester Williams Steele, a black fireman on the Louisville and Nashville Railroad since 1910, who had been discharged under the Washington Agreement. The FEPC found the Washington Agreement discriminatory and ordered the railroads and the unions to abandon it, but the Brotherhood refused to accept the ruling. Steele, represented by Charles Houston, a noted black attorney from Washington, D.C., brought suit against both the Louisville and Nashville and the Brotherhood of Locomotive Firemen and Enginemen in the U.S. District Court in Alabama. Defeated there, he

appealed to the Supreme Court, which reversed the lower court's verdict and ruled in Steele's favor.

December 1944 — The New York Telephone Company hired black women as telephone operators for the first time in response to pressure from the National Urban League and the FEPC.

January 1951 — The first agreement with the Bureau of Engraving outlawing segregation was signed by Ewart Guinier, secretary of the United Public Workers of America, CIO. Guinier was the leader of the Greater New York Negro Labor Council.

October 27, 1951 — The National Negro Labor Council was founded at a convention held in Cincinnati, Ohio, and attended by delegates, mostly black, from twenty-one cities. The convention adopted a Statement of Principles and a Program of Action, and pledged the NNLC would "work unitedly with the trade unions to bring about greater cooperation between all sections of the Negro people and the trade union movement; to bring the principles of trade unionism to the Negro workers everywhere; to aid the trade unions in the great unfinished work of organizing the South on the basis of fraternity, equality and unity; and to further unity between black and white workers everywhere." William R. Hood, president of Ford Local 600 of the UAW-CIO, was elected president; Coleman Young was elected executive secretary; Ernest Thompson of UE (United Electrical, Radio, and Machine Workers) was made director of organization; and Octavia Hawkins of Local 451 of the Amalgamated Clothing Workers in Chicago was named treasurer.

1957 — The Trade Union Leadership Council, comprising black trade union officials in Detroit, was founded to press for elimination of discrimination against Negroes in the AFL-CIO and the UAW.

August 1959 — A joint appeal by A. Philip Randolph and Walter Reuther to the AFL-CIO urged it to stress the elimination of racial discrimination in affiliated unions. The appeal brought no response.

October 1959 — A celebrated exchange between George Meany and A. Philip Randolph took place at the 1959 AFL-CIO convention. When Randolph, speaking for the resolution of the Brotherhood of Sleeping Car Porters, insisted that to maintain Jim Crow unionism because the members of segregated unions might want it was no more defensible than "maintain[ing] unions under Communist domination and corrupt influences on the ground that the members of said unions desired to keep them." The following exchange occurred:

> MEANY: Is this your idea of a democratic process, that you don't care what the Negro members think? You don't care if they want to maintain the

union they have had for so many years? I would like an answer to that.

> RANDOLPH: Yes.

> MEANY *(angrily):* That's not my policy. I am for the democratic rights of the Negro members. Who in the hell appointed you as guardian of the Negro members in America? You talk about tolerance.

May 1960 — The first convention of the Negro American Labor Council was held. A. Philip Randolph was elected president, and Cleveland Robinson of District 65, New York City, was elected vice president.

November 1962 — A March on Washington to take place in the late summer or fall of 1963 to demand jobs for blacks and an end to discrimination in industry and unions was first proposed at the convention of the Negro American Labor Alliance.

August 28, 1963 — At the first March on Washington for Jobs and Freedom, 250,000 people gathered in the largest mass assemblage in the history of the nation's capital. The keynote address was delivered by Martin Luther King, Jr., entitled "I Have a Dream." Though the AFL-CIO leadership refused to endorse the march, the AFL-CIO Industrial Union Department, headed by Walter Reuther, both endorsed and participated in it.

July 1, 1968 — The first "wildcat" strike of black bus drivers in Chicago was begun by Local 241, Amalgamated Transit Union, AFL-CIO. The strike was led by the Black Caucus: Concerned Transit Workers.

May 27, 1971 — The first suit against the Bethlehem Steel Company and the United Steelworkers charging racial discrimination in seniority was filed. It led to an order by Secretary of Labor James D. Hodgson to end the dual seniority system.

September 1972 — The Coalition of Black Trade Unionists was formed at a conference in Chicago attended by twelve hundred black workers. The workers participated in two days of discussion on the 1972 elections and on ways "to enhance Black influence and power in the American labor movement."

May 25, 1973 — The Coalition of Black Trade Unionists was formally established at a convention in Washington, D.C. attended by 1,141 delegates from thirty-three international and other unions, most of them affiliated with the AFL-CIO. The aim of the organization was to fight for first-class citizenship for black trade union members and to eliminate racism in American industry and organized labor.

March 24, 1976 — The U.S. Supreme Court, in a landmark civil rights ruling, decided five to three, that blacks who were denied jobs in violation of the Civil Rights Act of 1964 must be awarded retroactive seniority once they succeeded in getting those jobs. The court ruled that the blacks must be given the same seniority they would have enjoyed had they been hired initially, with all accompanying rights, including pension benefits, and in the event of layoffs, better job security than that possessed by workers with less seniority.

Boring-from-Within

January 1912 — The first Syndicalist Militant Minority League was formed in Chicago by former IWW members to "bore from within" the AFL for a progressive labor policy. The league was headed by William Z. Foster.

November 1920 — The Trade Union Educational League, headed by William Z. Foster, was founded to campaign within the AFL for industrial unionism, the amalgamation of craft unions, the organization of unorganized workers, independent political action by labor, and U.S. recognition of the Soviet Union.

Boycotts

1766 — The first American boycott was organized by the Sons of Liberty among workingmen, mechanics, and artisans. They determined not to buy any British goods until measures hostile to the American colonies were repealed. The boycott was successful, in large measure because the Daughters of Liberty pledged not to buy British goods.

1806 —The first mention of the word *boycott* occurred in a conspiracy trial in reference to the fact that cordwainers refused to eat at a boardinghouse where nonunion men boarded.

December 18, 1883 —The first boycott to attract national attention took place on this date. It was organized by the Typographical Union No. 6 of New York City against the *New York Tribune*. The boycott ended in 1892 when the officials of the newspaper announced that the *Tribune* "is now a strict union office."

February 1886 —The first boycott imposed on products that did not carry a union label was organized by the Cigar Makers' International Union.

July 2, 1886 —For the first time, labor leaders were imprisoned for sponsoring a boycott. Five leaders of the Carl Sahm Club (Knights of Labor) were sentenced to three years, two years, and ten months at hard labor in state prison for sponsoring the boycott against the "concert saloon" of George Theiss. The sentence was handed down by Judge George C. Barrett.

June 22, 1894 —In the first boycott by a railroad union, the American Railway Union boycotted Pullman Cars in support of the Pullman strikers.

1899 —The first campaign to boycott companies exploiting women and children was launched by the National Consumer's League.

1901 —The first action in the famous Danbury Hatters' Case took place this year when the United Hatters of North America called a strike and declared a boycott against the shop of Dietrich E. Lowe in Danbury, Connecticut. In 1903, Lowe filed suit against the union for triple damages of $240,000 plus $100,000. The decision led to the payment in 1915 of $52,130 in fines. The homes and bank accounts of the Danbury Hatters were attached to pay the fine.

1902 —The "Ladies Anti-Beef Trust Association" was formed by Jewish women, many of them garment workers on New York's East Side, to boycott kosher butchers who refused to pass lowered prices on to consumers. "Eat no meat while the Trust is taking meat from the bones of your children and women," read a Yiddish circular decorated with a skull and crossbones. When Rebecca Ablowitz, one of the boycotters, was asked by the magistrate after she was arrested why she had prevented nonboycotters from buying meat, she replied "We don't riot. But if all we did was to weep at home, nobody would notice it, so we have to do something to help ourselves."

December 19, 1903 — The first boycott of funerals occurred when striking Chicago teamsters boycotted livery carriages used in funeral processions.

August 21, 1904 — The Retail Kosher Butchers' Union conducted its first boycott against packinghouses in support of the striking packinghouse workers.

June 1912 — The first call for a worldwide boycott of American goods to obtain the release of political prisoners in the United States went out from socialists in Sweden. They urged such a boycott "until Ettor and Giovannitti are liberated." The two IWW leaders had been imprisoned and charged with murder during the Lawrence textile strike.

1936–1937 — Acting on a proposal by union president Ben Gold, the International Fur Workers Union became the first union to boycott goods made in Nazi Germany and Fascist Japan.

1966 — Farm workers, led by Cesar Chavez, struck the grape growers in and around Delano, California, joined the AFL-CIO, and marched three hundred miles from Delano to Sacramento to publicize their grievances and demands. Chavez called for a nationwide consumer boycott, first against Schenley Industries, which owned a large ranch in Delano, then against DiGiorgio products (S & W Foods and Treesweet) and the eleven-thousand-acre Giumarra vineyards, and finally against all California grapes. Because the farm workers were not covered by federal labor laws such as the Landrum-Griffin Act, they were unaffected by sections of the legislation that declared the secondary boycott illegal. The farm workers' boycott of nonunion grapes involved more Americans than any previous boycott, and was a significant factor in the union's final victory.

July 1976 — The International Longshoremen's and Warehousemen's Union, Local 10, in San Francisco voted to boycott South African cargo, and thus became the first U.S. union to condemn the apartheid racist government of South Africa and to back that condemnation with a boycott.

In August 1976, the International Typographical Union adopted a resolution at its 118th convention condemning the South African government for banning black workers from joining or forming unions, and pointing out that trade union organizations the world over had urged all trade unionists to condemn apartheid. The ITU convention therefore condemned "the racist system of apartheid which exists in South Africa and will have no official or cooperative efforts with the Trade Union Congress of South Africa until such time as they discontinue their support of the racist system of apartheid."

October 1980 — The nationwide boycott of products of J.P. Stevens and Company ended with the company, which had conducted a seventeen-year antiunion campaign, signing its first union contract with the Amalgamated Clothing and Textile Workers Union (ACTWU) covering thirty-five hundred workers at Roanoke Rapids, North Carolina. The boycott of Stevens products had been supported by the entire labor movement as well as by the National Organization of Women (NOW) and other groups.

Building Trades

1884 — The first Central Building Trades Council was established in New York City; it lasted until 1894. The first building trades council in Chicago was organized in 1888.

1885 — The first joint agreement achieved through collective bargaining in the building trades was signed by bricklayers.

December 1897 — The first federation of local building trades' councils, the National Building Trades Council of America, was formed.

October 1905 — The first industrywide confederation of building trade unions, the Structural Building Trades Alliance, was formed. It represented five national unions in the building trades.

1907 — The AFL established the first Building Trades Department.

July 1920 — The Lockwood Committee of the New York State legislature conducted the first legislative investigation of corruption involving unions and employers in the building trades. The committee concluded that "from structural steel and bricks to doorknobs and sandpaper, every article entering into building construction can be said to be under the control of merciless, gouging, monopolistic combines." The Building Trades' Employers' Association and Robert Brindell, head of the Building Trades Council, were charged with corruption and collusion in monopolistic practices. Brindell was sentenced to five to ten years in prison. A similar legislative exposé of corruption in the Chicago building trades was carried out by the Dailey Committee.

Bureau of Labor

July 27, 1884 — The Bureau of Labor was established in the Department of Interior. Its duty was to collect information on working people and on the "means of promoting their material, social, intellectual, and moral prosperity."

January 31, 1885 — The first commissioner of labor, Carroll D. Wright, was appointed by President Chester A. Arthur. Wright served until January 31, 1905, at a salary of $3,000 per year.

Bureau of Labor Statistics

August 22, 1866 —Labor's first demand for a bureau of labor statistics was presented by the National Labor Union.

June 23, 1869 —The first state labor bureau was established in Massachusetts. The Massachusetts Bureau of Statistics of Labor, under a chief and deputy, was "to collect, assort, systematize and present in annual reports to the Legislature . . . statistical details relating to all departments of labor in the Commonwealth." Henry Kemble Oliver was appointed the bureau's first chief. George McNeill (1836–1906), a shoemaker who was the president of the Boston Eight-Hour League, the author of *The Labor Movement* . . . (1887), and a leader in the movement that established the Massachusetts bureau, became its first deputy chief.

C

Child Day-Care Centers

1934 — The Works Progress Administration (WPA) established the first day-care centers on a national basis for the children of mothers receiving government assistance. WPA centers were closed to women who were regularly employed because they were primarily a relief effort and not designed to stimulate the employment of mothers.

1942 — The first WPA centers for the children of working mothers were established. They were also open to youngsters whose parents were in the armed forces.

August 31, 1942 — Child-care centers were established by the Federal Works Agency for the children of working mothers in defense industries. They were set up under the Lanham Act, which permitted federal financing of various community facilities and services in defense-impacted areas. Eventually there were hundreds of day-care centers in major production areas.

Child Labor

1619 — The first child workers arrived in Colonial America. They landed in Virginia.

1813 — Connecticut passed the first state law declaring that proprietors of manufacturing establishments should teach their child laborers "reading, writing and the first four rules of arithmetic."

1825 — Massachusetts conducted the first investigation into the relationship between child labor and school attendance. Actually, this was the first investigation by a state into *any* labor problem. Partly as a result of this investigation, Massachusetts passed a child labor law in 1836.

1833 — The issue of prohibiting the use of child labor in factories was considered for the first time in Pennsylvania, but no action was taken.

1836 — Massachusetts passed the first state law restricting child labor. The law stated that no child under the age of fifteen could work in "manufacturing establishments" unless that child attended school for at least three of the twelve months preceding any year of employment. In 1842, enforcement provisions were added to the law.

1842 — The first state law limiting the number of hours of employment for

35

children to ten per day was passed by Massachusetts. The act pertained to children under twelve.

1848 — The first state law setting a minimum age (twelve years) for child employment in factories was passed by Pennsylvania. The legislation prohibited child labor in cotton, woolen, silk, and flax factories. In 1849, the age was raised to thirteen and the act was broadened to cover the paper and bagging industries as well.

1878 — Massachusetts became the first state to require that employers submit evidence of both the age and the schooling of children they wished to employ in order to obtain employment certificates.

1879 — The first enforceable law limiting children and women workers to a ten-hour day was passed by Massachusetts.

1892 — Boston issued the first city ordinance regulating child labor in street trades. Children under ten were prohibited from selling newspapers or working as bootblacks in the streets or public places of Boston. Minors over ten years of age were required to have a license.

1902 — For the first time, the American Academy of Political and Social Science devoted a session to "The Child Labor Problem."

1903 — New York passed the first child labor law in the United States making

normal development, sound health, and physical fitness for a proposed job requirements for an employment certificate.

July 1903 — Mother Jones led the "March of the Mill Children" from Philadelphia to Oyster Bay, New York, to persuade President Theodore Roosevelt to speak out against child labor. The children carried banners with such slogans as: "We only ask for Justice," "We Want to Go to School," "We Want Time to Play." Though TR refused to see Mother Jones or the children, the crusade helped in passing child labor legislation in Pennsylvania.

1904 — The National Child Labor Committee was set up under the leadership of Dr. Felix Adler, noted educator and founder of the Ethical Culture Society (chairman of the board); Homer Folks, executive secretary of the New York State Charities Aid Association (vice chairman); and V. Everitt Macy, philanthropist and director of the Title Guarantee Trust Company (treasurer).

1907 — The first federal child labor bill was introduced into Congress under the sponsorship of Senator Albert Beveridge of Indiana. This measure was designed to prohibit the interstate transportation of articles produced in factories or mines that employed children under sixteen years of age. The bill was quickly defeated.

1908 — For the first time, Child Labor Day was observed in schools and churches throughout the country.

1908 — Montana became the first state to adopt a sixteen-year minimum age for children employed in manufacturing.

1910 — Massachusetts became the first state to require by law a physical examination of a child before he or she could receive an employment certificate.

1910 — For the first time a state (Massachusetts) empowered its board of health to determine whether or not a particular occupation was too hazardous to allow employment of minors under eighteen. Massachusetts had passed a similar law in 1894 applying to children under fourteen.

1912 — The Federal Children's Bureau was established by Congress within the Department of Commerce and Labor. Its first chief was Julia Clifford Lathrop. The bureau was directed to "investigate and report . . . upon all matters pertaining to the welfare of children and child life among all classes of our people."

September 1, 1916 — The first federal child labor law (Keating-Owen Law) was signed by President Woodrow Wilson. It forbade interstate commerce in the products of child labor. Because it focused on manufacturing, the law covered only 150,000 of the nation's 1,850,000 working children.

June 3, 1918 — The U.S. Supreme Court, in a five-to-four decision, ruled the federal child labor law unconstitutional because it transcended Congress's power over commerce and interfered in a purely local matter to which federal authority did not extend.

1919 — The first tax on the use of child labor was enacted, the Revenue Act of 1919. However, in 1923, the act was ruled unconstitutional.

June 1924 — The first constitutional amendment granting Congress the power to limit, regulate, and prohibit the labor of persons under eighteen years of age was passed. When submitted to the states, however, it failed to achieve ratification.

1938 — For the first time, a federal child labor law was ruled constitutional. The Supreme Court upheld the Walsh-Healey Act, which prohibited the employment of boys under sixteen and girls under eighteen in government contract work exceeding $10,000 in value.

Children and Strikes

1828 — The first children's strike took place in the summer of 1828 in Paterson, New Jersey, when child workers, including a large number of girls, marched out of the cotton mills after the mill owners tried to change their dinner hour from 12 to 1. "The children would not stand for it," said one observer, "for fear if they assented to this, the next thing would be to deprive them of eating at all." Parents supported their children, and joined by carpenters, masons, and machinists, the children extended their demands to include a ten-hour day. The militia was called out and the strike ended when the owners reestablished the 12 o'clock dinner hour.

October 1890 — During a Knights of Labor shoe workers' strike, school-children gathered around struck factories and threw rocks at windows and doors. This happened in Lynn, Massachusetts, where working-class children identified with the labor struggle from an early age. The police were called in to protect the property.

July 4–19, 1903 — The first march of children on strike to publicize the conditions of child labor and the inadequate enforcement of a state law prohibiting children under ten from working was led by Mother Jones. The children marched from Philadelphia to Oyster Bay, New York, to seek the support of President Theodore Roosevelt. The immediate issue was a strike of more than seventy-five thousand textile workers, under the leadership of the United Textile Workers, of whom about ten thousand were little children. President Roosevelt refused to see Mother Jones or any of the child marchers, and the strike was lost. However, the publicity forced Pennsylvania to enact an effective child labor law.

November 18, 1903 — The first strike by schoolchildren against a teacher occurred when students of Miss Ida Stodder of the Hendriks School in Chicago staged a strike to protest their teacher's use of a streetcar during a strike by streetcar workers. As reported in *The New York Times* (November 19, 1903): "A number of the boy pupils in Miss Stodder's class in the eighth grade revolted to-day. They took their stand near the school gate shortly before 9 o'clock, and tried to induce other members of the class to remain out of school." The *Times'* head read: "School-boys in Strike. Teacher Who Rode on City Railway Car Caused Trouble."

February 10, 1912 — This date marked the first removal of children of strikers to the homes of sympathizers during a strike in the United States. One hundred and nineteen children were taken from Lawrence, Massachusetts, during the IWW strike there, to the homes of sympathetic families in New York City.

December 24, 1913 — The first Christmas Eve tragedy during a strike occurred when seventy-two persons, most of them children, lost their lives in a fire in Calumet, Michigan, during a Christmas party given by the Women's Auxiliary of the Western Federation of Miners, which was conducting a strike against the copper companies. The children panicked when a person, said to be a sheriff's deputy, shouted "Fire!"

1926 — Groups of two to three hundred children of textile workers in Passaic, New Jersey, paraded the town streets to publicize strikers' demands and to call for public support of their parents' struggle.

1928 — Children played an important role in the textile strike in New Bedford, Massachusetts, when they formed clubs composed of boys and girls from five or six years old to ten or twelve to help the strikers. "Children are rapidly becoming an important element in the strike here," the New Bedford *Evening Standard* observed on May 2, 1928.

May 1933 — For the first time, the wife of a governor marched as a picket during a strike. Mrs. Gifford Pinchot of Pennsylvania won nationwide fame for marching regularly on the picket line during the "children's strike" in Allentown, Pennsylvania. The strike, part of the Amalgamated Clothing Workers' campaign to organize the cotton garment industry (mainly shirts), was won.

Children and Unions

November 27, 1894 — The first union of newsboys, the Seattle Newsboys Union, was founded.

April 1915 — The first organizations of boys and girls to aid trade unions, the Blue Cross Leagues, were formed in several eastern cities. Every child in the leagues subscribed to the following statement (*The New York Times,* April 13, 1915):

> I believe in unionism —
> Because the union helps my father to get higher wages and to work shorter hours, and these help him to provide a more comfortable home for my mother, my brothers and sisters and for me.
> Because the union wants all children to be kept in school and at play, and not to be driven to sweatshops and factories during school age.
> Because the union helps to get fair treatment, and I believe in fairness in play, work, wages and in everything.
> Because when I grow up, if I am a wage-earner, I intend to become a member of a union.

Church and Labor

September 1884 — The first condemnation of an American labor organization by the Holy See in Rome was issued against the Knights of Labor: "On account of the principles, organization, and statutes of the Knights of Labor association, that association is to be relegated among those which are prohibited by the Holy See. . . ." Every Catholic priest in North America was directed to dissuade his parishioners from belonging to the organization. The condemnation lasted until 1889, when the Holy office changed it to "conditional toleration."

April 28, 1886 — On this date came the first order from a Catholic bishop forbidding Catholics to join the Knights of Labor. Archbishop Tascheau of Montreal issued a mandament to be read in all Catholic churches: "We believe it our duty to remind you, dear brethren, that the church forbids any one to enroll himself in any Masonic society under the pain of excommunication." The archbishop declared further: "Under the pretext of protecting the poor workingmen against the rich and powerful who would oppress them, the heads and instigators of these societies seek to get rich and raise themselves in the world at the expense of these unfortunate and oftentimes too credulous workingmen."

November 1886 — Father Edward McGlynn became the first Catholic priest to be suspended for labor activities. Archbishop Corrigan suspended Father McGlynn for supporting Henry George, the candidate of the United Labor party, for mayor of New York City.

September 6, 1891 — The first prolabor church organization, the Church Association for the Advancement of the Interests of Labor, was founded in New York City.

April 6, 1905 — In the first move to bar clerical delegates from a central labor union, the socialists opposed two fraternal delegates from the Presbyterian Ministers Association to the Central Federated Union of New York City. Their objection was sustained.

April 1919 — Reverend A.J. Muste entered the labor movement during the textile strike for an eight-hour day in Lawrence, Massachusetts. Muste established the Amalgamated Textile Workers, an independent union modeled after the Amalgamated Clothing Workers.

Citizens' Alliances

1880 — The first "citizens' alliance" (antiunion organization of businessmen) was formed. It was called the Committee of Five Hundred of Leadville, Colorado.

April 1904 — The first statewide organization of antiunion citizens' alliances, the California Citizens' Alliance, made its major objective a campaign against union-labeled goods.

City Central Labor Unions

1827 — The first city federation of labor organizations was formed. The Mechanics Union of Trade Associations of Philadelphia was the first coordinated movement by several trades. Its objectives were "to avert . . . the desolating evils which must inevitably arise from a depreciaiton of the intrinsic value of human labor; . . . to raise the mechanical and productive classes to that condition of true independence and equality. . . ." The union only lasted until late 1828.

August 14, 1833 — The first citywide federation of unions in the 1830s, the New York General Trades' Union, was founded with Ely Moore as president.

April 1850 — The Central Committee of United Trades of New York City, the first central labor organization of German workers was founded by Wilhelm Weitling.

March 1863 — The first city central labor body of the Civil War period was created: the Trades' Assembly of Rochester, New York.

1863 — This year saw the first city central labor body on the Pacific Coast: the San Francisco Trades' Assembly.

April 16, 1882 — The first declaration of principles to be adopted by a city central labor body in the 1880s was issued by the Trades and Central Labor Union of New York City. The union's declaration asserted that since labor created all wealth, laborers were entitled to their full share of that wealth. It called for the adoption of the eight-hour workday; the prohibition of the employment of children under fourteen in workshops, mines, and so forth; the abolition of the contract system for public works; the abolition of the convict labor system; the requirement that manufacturers pay their workers in cash; the passage of a law giving workmen a first lien on their work for full wages; equal pay for equal work for both sexes; the creation of a bureau of labor statistics; sanitary inspection of mines, factories, and so on; the repeal of the conspiracy law; and a circulating medium of exchange issued directly to the people, without the intervention of banking corporations.

March 1883 — On March 25, 1883, the Central Labor Union of Greater New York and Vicinity became the first city central labor union to hold a memorial meeting for a socialist leader. The meeting was held at Cooper Union to honor Karl Marx, the father of scientific socialism, who had died on March 14. Beginning on March 16, the American flag atop the Brooklyn Labor Lyceum flew at half-mast in Marx's honor.

1888 — The United Hebrew Trades of New York City became the first central labor organization of Jewish workers.

March 1912 — The molders' union of Lawrence, Massachusetts, became the first AFL local to withdraw its delegate from a central labor union. The molders took this step in reaction to the charge made by John Golden, president of the United Textile Workers (AFL), that the IWW strike in Lawrence was a "revolution."

Civil Rights Act

June 1964 — For the first time, a civil rights act prohibited discrimination by both employers and unions. Title VII of the Civil Rights Act of 1964 forbade employers and unions with more than one hundred workers to discriminate in employment, membership, apprenticeship, or promotion "against any individual because of his race, color, religion, sex, or national origin."

Civil Rights Department

November 9, 1976 —The first civil rights department on a national level was established by the International Association of Machinists. It was financed by membership dues. The significance of the department lies in the fact that the IAM was one of the last industrial unions to retain a "whites only" clause in its constitution, which it did until 1950.

Closed Shop

1794 —The first closed shop was established when Philadelphia cordwainers compelled their employers to hire only union members.

1805 —The first labor organization to insert a closed-shop clause in its contract was the Journeymen Cordwainers' Union in New York City.

April 1850 —The United Society of Cordwainers of New York City became the first union to establish a fully closed shop.

1866 —Sixty years after the cordwainers' action in New York, the Iron

Molders' International Union became the first union to establish a closed shop in most of its industry.

June 21, 1912 —The Illinois Supreme Court became the first state supreme court to uphold the constitutionality of the closed shop.

1947 —Congress made the closed shop illegal with the Taft-Hartley Act.

Collective Bargaining

1792 —Collective bargaining was first used by an organization of Philadelphia cordwainers.

1799 —In the first successful use of collective bargaining, the Federal Society of Journeymen Cordwainers obtained a contract in Philadelphia.

1809 —The first clear-cut case of collective bargaining in the printing industry occurred when journeymen printers of New York City drew up a price list and submitted it to their employers for negotiation.

1912 —The Lloyd-LaFollette Act, the first federal legislation permitting federal employees to unionize and bargain collectively, was passed by Congress.

1923 —For the first time, the U.S. Supreme Court held a collective bargaining agreement illegal under the Sherman Anti-Trust Act. The court declared the agreement between the Chicago mill-work manufacturers and the Carpenters' Union unconstitutional.

1935 — The first national labor relations act, the Wagner Act, was passed. The Wagner Act was also the first federal labor legislation to protect the rights of workers to organize and to elect their representatives for collective bargaining. It has been called the "Magna Charta of the U.S. Labor Movement."

In 1976, roughly 150,000 collective-bargaining agreements were in force in the United States, and about 147,000 of these had been negotiated without a work stoppage or strike taking place.

Communist

1851 — Joseph Weydemeyer, who had been in close contact with Karl Marx in Europe, was the first communist leader to arrive in the United States. In 1852 Weydemeyer started the first communist paper in the United States, *Die Revolution.* It was succeeded a year later by *Die Reform.*

October 1857 — The first American communist club was formed in New York City. Its constitution required all members to "recognize the complete equality of all men — no matter of what color or sex."

May 16, 1937 — The first communist to be elected president of an international union, Ben Gold, was unanimously elected by the International Fur Workers Union at its eleventh biennial convention in Toronto.

Company Stores

1874 — The first anti-company store legislation was passed in Pennsylvania.

January 14, 1880 — The first strike caused by a company's attempt to get rid of unmarried miners took place when Consolidated Mining Company of Ohio discharged forty single men and the other miners struck to have them reinstated. The reason given by the operators for discharging single men was that they did not buy as much from the company store as did men with families to support.

September 10, 1897 — The first strike against a company store that aroused national attention was organized by miners at Hazelton and Lattimer, Pennsylvania, who marched along the highways to visit mines and persuade other miners to join them. Their action led to the "Lattimer Massacre," the cold-blooded murder of miners by a sheriff and one hundred armed deputies. Nineteen miners were killed and thirty-five wounded, most of them shot in the back while running from the armed lawmen.

Company Unions

1894 — The first factory club designed to prevent workers from joining a union was started by Western Electric Company in Chicago.

1901 — The first company union was created by the Nernst Lamp Company of Pittsburgh.

July 1913 — The Mitten Plan of the Philadelphia Rapid Transit Company established the first fully developed company union. Grievances were to be settled by a board of arbitration, but it was stipulated that there was to be no union involvement in the procedure. A Co-operative Welfare Association was set up to pay out death benefits, sick benefits, and pensions to employees over sixty-five. Dues were $1 a month, but the plan was financed largely by the company.

September 1915 — With the Colorado Industrial Plan, also known as the Rockefeller Employee Representation Plan, the first company union was established in the coal mining industry. The plan was prepared by Mackenzie King, who later became the premier of Canada, for the Colorado Fuel and Iron Company.

August 1916 — The first company union was established in New York City: the Brotherhood of Interborough Rapid Transit Company Employees.

1918 — The first company union at the Standard Oil Company was set up by Jersey Standard in Bayonne, New Jersey.

June 5, 1919 — The company union plan drawn up by Mackenzie King for the Standard Oil Company of Indiana was introduced.

1933 — The first free election at the Colorado Fuel and Iron Company took place under the auspices of the National Labor Board. It resulted in a victory for the United Mine Workers by a vote of 877 to 273.

Congress

1834 — Labor's first congressman — Ely Moore (1798– 1861), printer, founder and first president of the General Trades Union of New York City (1833– 1836), founder of the National Trades Union (1834– 1836), and political editor of the New York *Evening Post* — was elected as a Democrat and served in Congress from 1835 to 1839.

1867 — The first federal recognition of the importance of labor came when the House of Representatives created a standing committee on labor.

1878 — The first congressional committee to look into the causes of a general depression of business activity and its effect on labor, and to devise and propose measures for relief, was created by the Forty-fifth Congress. Abram S. Hewitt was the committee's chairman.

1878 — The first labor congressman to be elected after the Civil War was

Thomas March of Rockland, Maine, secretary of the National Granite Cutters' Union.

1882 — The first labor congressman of the 1880s — Martin A. Foran (1844–1921), a cooper who had organized the Coopers' International Union and was its first president (1872) — was elected and served from 1883 to 1889. Foran was also the first labor novelist: the initial installment of *The Other Side,* the first labor novel written in the United States, appeared in the September 28, 1872, issue of the *Workingman's Advocate* of Chicago.

November 1910 — For the first time, several trade unionists were elected to Congress in the same year: eleven Democrats, three Republicans, and one Socialist, Victor Berger of Milwaukee. Berger was the first Socialist ever to be elected to Congress.

November 1910 — A trade unionist member of Congress was appointed chairman of the House Labor Committee for the first time. This was William B. Wilson, who had been international secretary-treasurer of the United Mine Workers when he was elected as a Democrat to Congress.

March 23,1936 — Philip LaFollette, senator from Wisconsin, introduced a resolution into Congress "to make an investigation of violations of the rights of free speech and assembly and undue interference with the right of labor to organize and bargain collectively." This resolution led to the LaFollette Committee investigation that exposed widespread antilabor activities on the part of business, including violence, to discourage workers from joining unions of their own choosing.

June 25, 1943 — The Smith-Connolly Bill, the first antilabor measure to pass Congress in more than a generation, became law over President Roosevelt's veto. It gave the president the authority to take over any plant producing war materiel if its operation was threatened by a labor dispute. The law also prohibited labor unions from contributing to candidates running in national elections.

Conspiracy Cases

November 1, 1805 — A Philadelphia grand jury indicted eight members of the Philadelphia Journeymen Cordwainers' Society on charges of combining and conspiring to raise wages. The workers appealed to the public to uphold their right to combine, and to join them in resisting the establishment of a precedent that would be dangerous to all democratic movements: "Under whatever pretences the thing is done, the name of freedom is but a shadow . . . if we are to be torn from our friends for endeavouring to obtain a fair and just support for our families, and if we are to be treated as felons and murderers only for asserting the right to take or refuse whatever we deem an adequate reward for our labor." The jury set the precedent anyway, declaring the workers "guilty of a combination to raise wages." They were fined $8 plus costs.

1821 —The first legal action against masters for conspiracy was taken when the employers of makers of ladies' shoes were indicted for conspiring to reduce wages. In this case, *Commonwealth v. Carlisle*, the employers were acquitted.

June 1836 —William Cullen Bryant and John Greenleaf Whittier became the first American poets to support trade unions when they defended the New York Journeymen Tailors convicted of conspiracy and excoriated by Judge Edwards as "foreigners" who were introducing foreign ideas into the United States.

1842 —In a case decided in Massachusetts, a court asserted for the first time that workers had a legal right to organize and that such organization was not a criminal conspiracy. *Commonwealth v. Hunt* grew out of a citywide strike in Boston in November 1839, called by the Boston Journeymen's Bootmakers' Society to prevent employers from hiring bootmakers who would not join the society. Seven of the union leaders were indicted and charged with malicious intent to destroy the plaintiff's business. The constitution of the Boston Journeymen's Bootmakers' Society was introduced in court as evidence that the society's regulations amounted to a conspiracy, even though the regulations had never been fully enforced. When the case came before the Supreme Judicial Court of the state of Massachusetts, Chief Justice Lemuel Shaw reversed the lower court and ruled that associations may be entered into "that may have a tendency to impoverish another, that is, to diminish his gains and profits, and yet so far from being criminal and unlawful, the object may be highly meritorious and public spirited." Shaw concluded: "The legality of such an association will therefore depend upon the means to be used for its accomplishment. If it is carried into effect by fair or honorable and lawful means, it is to say the least, innocent; if by falsehood or by force, it may be stamped with the character of conspiracy."

Contract Labor

July 1864 —The first act of Congress approving a contract labor system and establishing the American Emigrant Company for the purpose of importing contract labor was passed.

February 2, 1885 —Congress passed the first law prohibiting the importation of contract labor. It resulted from lobbying by the Knights of Labor.

Convict Labor

1642 —The first convict labor law was passed in Colonial America, in Virginia.

1823 — The first public protest by labor against the competition of prison-made goods was made in New York City.

April 1891 — The first strike against contract prison labor took place when miners of Coal Creek struck the Tennessee Coal and Mining Company. This strike led eventually to the abolishment of the company's contract for prison labor.

Cooperatives

1827 — The first cooperative store organized by trade unionists, the Labour for Labour Association of Philadelphia, began to operate three barter stores dealing in general merchandise.

October 6, 1845 — Boston mechanics established the Working Men's Protective Union, the first of more than eight hundred protective unions in the United States and Canada, to create consumer cooperatives for groceries, fuel, and other goods.

Winter 1847–1848 — The first important producers' cooperative store, the Journeymen Molders' Union Foundry, a stove and hollow foundry, was established by Cincinnati iron molders. It' failed.

December 1863 — The first cooperative department store set up by a trade union for union members, the Workingmen's

Emporium, was established by the Troy (New York) Trades Assembly.

February 12, 1866 — Black ship caulkers of Baltimore founded the first black cooperative, the Chesapeake and Dry Dock Company. Isaac Myers was named president.

1866 — The first cooperative foundry was established by the Iron Molders' International Union. The Troy Cooperative Iron-Founders' Association proved successful.

1869 — The first cooperative formed by striking women workers, a laundry in Troy, New York, was established by members of the Troy Collar Laundry Union who were on strike for wage increases. Kate Mullaney was president of both the union and the Troy Cooperative Collar Company, which failed.

1874 — The first regional labor cooperative movement, the Order of Sovereigns of Industry, was organized throughout New England.

1886 — The Richmond Soap Factory, the first integrated cooperative, was established by black and white Knights of Labor in Richmond, Virginia.

Corruption

September 1903 — Sam Parks of the Housesmiths' Union in New York City became the first union leader to be imprisoned for corruption. Parks, whose union was a local of the International Association of Bridge and Structural Iron Workers, was found guilty of taking payoffs from employers and other forms of graft, and was sentenced to five years in jail.

Cost-of-Living

1948 — The first union contract that contained an "escalator clause" tied to the U.S. Bureau of Labor Statistics' cost-of-living index was won by the United Automobile Workers from the General Motors Corporation.

Criminal Prosecutions

1677 — The first criminal prosecution of strikers followed the refusal of New York cartmen to remove dirt from the streets for 3 pence a load.

September 30, 1892 — On this date occurred the first prosecution of strike leaders for the crime of treason. Henry C. Frick, chairman of the Carnegie Steel Company, swore out a warrant before the chief justice of the Pennsylvania Supreme Court for the arrest of the entire advisory board of the striking steel union at the Carnegie plant in Homestead for treason against the state. Twenty-nine strike leaders were charged with plotting "to incite insurrection, rebellion and war against the . . . Commonwealth of Pennsylvania. . . ."

December 23, 1908 — For the first time, top leaders of the AFL were sentenced to prison. Judge Daniel T. Wright found Samuel Gompers, John Mitchell, and Frank Morrison guilty of contempt for refusing to abide by court injunctions issued in the Bucks' Stove and Range Company case involving the "We Don't Patronize" list published in the *American Federationist*. Gompers was sentenced to twelve months in prison, Mitchell to nine months, and Morrison to six months. The sentences were later lifted by the U.S. Supreme Court on a technicality.

October 1, 1910 — Dynamiting became a nationwide issue in a labor struggle for the first time when the *Los Angeles Times* building, which housed the open-shop *Times* (owned by a leading open-shop employer, General Harrison Gray Otis), was blow up. Twenty men were killed and twelve were injured in the explosion. J.M. McNamara, secretary-treasurer of the International Association of Bridge and Structural Iron Workers, along with his brother, J.B., and another man named Ortie McManigal, were arrested and charged with the dynamiting. Under pressure from Clarence Darrow and Lincoln Steffens, the McNamara brothers changed their pleas from innocent to guilty. J.B. was sentenced to life imprisonment and his brother to fifteen years. The McNamaras' guilty plea stunned and shocked the labor movement, which had rallied to their defense.

December 28, 1912 — In an unprecedented case, nearly all the officers of a union were convicted of a crime. Fifty-four officers of the International Association of Bridge and Structural Iron Workers were tried in a federal court in Indianapolis on a charge of conspiracy to transport dynamite and other explosives. Those indicted included the international president, the vice president, and all present and former members of the executive board. Forty men were tried in all, and the jury found thirty-eight of them guilty. International President Frank Ryan was sentenced to seven years in prison.

March 1913 — For the first time, an international president of a union who had been sentenced to prison was reelected. Frank Ryan, of the International Association of Bridge and Iron Structural Workers, was reelected by the union convention after being sentenced to seven years in prison.

August 17, 1918 — Large numbers of unionists were sentenced to federal prison for the first time when one hundred IWW members were found guilty of violating the Espionage Act. Fifteen of these men received twenty years, thirty-five got ten years, and twelve got one year, while one was let off with a reprimand. The fines totaled $2,300,000.

May 1922 — William Buzzard became the first union leader to be tried for treason. Buzzard was the United Mine Workers' leader in the West Virginia coal strike of 1920, which ended with the indictment of 325 miners for treason. Buzzard's trial, which lasted for five weeks, ended in his acquittal. The cases against the other defendants were dismissed.

Criminal Syndicalist Laws

March 14, 1917 — Idaho passed the first state criminal syndicalist law calling for imprisonment of anyone found guilty of sabotage or violence in a labor dispute. The law was directed against the IWW.

December 1918 — At the first "silent defense," forty-three of the forty-six IWW defendants in the Sacramento, California, criminal syndicalist trial, convinced that they could not obtain a fair trial, refused to enter any defense. They were sentenced to from one to ten years in prison.

Culture

1870 — Cigarmakers in Tampa and New York City initiated the reading of poetry and socialist works in the shops. The practice was for one of the cigar workers to read aloud while the others sat in a circle, rolling cigars.

September 28, 1872 — The first installment of *The Other Side,* by Martin A. Foran, president of the Coopers' International Union, was printed in the *Workingman's Advocate* of Chicago. This was the first novel by a trade union leader, and probably the first working-class novel ever published in the United States. *The Other Side,* which came out in book form in 1886, was written to defend labor from an anti-trade union English romance serialized in the literary magazine *Galaxy* — Charles Reade's "Put Yourself in His Place."

January 1979 — The first comprehensive national program undertaken by a U.S. union to bring culture to its members was launched by District 1199 of the National Union of Hospital and Health Care Employees. The $1.3 million two-year program included musical and dramatic performances and art and photographic exhibitions at the union's New York City headquarters and at its sixteen-hundred-family cooperative housing development in the city, and eight dramatic, musical, and poetry programs by both professionals and union members at some thirty hospitals and nursing homes employing District 1199 members. The project was financed by federal and state cultural agencies (there was a $300,000 grant from the National Endowment for the Humanities) and by private foundations and church groups. The program, directed by Moe Foner, executive secretary of District 1199, was named Bread and Roses, a phrase from James Oppenheim's poem, which was written during the Lawrence (Massachusetts) textile workers strike of 1912 when young female mill workers had carried a banner reading: "We want bread and roses, too." No other union has ever tried to involve its members in the arts and humanities on such a massive scale.

Department of Labor

September 1868 — The first resolution calling for the establishment of a federal Department of Labor was introduced by William H. Sylvis at the 1868 convention of the National Labor Union. The resolution was adopted.

March 21, 1888 — The first Department of Labor was created by an act of Congress. The act called for naming a commissioner of labor with a salary of $5,000 a year. Labor's demand for Cabinet status for the department was not incorporated in the act.

1901 — New York became the first state to set up a department of labor.

March 4, 1913 — Cabinet status was first granted to the Department of Labor in an act signed by President William Howard Taft on his last day in office. The act stated: "The purpose of the Department of Labor shall be to foster, promote, and develop the welfare of the wage earners of the United States, to improve their working conditions, and to advance their opportunities for profitable employment." The first secretary of labor, appointed by President Woodrow Wilson, was William B. Wilson, who was the leader of the United Mine Workers and a labor congressman. Wilson served as secretary until 1921.

June 5, 1920 — The first Women's Bureau in the Department of Labor was set up by an act of Congress, which gave the bureau a mandate to "formulate standards and policies which shall promote the welfare of wage-earning women, improve their working conditions, increase their efficiency, and advance their opportunities for profitable employment." The first director was Mary Anderson, who headed the bureau for a quarter of a century.

December 9, 1930 — The first secretary of labor who was not a member of the AFL was sworn into office. William Nuckles Doak, appointed by President Herbert Hoover, was a member of the Brotherhood of Railroad Trainmen.

1933 — Frances Perkins became the first woman secretary of labor and the first woman cabinet officer when she was appointed to office by President Franklin D. Roosevelt.

Departments

July 1908 — The first Metal Trades' Department was established by the AFL.

November 1908 — The first Railway Employees' Department was established by the AFL.

1912 — The first Mining Department was created by the AFL to combine the United Mine Workers and the Western Federation of Miners.

Discrimination

1903 — The first state antidiscrimination law to protect the elderly was passed by Colorado.

July 1944 — The National Maritime Union (CIO) obtained the first contract in the shipping industry that contained an antidiscrimination clause. The contract with 125 ship companies included a clause barring discrimination because of race, creed, or color.

March 12, 1945 — The first state commission to combat discrimination in employment, the New York State Commission Against Discrimination, was established "to formulate policies to eliminate and prevent discrimination in employment because of race, creed, color, or national origin, either by employers, labor organizations, employment agencies or other persons." It consisted offive commissioners, who were appointed on July 1, 1945, with Henry C. Turner as chairman.

Dual Unions

April 1884 — The first major complaint against dual unionism was made by the Cigar Makers' International Union against the Progressive Cigar Makers Union of the Knights of Labor. "Dual unionism" refers to encroachment by a labor organization on the jurisdiction of an existing union.

December 10, 1895 — The first dual labor union center, the Socialist Trades and Labor Alliance, was founded by Daniel De Leon, leader of the Socialist Labor party, with the aim of destroying the AFL. De Leon called on all members of the SLP to withdraw from the AFL unions and to join the STLA.

1908 — The Detroit IWW was organized by Daniel De Leon and his followers after De Leon was rejected as a delegate by the 1908 IWW convention's credentials committee. The Detroit IWW, with headquarters in that city, was composed mainly of De Leon's followers in the Socialist Labor party. In September 1915, at its eighth convention, it changed its name to the Workers' International Industrial Union.

September 1928 — The National Miners Union became the first dual union organized by the Trade Union Educational League. The justification was that the National Miners would organize in areas untouched by the United Mine Workers.

E

Education

1639 — The first tax-supported public school was set up in Dorchester, Massachusetts.

1827 — Labor made its first organized demand for free public education, open to children of all economic classes. The Philadelphia trade unions formed a committee to study the process of education in Pennsylvania, and set about surveying candidates for the state legislature on their views toward "an equal and general system of education." The committee drew up plans for statewide public education supported by taxes and governed by elected school boards in each community school district.

1828 — The Philadelphia trade unions submitted a questionnaire to all candidates for the state legislature asking them where they stood on the matter of "an equal and general system of education."

February 6, 1830 — Labor made its first proposal for compulsory education in an editorial in the *Mechanics' Free Press.*

1830 — The Philadelphia trade union committee issued a report calling for free public schools in every part of the state, to be governed by publicly elected school boards.

1834 — The first national demand for free education by labor came at a national convention of unionists in New York. The delegates called for "an equal, universal, republican system of education."

1834 — Pennsylvania began a system of public education.

1835 — The first society organized to further the cause of working-class education, the Society for the Diffusion of Knowledge Among the Working Classes, was formed in Philadelphia. It published its plan in the *National Laborer.*

1852 — Massachusetts passed the first law requiring school attendance by children. Under its provisions, children between the ages of eight and fourteen were compelled to attend school for at least twelve weeks a year.

1869 — The Knights of Labor became the first labor organization to require its members to learn to write when it stipulated that a member had to be able to write his name in order to obtain entrance to the meeting room.

1899 — A national school for workers was first projected by the General Assembly of the Knights of Labor. The assembly outlined a plan to form "The People's Institute of Civics" under the "jurisdiction and control of the Knights of Labor." At the school, which was to be located in Washington, D.C., young men were to be taught political science, history, oratory, and composition so they might "defend our principles and study the problems of the present and future." The course was to last three years and provision was made for postgraduate work "for the benefit of those who desire to become organizers, speakers, and agitators."

February 1914 — The first commission to study federal aid for vocational education was appointed by President Woodrow Wilson.

1915 — In Chicago, the first school for active workers in the labor movement was set up.

1916 — The AFL first proposed federal support of the public school system.

1916 — The first courses for workers were set up at various locations in New York City called Unity Centers by Dress and Waistmakers Union No. 25 of the International Ladies' Garment Workers' Union. The New York City Board of Education supplied the teachers, and the union paid their salaries. The Unity Centers offered courses in English, the labor movement, and economics, and instituted lectures on health and hygiene. The program eventually led to the formation of the Workers' University.

April 7, 1919 — The Boston Labor Council became the first AFL affiliate to establish a labor college. It opened the Trade Union College because "progress for organized wage-workers can be assured only by social and industrial policies shaped by their own right thinking and . . . their ambitions for self-betterment must therefore include a concern for the higher training of the mind." Among the teachers were Harold J. Laski, the British socialist, and Professor Roscoe Pound, later dean of the Harvard Law School. That same year, the Seattle Labor Council also established a labor college, with Reverend Sidney Strong as educational director. It lasted until 1932.

October 6, 1921 — Brookwood Labor College was founded in Westchester County, New York, under the direction of Reverend A.J. Muste with a board composed of trade union representatives. Its two-year course prepared students for such functions as union organization, labor journalism, compilation of labor statistics, and workers' education. Most of the college's graduates became organizers who spread the message of unionism among unorganized workers. The school came under attack from AFL leaders because of its "radicalism."

1921 — At the first National Workers' Educational Conference, it was reported that twenty-four workers' colleges and schools existed in twenty-two cities.

1921 — The first labor educational organization formed by trade unionists and educators, the Workers' Education Bureau, began to conduct labor classes. The bureau was sponsored by the California Federation of Labor and the University of California.

April 1923 — Commonwealth College, for the education of workers and farmers in the Southwest, was opened. After eighteen years, it was forced to close its doors in 1941. Commonwealth College was organized on a cooperative basis; students shared in manual labor, farm work, and study. The faculty served without salary, taking only the subsistence provided by the products of the school's labor and by small bequests. The college was under constant attack for alleged radicalism.

December 1928 — The first Commission on Workers' Education was formed by the AFL to investigate left-wing influence in the Workers' Education Bureau and Brookwood Labor College.

July 1930 — The first member of organized labor who was elected to a board of education in the South was Raymond E. Thomason, secretary of the Brotherhood of Railway Clerks. Thomason was elected to the board of education of Jefferson County (Birmingham), Alabama, on a platform calling for elimination of the requirement that pupils unable to pay fees be denied their diplomas until their parents took a "pauper's oath." Thomason took the position that schools were public institutions, and that no one should be forced to declare himself a pauper in order to educate his children. He was elected by a nearly two-to-one majority over his nearest rival.

1932 — Highlander Folk School was begun by Myles Horton and Don West in Tennessee to conduct workers' education. It provided native leadership for the southern trade union movement and for organizational work among the farmers.

1933 — An AFL convention proposed that the federal government provide 50 percent of the funds needed to maintain the free public school system. "We cannot simply sit by and watch the passing of the free public school," the convention declared. "The nation's responsibility is clearly set out. . . . Federal aid in education is not federal control."

Elections

November 7, 1829 — Ebenezer Ford, president of the Carpenters' Union, became the first labor union member elected to public office. He polled 6,166 votes when he ran for the New York State Assembly as a candidate of the New York Working Men's party.

1830 — The first member of Congress elected as a result of labor's support was Stephen Simpson, candidate of the Working Men's party of Philadelphia.

1834 — The first labor congressman, Ely Moore, president of the General Trades Union of New York City, was elected.

November 1836 — William English, president of the Philadelphia Trades' Union, became the first labor representative elected to the Pennsylvania legislature.

Employers' Liability

1856 — Georgia enacted the first employers' liability law. It applied only to railroad workers.

1902 — New York passed the first full employers' liability law.

1906 — Congress passed the first federal employers' liability law. It was soon declared unconstitutional.

1908 — A revised federal employers' liability law, designed to correct the problems that had led to the 1906 law's being declared unconstitutional, was passed. This was the first federal employers' liability law to be upheld.

Employers' Offensive

July 1863 — In the first widespread antilabor offensive, employers formed associations in major northern and western cities to destroy unions and break strikes.

May 3, 1866 — The event that precipitated the Haymarket tragedy of 1886 took place when fourteen hundred locked-out workers at the McCormick Harvester factory in Chicago, members of Labor Assembly 582 of the Knights of Labor who were striking for an eight-hour day and a $2 daily wage, combated both scabs and police. Four workers were killed, and a protest meeting was called for Haymarket Square on May 4.

May 5, 1886 — The first nationwide employers' offensive against the labor movement was organized after a bomb explosion at the Haymarket Square meeting, which killed six policemen. Trade unions and the eight-hour movement were attacked as "anarchistic," and unionists as "dynamiters."

1900 — The first citywide antiunion employers' association was founded in Dayton, Ohio. Thirty-eight firms became charter members.

Employment Offices

1834 — The first private employment office was set up in New York City.

1890 — Ohio established the first permanent public exchanges to provide job information. The exchange constituted the first state employment service.

1894 — The first municipal employment service was created in Seattle, Washington.

July 18, 1896 — New York City set up the first free employment bureau.

1907 — The first U.S. employment service was established under the Bureau of Immigration.

1911 — Massachusetts established the first free state employment bureau. Actually, three bureaus were set up, in Boston, Springfield, and Fall River.

1918 — The U.S. Employment Service, the first government organization to provide job information for men and women, was created within the Department of Labor. It was disbanded after World War I.

February 24, 1931 — The first congressional act to establish a U.S. Employment Service in the Department of Labor was passed. The purpose of the service was to publish information on employment opportunities. President Hoover vetoed the act on March 7.

June 6, 1933 — The Wagner-Peyser Act finally established the first national employment service, the U.S. Employment Service, as a division of the Department of Labor. The act provided for matching federal funds with state funds if a state would operate public employment offices. It also created the basis for the present public employment service system under the Department of Labor.

Equal Pay for Equal Work

1866 — The first labor group to come out for equal pay for equal work for men and women alike was the National Labor Union.

November 24, 1942 — For the first time, the federal government upheld the principle of equal pay for equal work when the War Labor Board adopted an official policy of equal pay for equal work for men and women.

1953 — The federal Equal Rights Act, mandating equal pay for equal work for men and women, was passed.

July 5–15, 1981 — In the nation's first strike for equal pay for comparable work, municipal employees in San Jose, California (known as the "feminist capital" of the United States because a majority of City Council members are women and the mayor is a woman), struck for equal pay for women performing jobs comparable to those held by men. The strikers (most of whom were women) demanded an end to the classification of certain jobs as "women's jobs" — with substantially lower pay than many "men's jobs" that required no more (and sometimes less) skill and education — and pay based on job evaluation. The strikers made two specific demands: a general 10 percent raise and a $3.2 million fund to be used over a four-year period to adjust municipal workers' pay scales so that those holding jobs of comparable value would receive approximately equal pay. The strike ended after a ten-day struggle with the municipal workers winning a two-year contract that narrowed the wage gap between male and female workers.

Equal Rights Amendment

February 1923 — The Senate Judiciary Committee held the first congressional hearings on the Lucretia Mott or Equal Rights Amendment, which was sponsored by the National Woman's party. The amendment read: "No political, civil or legal disabilities or inequalities on account of sex nor on account of marriage, unless applying equally to both sexes, shall exist within the United States or any territory thereof." The ERA was opposed by nearly all labor organizations on the ground that it would destroy all protective labor legislation in favor of women workers.

1976–1977 — For the first time labor organizations, including the AFL-CIO, came out in favor of the Equal Rights Amendment. A Labor Committee for ERA, representing fifteen national unions, worked with ERAmerica, a national organization set up to spearhead the campaign for ratification of the amendment, as did the AFL-CIO itself.

Expulsions

July 16, 1922 — In the AFL's first expulsion of a union for association with the Trade Union Educational League, the Bookkeepers', Stenographers', and Accountants' Union No. 12646 of New York City had its charter revoked.

March 2, 1927 — For the first time, the AFL expelled the majority of a union, dissolved it and its locals, and put the union into receivership. It expelled thirty-seven officers of the Joint Board of the Fur Workers Union in New York City — the left-wing leadership headed by Ben Gold — dissolved the New York Joint Board and its locals, and ordered all union property turned over to a newly set up Joint Council. The AFL cited as the reason for its action "communist domination" of the Joint Board.

August 4, 1936 — In its first ultimatum to unions associated with the CIO, the AFL Executive Council gave the unions until September 5 to sever their connections with the CIO. When the unions did not comply with the order, they were automatically suspended. In November 1936, the Tampa convention of the AFL sustained the Executive Council's suspension order by a vote of 21,679 to 2,043. The suspended CIO unions were not present at the convention to vote.

October 1937 — The Denver convention of the AFL authorized the Executive Council to revoke the charters of all CIO unions at its discretion. The vote was 25,616 to 1,227.

January 1938 — The AFL Executive Council revoked the charters of three CIO unions. Three months later, four others had their charters revoked.

November 15, 1946 — The CIO Executive Board gave President Philip Murray the authority for the first time to take over the funds and property of local and state Industrial Union Councils that failed to conform to CIO policy as Murray interpreted it.

November 1949 — The CIO issued its first expulsion orders aimed at international unions. Eleven international unions, with almost one million members, were expelled on the ground that they adhered to the policies of the Communist party. The unions expelled were the United Electrical, Radio, and Machine Workers (UE); the International Fur and Leather Workers Union; the International Union of Mine, Mill, and Smelter Workers; the International Longshoremen's and Warehousemen's Union; the United Farm Equipment Workers; the Food, Tobacco, and Agricultural Workers; the United Office and Professional Workers; the United Public Workers; the American Communications Association; the National Union of Marine Cooks and Stewards; and the International Fishermen and Allied Workers.

F

Factory Inspection

April 30, 1879 — The first factory inspection law was enacted in Massachusetts. It directed the governor to appoint two or more of the district police to act as inspectors of factories and public buildings.

Factory Workers

October 1834 — Labor's first demand for regulation of factory labor, "Address to the Workingmen of Massachusetts," was issued by the convention of the New England Association of Farmers, Mechanics, and Other Working Men.

December 1836 — In the first effort to establish a national union of factory workers, the Cotton and Woolen Spinners' Society of Philadelphia issued a call to "Factory Workers in General Throughout the United States." The attempt failed.

Fair Employment Practices Committee

1942 — The first Fair Employment Practices Committee to be established by the U.S. government was directed to eliminate discrimination in war industries based on race, creed, or national origin. The committee was created by President Franklin D. Roosevelt to head off a March on Washington that was being organized under the leadership of A. Philip Randolph to protest discrimination against blacks.

Fair Practices Clause

1950 — The first fair practices clause banning discrimination by religion, race, or marital status was included in a national contract. After twelve years of struggle, the United Electrical, Radio, and Machine Workers of America (UE) finally won agreement to such a clause in its contract with General Electric.

Farmer-Labor Party

1830 — The first farmer-labor parties were established: the Farmer and Mechanics' Party of Salina, New York, and the Farmer and Mechanics' Party of Albany, New York. The emblem of the Albany party was an arm and hammer superimposed on a plow.

November 1834 —The first Labor-Populist ticket was put up in Illinois.

July 11, 1920 —The first farmer-labor party of the twentieth century, the Farmer-Labor party, nominated Parley Christensen of Utah for president. He received 300,000 votes.

July 4, 1924 —For the first time, the AFL Executive Council endorsed a farmer-labor party: the La Follette-Wheeler national ticket of the Progressive (Farmer-Labor) party. This was also the first year that the railroad brotherhoods endorsed a farmer-labor party.

Federal Troops and Labor Disputes

1779 —The first use of federal troops in a strike came when 150 mariners at the port of Philadelphia struck for higher wages. The government of the Confederation used federal troops to back up state authorities, who had the leaders of the strike arraigned before the magistrates.

January 29, 1834 —President Andrew Jackson ordered the first use of federal troops during a strike. At the request of the Maryland legislature, he dispatched troops to end a labor disturbance among workers on the Chesapeake and Ohio Canal.

April, 1864 —The first U.S. Army order prohibiting unionization of workers, General Order No. 65, was issued by Major General William Rosecrans in St. Louis.

July 1864 —The U.S. Army first assigned soldiers to take over strikers' jobs when Major General William Rosecrans dispatched troops to replace striking printers at St. Louis newspapers.

July 16–30, 1877 —This date marks the first use of federal troops against a strike in more than one state. In response to requests from several governors, including those of West Virginia, Maryland, and Pennsylvania, President Rutherford B. Hayes called out federal troops during the great railroad strike. The strike was crushed by the soldiers, state militia, and local police. Over one hundred workers were killed.

1892 —A "bull pen" or stockade was first used by the U.S. Army to imprison union men during a strike: during the Coeur d'Alene strike by the western miners.

July 5, 1894 —John Peter Altgeld became the first governor to protest the sending of federal troops by a president of the United States during a strike. In a telegram to President Grover Cleveland, the Illinois governor protested that neither he nor the legislature had applied for federal troops in the Pullman strike, and charged that newspaper accounts of violence by strikers preventing the trains from operating were "pure fabrications."

June 1904 — The first deportation of union members during a strike came when twenty-seven members of the Western Federation of Miners were forcibly removed from Cripple Creek to Colorado Springs by the U.S. Army, sheriffs, and militia. The men were instructed not to return to their homes. On June 10, General Sherman Bell deported seventy-nine men to Kansas and ordered them never to return to Colorado.

December 1907 — A federal commission condemned the sending of federal troops on a strike-breaking mission for the first time after President Theodore Roosevelt dispatched troops to Goldfield, Nevada, to break the IWW strike there.

December 1914 — For the first time, federal troops were used to prohibit the importation of strikebreakers from other states when President Wilson sent soldiers to Colorado during the United Mine Workers' strike against the Colorado Fuel and Iron Company.

December 1943 — Federal troops were used for the first time to put down a "hate strike." The strike took place at the Point Breeze, New York, plant of the Western Electric Company over a demand by white workers for separate toilet facilities. The United Electrical, Radio, and Machine Workers (UE), with the endorsement of the CIO Industrial Union Council, urged the strikers to return to work, and when they refused, called upon President Roosevelt to intervene on the ground that the race issue was being exploited "in the interests of the nation's enemies." Roosevelt ordered the army to take over the plant, and the strikers returned to work.

April 26, 1944 — For the first time, a president of a company was forcibly removed from his office by troops for refusing to obey an order of the War Labor Board to recognize a union of his employees. President Roosevelt ordered the seizure of Montgomery Ward in Chicago and the bodily removal from the building of company president Sewell Avery.

Foreign Governments

October 13, 1897 — For the first time, a foreign government charged that its nationals' rights had been violated in a labor struggle in the United States. The Austrian minister in Washington complained to the State Department that the rights of Austrian subjects had been violated in the massacre of peaceful miners at Lattimer, Pennsylvania. The Austrian government demanded indemnity for the families of the Hungarian strikers killed, but the demand was rejected by the State Department: "To reward the wounded living and the heirs of those slain . . . would be offering a premium to lawlessness and inviting renewed outbreaks and riots. This Government is therefore unable to admit the justice of the claim."

August 1909 — In the first complaint by a foreign government that its nationals were being mistreated in U.S. industrial plants, Austria's vice-consul protested the peonage imposed on Austro-Hungarians who had been brought to McKees Rocks, Pennsylvania, under misrepresentation, and then forcibly detained against their will in a plant there after they learned they were being used as strikebreakers during a strike led by the IWW against the Pressed Steel Car Company.

Fourth of July

July 4, 1865 — This was the first labor celebration of the Fourth of July in which all U.S. workers enjoyed freedom, as a result of the abolition of slavery by the Thirteenth Amendment.

July 4, 1897 — The first Fourth of July general strike in an industry occurred with the general stoppage by bituminous coal miners, who were members of the United Mine Workers. One hundred thousand miners went out on this strike, which ended in victory for the union everywhere but in West Virginia.

July 4, 1934 — The first Fourth of July parade to demonstrate labor-farmer solidarity marched in Minneapolis. The strikers and farmers paraded in the city to support a strike by Local 574.

Free Speech Fights

August 1906 — The first IWW free speech fight occurred in Toronto, Canada, after the banning of street-corner meetings.

September 30, 1909 — The first notice appeared in the *Industrial Worker* of an IWW free speech fight. It appealed to all IWW members to join the free speech fighters in Missoula, Montana.

March 5, 1910 — Spokane, Washington, was the site of the first agreement between city officials and IWW free speech fighters ending a free speech fight. On March 9, the City Council repealed the law banning street speaking.

February 11, 1912 —The first use of a boat to address workers on shore after street meetings had been banned was made during the IWW free speech fight in Vancouver, Canada.

G

Gangsters

April 24, 1933 — The left-wing Joint Board of the Fur Workers' Union smashed a takeover attempt by the Lepke-Gurrah mob, which had already seized control of locals of the ILGWU and of entire sections of the garment industry. In this first successful union effort to beat back a gangster takeover, the rank-and-file fur workers battled gangsters and left them helpless on the streets of the fur market district in New York.

October 27–30, 1936 — Irving Potash and Sam Burt of the left-wing fur workers' union became the first trade unionists to testify against gangsters. For three days in court they exposed the Lepke-Gurrah gang in the fur industry. Their testimony put Lepke and Gurrah behind prison bars, and helped to smash the Lepke-Gurrah rackets.

General Strike

June 1835 — The first general strike in American history took place in Philadelphia. The issue was the ten-hour day. The strike, which was successful, began with city employees and spread to other

trades. This was also the first strike by public employees.

February 1846 — The first plan for a general strike for the ten-hour day was advanced by John C. Cluer. He based his plan on British labor experience and called for a general strike on July 4, 1846, to signal the Second Independence Day. The strike did not materialize.

November 1892 — New Orleans witnessed the first general strike of unions affiliated with the AFL. It lasted four days and the basic issue was the preferential union shop. Though the strikers did not win their demand, they did achieve an agreement that stipulated there would be "no discrimination against union men." This was the first general strike in which white and black workers participated.

May 16, 1903 — The first general strike in the Rocky Mountain area took place when eight thousand workers in thirty-seven organized trades struck in Denver, Colorado.

June 1905 — The first discussion of a nationwide general strike at a labor convention took place when Lucy

Parsons, the widow of Haymarket martyr Albert R. Parsons, proposed the idea at the founding convention of the IWW. The idea was endorsed by the Industrial Workers' Club of Chicago, but was not adopted by the convention.

March 4, 1910 —The first general strike of the twentieth century in an American city was called by the Central Labor Union of Philadelphia in support of a strike by the Amalgamated Association of Street Car Employees against the Philadelphia Transit Company. Within a week, 146,000 workers were out. The strike ended in defeat on March 27.

March 15, 1910 —For the first time, unions urged their members to withdraw their savings from antilabor banks. The proposal came from the Philadelphia Central Labor Union during its general strike.

March 17, 1910 —A statewide general strike was approved for the first time. The state convention of the Pennsylvania State Federation of Labor adopted a resolution calling for a statewide general strike in support of the Philadelphia general strike, but it was not carried out.

September 27, 1916 —For the first time, a citywide general strike that was called failed to materialize. The New York Central Federated Union called a general strike of all New York City unions in support of striking workers on the elevated, subway, and surface lines. Only the brewery workers responded, went out, and remained on strike until October 1, when the general strike was called off. The transit workers', strike itself was defeated.

February 6, 1919 —The first general strike after World War I took place in Seattle, Washington, when sixty-thousand organized workers went out on strike and shut down Seattle completely. The strike ended in failure on February 11.

July 7, 1934 —The first general strike in California occurred in San Francisco and involved 125,000 workers. Every union but two walked out in support of the longshoremen, whose strike was led by Harry Bridges. The event that triggered the general strike occurred on July 5 ("Bloody Thursday"), when two workers (Howard Sperry, a longshoreman and war veteran, and Nick Bordoise, a member of the Cooks Union and the Communist party) were killed and hundreds were injured by the police. The strike ended on July 19 in a victory for the longshoremen.

May 28, 1946 —The first general strike to be called after World War II took place in Rochester, New York. It was called by a committee of the AFL Central Labor Council and the CIO when the city administration tried to prevent workers in the Division of Public Works from joining a union. The strike lasted one day and ended with the city administration agreeing not to interfere with the right of public works employees to join a union.

Government Ownership

December 1892 — The AFL adopted its first resolution favoring government ownership of the telegraph and telephone systems.

December 1893 — The AFL adopted its first resolution calling for collective ownership of all means of production and distribution. This was Plank 10 of the "Political Programme" passed by the AFL convention.

December 28, 1917 — The federal government took over the operation of all railroad and water transport lines for the first time.

1919 — Railroad workers issued their first demand for government ownership and operation of the railroads. The Plumb Plan called for government retention of the railroads it had taken over during World War I. Though the Railroad Brotherhoods and the AFL Railway Employees' Department repeatedly urged Congress to support the Plumb Plan, Congress returned the roads to the private owners in the Transportation Act of 1920.

Grievance Procedure

1961 — The first grievance procedures for federal employees were set up by Executive Order 10988.

October 1976 — The United Steel Workers put forth their first demand for major reform in grievance procedures. The proposal, made for the 1977 contract, provided that workers discharged or suspended for disciplinary reasons could stay on the job until their cases had been fully reviewed. Present practice provides for the discharge to become effective immediately, with the worker entitled to subsequent reinstatement with back pay if the discipline is found unjustifiable.

Guaranteed Employment

1896 — The wallpaper industry became the first industry to guarantee union members twelve months' work.

1923 — The first guaranteed employment plan was offered by the Proctor and Gamble Company, which promised forty-eight weeks of work, or its time equivalent, each year to those hourly factory employees who had worked for Proctor and Gamble at least two years.

May 9, 1944 — The first labor proposal for a guaranteed weekly and annual wage was made by Philip Murray at the United Steel Workers convention.

1964 — The first guaranteed annual wage for longshoremen in the Port of New York was offered and accepted in exchange for the employers' right to use automated cargo-loading equipment.

October 1976 — The United Steel Workers incorporated their first demand for guaranteed lifetime job security in the union's proposals for its 1977 contract.

Guilds

1640s — The General Court of Massachusetts authorized the chartering of guildlike associations in the cooperage, shoemaking, and shipbuilding trades.

1648 — The first labor organization was formed when Boston shoemakers' and coopers' (barrel makers) guilds obtained a three-year charter. Partially because of protests by local rural artisans, who considered the guilds a hindrance to free trade, the charters were not renewed.

1724 — The first labor organization in the building trades was founded in Philadelphia when the house carpenters created the Carpenters' Company of the City and County of Philadelphia to establish a "book of prices" for the payment for their work "so that workmen should receive the worth of their money." It seems that this organization consisted of master carpenters. Their "Rules of Work" called for "a price scale bearing a proper proportion to the price of labor with due regard to the increased cost of living." It was at their meeting house — Carpenters' Hall — that the First Continental Congress met in 1774. The Carpenters' Company of Philadelphia was the best known guild in Colonial America.

H

Health and Safety

1837 — The first report on occupational health hazards, B. W. M'Cready's "On the Influence of Trades, Professions and Occupations in the United States in the Production of Diseases," was published in an 1837 edition of *Transactions,* put out by the Medical Society of New York.

1850 — The first state report on occupational hazards, *Massachusetts House Document No. 153,* was published.

1883 — New Jersey put out the first report on workers' health by a state labor bureau, the *Sixth Annual Report, New Jersey Bureau of Labor Statistics of Labor and Industries, 1883.*

1887 — The Homestate Mining Company in North Dakota set up the first company-financed medical department with a full-time staff.

1903 — The first federal report on industrial hygiene, C. F. W. Doehring's *Factory Sanitation and Labor Protection,* was published by the U.S. Bureau of Labor.

1906 — Massachusetts became the first state to appoint health inspectors to inspect factories, workshops, schools, tenements, and similar buildings. The inspectors presented their first report in 1907, entitled *First Annual Report of the State Inspectors of Health,* and it was published in Boston by the Massachusetts State Board of Health in 1907.

1908 — The first two federal reports on health hazards in a number of industries appeared. These were Dr. George M. Kober's report for the Committee on Social Betterment of the President's Home Commission, and Frederick L. Hoffman's study of "Mortality from Consumption in Dusty Trades," published as *U.S. Bureau of Labor Bulletin No. 79* in November 1908.

January 28, 1911 — A patent was canceled for the first time because it was dangerous to health when President William Howard Taft voided a patent issued to the Diamond Match Company.

February 11, 1911 — The first recommendation to move factories to the suburbs and form industrial towns to solve the problems of housing congestion was made by the New York City Mayor's Committee.

1911 — The first state factory investigating commission to study safety and health conditions was set up in New York. The commission originated out of the Triangle Waist Company fire in New York City in which 154 workers, mostly young women, died. It pressed the legislature into passing the first serious safety laws for working people.

December 29, 1970 — The Occupational Safety and Health Act, the first major federal legislation pertaining to workers' health and safety, was signed into law by President Richard Nixon. It required employers to provide a workplace "free from recognized hazards that are causing or are likely to cause death or serious physical harm to employees," and to meet specific standards promulgated by the Department of Labor's Occupational Safety and Health Administration (OSHA). The law gave OSHA the power to inspect workplaces, make citations for violations, and propose penalties. In situations of "imminent danger," the Labor Department was authorized to seek an injunction in federal court to shut down the offending operation. The act explicitly provided that workers could call in inspectors without giving their employers advance warning, and that they had the right to "walk around" with OSHA compliance officers in order to point out suspected violations. Employer reprisals against workers who take these actions were forbidden.

The strongest support for this precedent-setting law came from the Oil, Chemical, and Atomic Workers, the Steelworkers, the AFL-CIO, the United Auto Workers, and Ralph Nader's Study Group on Disease and Injury on the Job.

1972 — The first Black Lung Benefits Act was passed. In February 1969, forty-two thousand of West Virginia's forty-four thousand coal miners had participated in a wildcat strike lasting three weeks and had marched on the state capital to demand a black lung compensation bill. The miners' agitation led to congressional passage of the Coal Mine Health and Safety Act of 1969 and the Black Lung Benefits Act of 1972 to aid miners who had contracted black lung disease from inhaling coal dust while working in the mines.

May 2, 1976 — The first announcement that unions would seek to eliminate excessive noise in factories in industry contracts appeared in a front-page story in *The New York Times,* which reported: "Excessive noise, not in products but in the factories where they are made, is the target of organized labor's latest crusade — a campaign with some of the historic dimensions of the battles over child labor and the eight-hour day."

October 24, 1977 — The first announcement that factory heat would become an issue in union contracts appeared in a *New York Times* story. The story quoted Marc Stepp, United Automobile Workers vice president, as stating "that the heat wave last summer that led to several wildcat walkouts at area automobile plants dramatized the need for contract language in 1979 to protect workers from unbearable conditions. Workers walked out at several Chrysler plants last summer when temperatures reached over 100 degrees in the plants."

April 1981 — The first strike over inadequate protection from uranium contamination occurred when members of the Oil, Chemical, and Atomic Workers International Union struck the TNS Corporation. TNS, which makes armor-piercing artillery shells out of depleted uranium in a plant near Jonesboro, Tennessee, had offered a 25 percent wage increase over one year, plus increased benefits, including an additional holiday, when the union contract expired on April 21. But the plant's one hundred workers believed their health was more important than money and refused to return to work until the company agreed to take adequate steps to protect them from uranium contamination. "Union officials," reported *The New York Times* on June 11, 1981, "say they believed this was the first strike in recent times in which the major issue was the workers' health and safety."

High Cost of Living

March 1837 — The first labor meeting to protest the high cost of living was held in New York City. The slogan of the meeting was: "Bread! Meat! Rent! Fuel! Their prices must come down!"

Hiring Hall

April 1850 — The New York Operative Bakers' Union set up the first hiring office established by a union.

Hours of Work

May 1791 — Incensed by their employers' practice of paying a flat daily wage for the long summer shift and resorting to piece rates during the short winter days, a group of Philadelphia carpenters started the first strike in American history for the ten-hour day.

1802 — The first petition to a state legislature for a shorter working day was presented by carpenters in Georgia, who sought to place their profession "upon a more respectable and recognized social footing."

1825 — The first large-scale strike for a ten-hour day took place when six hundred journeymen carpenters walked off their jobs in Boston. The strike was lost.

March 1835 — The first labor publication that stimulated a national movement, the *Ten-Hour Circular,* was issued during the Boston ten-hour strike. It had a profound effect on the national ten-hour movement.

1835 — The first general strike for the ten-hour day took place when all workers in Philadelphia, including public employees, turned out. The strike ended in victory for the workers.

1836 — Congress passed the first federal act regulating the hours of work in federal employment. It declared government offices would be open for the transaction of public business at least eight hours a day during the winter months (October 1–April 1) and ten hours in the summer months (April 1–October 1). Thus government office workers were assured that their workday would be eight and ten hours for half the year each.

January 2, 1840 — The first authorization of a ten-hour day for federal employees was President Martin Van Buren's executive order giving navy yard workers a ten-hour day without a reduction in pay.

1840 — The building trades became the first trade unions to win a sixty-hour week. It was established in most of the United States.

1841 — Governor Fort of New Jersey became the first governor to recommend a ten-hour workday.

1842 — Lowell workers and their sympathizers brought the first petition to the Massachusetts legislature for the ten-hour day.

1842 — The first adoption of the eight-hour day was achieved by ship carpenters and caulkers at the Charlestown (Massachusetts) Navy Yard.

1846 — The first employer to grant the ten-hour day without being compelled to do so was Knapp and Totten of Pittsburgh.

July 9, 1847 — New Hampshire became the first state to establish the ten-hour day for all workers. The committee investigating the matter believed that "a proper reduction in hours of labor would be found advantageous to all parties. Employers would realize a greater profit, even in less time, from labourers more vigorous and better able to work, from having had suitable time to rest; while operatives would be allowed that time for intellectual and moral culture, which duty to themselves and others most imperatively demand." The law provided that "in all contracts relating to labor, ten hours shall be taken to be a day's work unless otherwise agreed by the parties." It went into effect on September 15, 1847, by which time employers had forced many workers to sign agreements to work longer than ten hours as a condition of employment.

1849 — Ship carpenters and caulkers in New York City won the eight-hour day for all repair work.

1851 — The first labor organization was founded for the purpose of winning the eight-hour day. It was called the Assembly of Associated Mechanics and Workingmen of Philadelphia.

1853 —The first ten-hour law on the Pacific Coast went into effect in California.

1853 — New York became the first state to pass a law declaring ten hours to be a day's work in all public works. The law did permit employer-employee agreements for longer hours.

May 1854 —The Boston caulkers became the first union to adopt the eight-hour system.

1856 —The first agreement for shorter hours in the South was achieved by New Orleans ship carpenters, who won the ten-hour day.

1859 — Ira Steward introduced the first demand by a labor union for an eight-hour day for all workers at the convention of the National Union of Machinists and Blacksmiths in Philadelphia.

September 1863 —The first significant labor action to secure the eight-hour day was taken when the National Union of Machinists and Blacksmiths and Boston Trades' Assembly jointly endorsed the eight-hour day.

1864 —The Workingmen's Convention of Boston, the first eight-hour organization, was established by Ira Steward, "Father of the Eight-Hour Day."

1865 —The first of the eight-hour leagues, the Grand Eight-Hour League of Massachusetts, was started.

September 1865 —The Republican party of Massachusetts became the first political party to insert a demand for the eight-hour day in its party platform.

December 1865 —The first resolution calling for the investigation of the need for an eight-hour day on all government work was introduced into Congress.

March 1866 —The first bill providing for an eight-hour day for all laborers, workmen, and mechanics employed by or on behalf of the government was introduced into Congress. It failed to pass.

August 23, 1866 —The first unified call for an eight-hour day was issued by the National Labor Union at its convention in Baltimore.

August 24, 1866 —A delegation of the National Labor Union made the first presentation of an eight-hour demand to the president of the United States when it brought its petition to Andrew Johnson in the White House.

March 5, 1867 —Illinois became the first state to pass a law establishing eight hours as a legal day's work for all nonagricultural labor. The law pertained to workers hired on or after May 1, 1867. However, escape clauses rendered it ineffective.

June 8, 1867 —The eight-hour day was instituted in San Francisco city government.

July 25, 1868 — The first act of Congress declaring that eight hours should constitute a day's work for laborers, mechanics, and all other workmen in federal employ was signed by President Ulysses S. Grant. It was never fully enforced.

May 19, 1869 — President Ulysses S. Grant became the first U.S. president to enforce an eight-hour law when he issued a proclamation directing that there be no reduction in wages paid to laborers, workmen, and mechanics in the employ of the United States because of any reduction of working hours.

1870 — New York enacted the first eight-hour law for state and municipal workers.

May 19–June 30, 1872 — The first wave of eight-hour strikes occurred in a number of cities. By May 22, there was a victory in New York City against private employers.

August 23, 1873 — The first delegation of postal workers came to Washington to seek back pay for the eight-hour day under the law.

1874 — The Massachusetts legislature passed first state ten-hour law that did not make an exception of contracts between workers and employers. The law was rather weak, but it was strengthened in 1879 and became the first effective state law limiting hours of work.

April 13, 1875 — The Industrial Congress and Industrial Brotherhood issued the first call for a nationwide movement for the eight-hour day. July 4, 1876, was designated as the date to inaugurate the eight-hour day. It was not realized.

1876 — In the first court decision on a law relating to hours of work, the Massachusetts Supreme Court upheld the ten-hour law for women, which had been passed in 1874.

1879 — Massachusetts enacted the first enforceable ten-hour law covering women and children working in factories.

May 22, 1880 — The first Early Closing Association of Sales Clerks and Department Store Workers was founded in New York City. It demanded a shorter working day in all retail and department stores.

1884 — The Federation of Organized Trades and Labor Unions of the United States and Canada (later the American Federation of Labor) issued the first call for a general strike, on May 1, 1886, for the eight-hour day.

May 1, 1886 — In this first celebration of May Day as a day for labor, about 350,000 workers in 11,562 establishments across the country went on strike for the eight-hour day. Chicago was paralyzed by the eight-hour strikes. In New York City, close to 25,000 workers marched in a torchlight procession for the eight-hour day. It was estimated that 185,000 out of the 350,000 workers who struck for the eight-hour day gained their demand on May 1 and the days following.

1888 — The first eight-hour law for workers in the Government Printing Office was enacted.

February 22, 1889 — Under the leadership of the AFL, the first mass meetings since 1886 for the eight-hour day were held. These meetings took place in 240 cities.

1889 — The eight-hour day was internationalized with the adoption of a resolution at the International Workingmen's Congress in Paris, establishing the Second International. The resolution set May Day as international labor day for the struggle for the eight-hour day.

May 1, 1890 — The first international labor day was celebrated, with the eight-hour day as the issue. It was called "Labor's Emancipation Day."

1890 — Ohio enacted the first law providing that no worker engaged in operating trains should remain on duty for more than twenty-four consecutive hours, at the end of which period he must have a rest period of no less than eight hours. In 1892, the maximum duty was shortened to fifteen hours.

1892 — The first federal eight-hour law covering all workers and mechanics employed by the United States and the District of Columbia government on public works was passed.

1893 — Illinois passed the first enforceable eight-hour law for women. Mrs. Florence Kelley, who played a leading role in obtaining passage, was appointed factory inspector to enforce the law. This legislation was declared unconstitutional by the Illinois Supreme Court in 1895.

1897 — The House Committee on Labor introduced the Phillips Bill to extend the eight-hour law to contractors and subcontractors with government agreements. It was passed by the House but defeated in the Senate.

1899 — The first state law making it unlawful for an employee to work longer than eight hours on public works was passed by California. It was upheld by the U.S. Supreme Court in 1903.

1905 — The first U.S. Supreme Court decision declaring a statute aimed at protecting labor unconstitutional was handed down in *Lochner v. New York*. The case in question was a New York law limiting the hours of bakers to ten per day and sixty per week.

1907 — Congress passed the first act providing for ten hours' rest after sixteen consecutive hours of work for trainmen. The law also stipulated a nine-hour working day for train dispatchers.

February 28, 1908 — The eight-hour day was introduced throughout the entire printing industry under union contracts.

1908 — For the first time, the U.S. Supreme Court ruled women's maximum-hour legislation constitutional in *Muller v. Oregon.*

January 5, 1914 — Henry Ford became the first American industrialist to institute a $5 daily wage and the eight-hour day.

1916 — The Adamson Act became the first federal law to provide an eight-hour day for those employed in the operation of the railroads, with extra pay for hours worked beyond the normal eight. It did not, however, include the nonoperating workers.

January 1, 1917 — On this date, the eight-hour day for all railway transportation workers was scheduled to go into effect. However, the railroads delayed instituting the eight-hour day because they wanted to test the Adamson Act, which mandated it, in the courts. The railroad workers threatened a general strike, and on March 28, 1917, the railroad managers agreed to institute the eight-hour day. The Adamson Act was the first federal legislation granting the eight-hour day to workers in the private sector.

September 1917 — The first "on-the-job strike" for the eight-hour day was led by the IWW in the Pacific lumber industry. The Wobblies hired out for ten hours, but left the job after eight hours to underscore their demand for an eight-hour day.

1917 — The first eight-hour law prohibiting salaried workers, as well as blue-collar workers, from working more than eight hours a day was enacted in Alaska. It was declared unconstitutional by the U.S. District Court for Alaska.

March 1, 1918 — The first eight-hour day in the Northwest lumber industry was won by the IWW.

June 14, 1918 — For the first time, the AFL adopted a resolution calling upon the president of the United States to issue a proclamation establishing the eight-hour day throughout the country. The resolution was submitted to President Woodrow Wilson.

June 1918 — The first call for the organization of the steel industry for union recognition and the eight-hour day was issued by William Z. Foster, on behalf of the Chicago Federation of Labor, at an AFL convention. On August 1, 1918, the National Committee for Organizing the Iron and Steel Industry was created with representatives from each international union. Samuel Gompers was named chairman; John Fitzpatrick, president of the Chicago Federation of Labor, was made vice chairman; and William Z. Foster was named secretary.

September 18, 1918 — The War Labor Board upheld the eight-hour day for the first time in the case of the Wheeling Mold and Foundry Company.

January 1, 1919 — Cleveland firemen instituted the eight-hour day in defiance of the city authorities.

January 28, 1919 — The first forty-four-hour week was established nationally by the Amalgamated Clothing Workers in shops of the National Association of Clothing Manufacturers.

February 7, 1919 — An award handed down by federal Judge Samuel Alschaler, administrator of labor relations for the industry, forced the meat-packing industry to institute the eight-hour day.

February 1919 — In the first widespread application of the "on-the-job strike" for the eight-hour day, workers arrived at silk mills a half hour later than usual and quit at the usual hour. The action led to the lockout of thirty thousand workers.

1923 — The twelve-hour day was ended in the steel industry, and the eight-hour day was instituted.

June 11, 1926 — The first five-day, forty-hour week was won by New York fur workers, under the leadership of Ben Gold, head of the New York Joint Board, after a seventeen-week strike. The fur workers also won a 10 percent wage increase over the existing minimum wage scale, ten legal holidays (seven of them paid), and the provision that no overtime work would be allowed except during the four months from September through December, when shops could work for four hours extra on Saturday, with extra pay.

November 1930 — The five-hour day was first proposed and the Metal Trades Department of the AFL endorsed the demand. The 1930 AFL convention voted to refer the proposal to the Executive Council for "immediate and thorough consideration." The 1932 convention went on record for the five-day week and the six-hour day with no reduction in weekly wages.

November 1932 — For the first time, the AFL endorsed the reduction of working hours through legislation rather than through collective bargaining. The 1932 convention endorsed "an immediate reduction in the hours of labor as a condition absolutely essential to the restoration and maintenance of prosperity." The Executive Council was instructed to draft legislation to be presented to the incoming Congress. Its work led to the introduction of the Black Bill for a thirty-hour week.

December 21, 1932 — Senator Hugo L. Black introduced the first thirty-hour bill into Congress. The bill would have denied the channels of interstate and foreign commerce to articles produced in establishments "in which any person was employed or permitted to work more than five days in any week or more than six hours in any day." The bill was not voted upon in the Seventy-second Congress during its regular session, but in the special session called by President Franklin D. Roosevelt, it passed the Senate on April 6, 1933. It was expected to pass in the House when opposition by industry and the Roosevelt administration caused it to be buried in the Rules Committee.

September 5, 1933 — The Fur Division of the Needle Trades Workers' Industrial Union became the first union to win a thirty-five-hour week at the same pay as for forty hours.

June 30, 1936 — The first federal forty-hour week law, the Walsh-Healy Act was passed by Congress. Starting September 28, 1936, workers on government contracts worth over $10,000 were required to receive overtime compensation at the rate of not less than time-and-one-half for hours worked in excess of forty. The act also provided for overtime pay for work in excess of eight hours in any one day, if such compensation yielded a greater amount than the worker would receive on the weekly forty-hour basis. Workers under government contracts were not to be paid less than the prevailing local industry wage. This, the first federal legislation to set minimum wages for those working under government contracts, included child and convict labor measures, safety and health provisions,

and was the first federal legislation to establish safety and health standards. The Walsh-Healy Act was also the first child-labor law to be ruled constitutional. It prohibited the employment of boys under sixteen and girls under eighteen in government contract work exceeding $10,000.

1938 — The Fair Labor Standards Act established the five-day, forty-hour basic schedule throughout interstate industry.

September 7, 1945 — The CIO Oil Workers Industrial Union called the first postwar strike: "52-40 or Fight." Strikers demanded a forty-hour week at fifty-two hours' pay, or a 30 percent increase in wages. When forty-three thousand refinery workers in twenty states struck for this demand, President Harry S. Truman ordered the Navy Department to operate the struck refineries.

1962 — The first union contract establishing a twenty-five-hour basic work week in an industry was negotiated by Harry Van Arsdale, Jr., head of the New York City electrical workers' union. The agreement also provided for five hours of built-in overtime for each worker.

October 1976 — The first step toward achieving a four-day, thirty-two-hour work week in basic industry was taken in an agreement reached between the United Automobile Workers and the Ford Motor Company. It provided that in the second year of the contract, each worker would have five four-day weeks in the course of the year. The total was scheduled to rise to seven in the third year.

Housing

1922 — The Minneapolis Central Labor Union became the first union to make construction loans available to members through union-owned home loan companies when it established the Union Building and Loan Association of Minneapolis. By 1928, eight of these companies were in operation.

1927 — The Amalgamated Clothing Workers began construction of extensive cooperative apartment houses in the Bronx, New York City, and thus inaugurated the first low-rent housing built by a union.

The Hosiery Workers were second in 1930 with a housing project in Philadelphia. By 1969, over two hundred union-sponsored housing projects were either completed or under way.

1935 — The first AFL Housing Committee was established to research housing needs, provide public information, promote legislation, develop projects, and protect the interests of labor and consumers in the housing movement.

1937 — The U.S. Housing Act established a low-rent public housing program. The object was to provide decent,

safe, and sanitary housing for low-income workers with the aid of federal subsidy payments. The act stipulated that a substandard dwelling unit was to be eliminated for every new public housing unit created.

1938 — The first convention of the Congress of Industrial Organizations (CIO) established the CIO Committee on Housing and called for the construction of a million units a year for the next ten years.

1949 — A national housing policy was proclaimed in the Housing Act. One of its goals was "the realization as soon as feasible of the goal of a decent home and a suitable living environment for every American family."

1955 — The first convention of the newly merged AFL-CIO announced: "We believe all housing units built with the aid of federal funds or credit or any other form of financial assistance should be made available to minority families on an equal basis with all other families."

1964 — The AFL-CIO took the first step toward achieving massive housing for workers by establishing the Mortgage Investment Trust to invest union pension funds in government-insured mortgages, and thus initiate a flow of union capital into the housing industry. The AFL-CIO also established a Department of Urban Affairs to coordinate the federation's work in such areas as housing, urban environment, mass transit, and manpower, including minority job training and job development programs.

1968 — The Federal Housing Act set a national housing goal for the next decade: the provision of twenty-six million standard housing units through new construction and rehabilitation, including six million subsidized units for low- and moderate-income families.

I

Immigrants

July 1883 — What was described in the press as the "first immigrant strike" took place when 750 Jewish immigrants walked off their jobs. They were led by the newly organized Dress and Cloak Makers' Union, which was affiliated with the Knights of Labor and the Central Labor Union. After two weeks, the workers won their principal demands of $2.50 per day and a working day from 8 a.m. to 6 p.m.

February 1885 — For the first time, a U.S. labor group included the word "Jewish" in its name. The Russian-Jewish Workers' Farein was organized in New York City by members of the Socialist Labor party to spread socialist propaganda in Yiddish.

April 19, 1885 — The Jewish Workingmen's Union (Der Idisher Arbeiter Farein), the first Jewish general labor body organized to help build trade unions among Jewish workers, was formed in New York City. By May 1886, it had organized about fourteen unions.

October 14, 1885 — What is considered to be the first labor leaflet in Yiddish was issued by the Jewish Workingmen's Union of New York City. It dealt with the demand for the eight-hour working day and was written by Jacob Schoen.

October 1888 — The first and only permanent organization center for Jewish workers in the United States, the United Hebrew Trades was founded. By March 1890, it had twenty-two unions affiliated with it representing six thousand members.

April 1891 — The United Garment Workers became the first national union to call for a literacy test to limit immigration.

1902 — The AFL gave its support for the first time to the movement to use literacy tests to restrict immigration from southeastern Europe.

1912 — *Immigration and Labor* by Dr. Isaac Hourwich was published. This was the first book to demonstrate that the immigrants from southern and eastern Europe — the so-called new immigrants, who were viewed by many AFL leaders as unsuitable material for unionization — had actually encouraged labor organization.

May 19, 1921 — Congress passed the first quota law to curb immigration. It had been demanded by the AFL.

Incorporation of Trade Unions

1809 — The Philadelphia Typographical Society incorporated to protect its benefit funds. However, the society's charter preserved its wage-fixing activities in a clause that reserved to the society "its power of making laws."

1816 — The New York Typographical Society also sought to incorporate in order to protect its benefit funds. But when the state Senate amended a bill of incorporation passed by the Assembly by adding a clause that prohibited the Typographical Society from concerning itself with trade matters or attempting to regulate wages, the society refused to accept the condition.

1883 — The first bill providing for the incorporation of trade unions was introduced into Congress. It was sponsored by the Knights of Labor and failed to pass.

Industrial Congress

October 12, 1845 — The first Industrial Congress of the United States met in New York City. William E. Wait of Illinois was elected president. Annual meetings were held until 1856.

Industrial Statistics

September 1868 — The first labor resolution demanding that industrial statistics be included in the Federal Census was adopted by the 1868 convention of the National Labor Union.

Industrial Unionism

1869 — The Knights of Labor, the first national labor federation to unite skilled and unskilled workers according to the principles of industrial unionism, was founded in Philadelphia. At first the Knights organized only skilled workers, but in keeping with the principle that "An injury to one is the concern of all," emphasized by its founder, Uriah S. Stephens, it began to unite the skilled and unskilled, and eventually blacks and whites, men and women, native-born and foreign-born workers. The only group the Knights excluded was the Chinese. The first industrial union to admit Chinese and Japanese workers was the Industrial Workers of the World (IWW). After first excluding them, the United Mine Workers organized Oriental miners in the United States.

June 20, 1893 — The American Railway Union, the first industrial union of railroad workers, was formed at a convention in Chicago where Eugene V. Debs was elected president. Within one year, the union had 150,000 members.

August 10, 1893 — The first lodge of the American Railway Union was formed in Fort Madison, Iowa.

January 27, 1901 — The first union to be chartered by the American Labor Union was the United Brotherhood of Railway Employees. This was an industrial union of all workers in the railroad industry from track laborers to engineers. They were organized into separate locals but were united in a division covering an entire railroad system.

1901 — The AFL made its first declaration on the form of organization of its affiliates. The Scranton Declaration declared "craft autonomy" the cornerstone of the federation, but permitted the organization of an industrial union in isolated areas where it was more feasible to enroll all workers in "the paramount organization." The references to "isolated area" and "paramount organization" were obviously intended to apply to the United Mine Workers and to no other industry or union.

June 27, 1905 — The Industrial Workers of the World (IWW) was founded at a convention in Chicago. It was the first labor federation of the twentieth century dedicated to organizing the unorganized on the basis of industrial unionism and the unity of all workers regardless of race, sex, or nationality.

March 30, 1906 — The first new industrial union organized by the IWW

was the General Electric Industrial Workers' Union at the General Electric plant in Schenectady, New York.

1912 — The first resolution calling for industrial unionism to come before an AFL convention was introduced by delegates of the United Mine Workers. It was defeated 10,934 to 5,929.

March 19, 1922 — For the first time, a city central labor union endorsed the cause of industrial unionism. The Chicago Federation of Labor came out in favor of it and requested the AFL to call a conference of international unions for its adoption.

November 1934 — The AFL conceded for the first time that mass-production methods, the vast size of antilabor industrial and financial organizations, and the difficulty if not impossibility of organizing the unorganized into craft unions had made it necessary to adopt a new organization policy. The report of the Committee on Resolutions at the AFL convention in San Francisco declared that while craft organization was "most effective" in industries where "the lines of demarcation between crafts are distinguishable," it realized that in many of the industries in which thousands of workers were employed, "a new condition exists requiring organization upon a different basis to be most effective." To meet this "new condition," the Executive Council was instructed to charter new national or international unions in the automobile, cement, and aluminum industries, and in "such other mass production and miscellaneous industries" as the council felt necessary. The new unions were to be put under the provisional direction and administration of the AFL. The Executive Council was also instructed to inaugurate an organizing drive in the iron and steel industry at the earliest possible moment.

While the resolution did not make clear just what type of unions would be used in organizing, the AFL Executive Council was increased in size from eleven to eighteen members, with three advocates of industrial unionism added to the body: John L. Lewis of the United Mine Workers, David Dubinsky of the International Ladies' Garment Workers' Union, and George Berry of the Printing Pressmen. However, the craft unions still controlled the Council.

October 15, 1935 — The greatest debate in the history of the AFL came at its Atlantic City convention over the report by the Committee on Resolutions on industrial unionism. A majority of the committee recommended nonconcurrence with resolutions favoring industrial unionism, while a minority report directed the Executive Council to initiate aggressive organizing campaigns in industries that were still largely unorganized, using the form of industrial unionism rather than craft unionism in chartering the new unions. After seven and one-half hours of debate on whether to accept or reject the minority report, the convention defeated it by a vote of 18,824 to 10,933 with 788 not voting.

1935–1936 — The Committee of Industrial Organization was formed after American Federation of Labor, at its 1935 convention, rejected a resolution calling for the organization of the mass production industries. In 1938, the CIO became an independent industrial union national federation under the name of Congress of Industrial Organizations.

Injunctions

July 1, 1894 — The first antilabor injunction based on the Sherman Anti-Trust Act was handed down by a federal court in the Pullman strike. Eugene V. Debs, president of the American Railway Union, was sentenced to six months in prison for refusing to abide by the injunction and was confined in the McHenry County Jail in Woodstock, Illinois.

1903 — For the first time, an anti-injunction bill passed one house of Congress: the House of Representatives. It then was defeated in the Senate.

December 18, 1907 — The first injunction against the AFL and its entire leadership was issued by a federal court to restrain the federation from publishing the name of Bucks' Stove and Range Company in the "We Don't Patronize" list of the *American Federationist*. The injunction was made permanent on March 23, 1908.

March 1908 — AFL leaders held their first meeting with farmers' organizations. Its purpose was to protest injunctions in labor disputes and to urge Congress to grant relief to labor.

November 29, 1921 — In the first injunction ever obtained by a trade union, the Joint Board of Cloak, Skirt, and Reefers' Makers' Unions (ILGWU) got an injunction forbidding the Protective Association of New York to encourage any member to violate its agreement with the union. The action was disapproved of by many unions.

1921 — For the first time, the U.S. Supreme Court declared a law forbidding the issuance of an injunction prohibiting peaceful picketing unconstitutional. In *Truax v. Corrigan,* the court declared an antipicketing Arizona statute unconstitutional.

1932 — Congress passed the first law prohibiting federal courts from issuing injunctions against unions. This was the Norris-LaGuardia Act.

Insurance

October 19, 1854 — The first national workers' insurance company was organized by German socialists and incorporated as the Workmen's Sick and Death Benefit Fund of the United States under the laws of New York State. In 1916, the fund had 329 branches in 28 states, and 51,997 beneficiary members.

1867 — The Locomotive Mutual Life Insurance Association became the first mutual life insurance plan for railroad workers. It was open only to members of the Brotherhood of Locomotive Engineers.

1925 — The first union insurance company was established: Union Labor Insurance Company, founded at a conference of about fifty international unions called by AFL President William Green. AFL Vice President Matthew Woll was named president of the company.

International Labor Solidarity

1827 — The Philadelphia Typographical Society contributed $90 to assist the Greek people in their struggle for independence. This was the first example of international labor solidarity.

September 1830 — The first message from workers of the United States to workers of another country was sent by mechanics and workingmen of New York City to the workers of Paris after the French Revolution of 1830. It read: "Fellow laborers! We owe you our grateful thanks. And not we only, but the industrial classes — the *people* of every nation. In defending your own rights, you have vindicated ours."

September 13, 1834 — The first proposal for an international alliance of labor in all countries was made in an editorial published in the *National Trades' Union*, the organ of the New York General Trades' Union.

April 22, 1858 — The first meeting whose purpose was to establish an international labor association in cooperation with similar movements in Europe was held in New York City.

1867 — The first effort to regulate international competition of labor was made by the National Labor Union and the International Workingmen's Association.

1867 — Richard Trevellick became the first American labor delegate appointed to attend an international labor congress. He was designated by the National Labor Union to attend the congress of the International Workingmen's Association in Europe, but was unable to attend.

November 1868 — The first section of the International Workingmen's Association (First International) was formed in New York City with Friedrich A. Sorge as secretary.

April 1869 — The New York Compositors' Union was the first American union to ask for aid from a European labor federation to prevent the importation of strikebreakers. The compositors sent their request to the General Council of the International Workingmen's Association, which complied with it.

1869 — The first American delegate to actually attend the convention of the International Workingmen's Association was Andrew C. Cameron. He went to the Basle Convention as a delegate of the National Labor Union.

1870 — For the first time, an American labor federation endorsed affiliation with a European labor body. The National Labor Union adopted a resolution favoring affiliation with the International Workingmen's Association, though it never actually affiliated.

April 6, 1886 — The first address to the workingmen of the world by an American labor organization was issued by the Joint Executive Board of Assemblies Nos. 101, 93, and 17 of the Knights of Labor. The address came out of St. Louis and read, in part:

> *To the Workingmen of the World:*
> FRIENDS AND BROTHERS: Hear us, for we plead for our right. Men of equity, look upon us, for we struggle against giants of wrong. Mad with the frenzy of pride and self-adulation, begotten as it is of the success of outrage and infamy, there stands before us a giant of aggregated and incorporated wealth, every dollar of which is built upon blood, injustice, and outrage. . . .
> Fellow-workmen, Gould must be overthrown. His giant power must be broken, or you and I must be slaves forever. The Knights of Labor alone have dared to be a David to this Goliath. The battle is not for to-day, the battle is not for to-morrow, but for the trooping generations in the coming

ages of the world, for our children and our children's children. 'Tis the great question of the ages. Shall we in the coming ages be a nation of free men or a nation of slaves? The question must be decided now. The chains are already forged that are to bind us. Shall we await until they are riveted upon our limbs? Nay, God forbid. . . .

October 1887 — In the first international labor defense movement affecting American labor, London workers condemned the death sentences meted out to Albert R. Parsons, August Spies, Adolph Fischer, George Engel, and Louis Lingg in the Haymarket Affair. Among the speakers at the meeting that called for a pardon were William Morris and George Bernard Shaw.

1893 — The first AFL-sponsored labor conference for foreign labor editors was held in conjunction with the Columbia Exposition commemorating the Four Hundreth Anniversary of America.

1894 — The British Trades Union Congress sent its first fraternal delegation to an AFL convention.

1895 — The AFL sent its first fraternal delegation to attend a convention of the British Trades Union Congress.

July 19, 1896 — The United Hebrew Trades called its first meeting to express support for a strike in another country. At a mass meeting, Russian Hebrew workingmen expressed "sympathy with the 86,000 striking workingmen of St. Petersburg, Russia."

January 22, 1906 — American labor called its first demonstrations in support of strikes in other countries. The IWW sponsored walkouts to express solidarity with striking Russian workers, and the Socialist party supported the demonstrations.

1909 — The AFL made its first appeal to affiliated unions for financial assistance to unions of another country. The appeal went out on behalf of the Swedish trade unions in their general strike and lockout.

1911 — The AFL sent its first delegation to an international labor body. The delegates went to Budapest for a meeting of the new International Federation of Trade Unions (originally called the International Secretariat).

July 7, 1916 — Samuel Gompers issued his first appeal to Latin American workers to join the Pan-American Labor League, which he had founded.

April 24, 1917 — For the first time, a demonstration in a foreign country succeeded in preventing the execution of an American labor leader. Russian workers and others demonstrated before the American Embassy in Petrograd to protest the impending execution of Tom Mooney, who had been convicted of bomb-throwing at a San Francisco World War I Preparedness Rally in

1916. *The New York Times* reported on April 25, 1917: "The demonstration was led by Nikolai Lenin, the radical Socialist leader. . . ." *The New Republic* commented on May 5, 1917: "Is it not a remarkable commentary upon the attitude of the American press toward labor that one of the most significant and dramatic events should have come to the attention of American newspaper readers through a mass meeting in the Nevsky Prospect?" When President Wilson appealed to the governor of California to commute Mooney's sentence to life imprisonment, the governor stayed the execution and commuted the sentence.

November 1918 — The first Pan-American Labor Conference was held. It established the Pan-American Federation of Labor.

October 1919 — The first meeting of the International Labor Organization was held in Washington, D.C., with Secretary of Labor William B. Wilson presiding. The organization had been formed earlier in the year under the name of the International Labor Bureau.

1922 — The Russian-American Industrial Corporation, established by the Amalgamated Clothing Workers, was the first American trade union corporation to assist in developing an industry in another country. It was intended to help develop the clothing industry in the Soviet Union.

1934 — For the first time, the U.S. government accepted membership in the International Labor Office (ILO).

October 1945 — The first World Federation of Trade Unions was organized. The CIO affiliated, and the 1947 CIO convention endorsed this affiliation.

1948 — The Inter-American Confederation of Workers was formed in Peru to replace the Pan-American Federation of Labor.

1964 — The first World Auto Workers Conference convened in Frankfurt, Germany, on the initiative of the UAW.

April 26, 1976 — For the first time, workers in foreign subsidiaries of U.S. corporations demonstrated solidarity with U.S. workers by refusing to accept overtime while the U.S. workers were on strike. The action took place in subsidiaries of the large U.S. tire manufacturing companies and represented the first international union action in support of the seventy thousand striking American rubber workers, members of the United Rubber Workers. They had gone on strike against the Big Four rubber companies on April 21.

J

Job Control

1903 — The first union to win complete job control in the building trades was the Housesmiths Union of New York City.

Judges

1854 — Ellis Lewis was the first trade unionist to become a judge. A union printer, Lewis was appointed chief justice of the Pennsylvania Supreme Court and held office until December 7, 1857.

April 30, 1886 — The first judge to be censured by a grand jury for refusing to take an antilabor stand was Police Justice Weide of New York City. He was censured for releasing workers "engaged in parading before the doors of Messrs. Cavanagh, Sandford & Co. with boycott placards hung upon their necks and breasts, and distributing boycott circulars detrimental to the business of the complainants." As a result, the grand jury charged, "the disgraceful and unlawful practices of the boycotters were continued for nine days without the slightest interference by the police. . . ."

July 31, 1976 — The first federal judge to reverse a decision of his own that had resulted in a strike was federal District Judge Dennis R. Knapp. He said that he would not impose fines and jail terms pending against members of the United Mine Workers Local 1759 in West Virginia if the wildcat strikers returned to work "in a reasonable time."

Jurisdiction

August 1835 — In the first promulgation of exclusive jurisdiction for a union, the New York General Trades' Union rejected affiliation with the New York Weavers' Society on the ground that the weavers' constitution forbade receiving "two sets of delegates from one Trade or Art."

1888 — The first jurisdictional dispute involving an AFL union came when the carpenters' and furniture workers' unions battled over work to be done on the Exposition Building in Pittsburgh.

Labor Banks

May 16, 1920 — The first labor bank, the International Association of Machinists' Bank, was started with capital of $160,000. By the end of 1922, ten labor banks had been established. The top number of thirty-six was reached in 1926, with over $13 million in capital invested. However, many of the labor banks failed after the crash of 1929, and by 1930, only fourteen still survived.

Labor Conditions

1832 — Committees appointed by the New England Association of Farmers, Mechanics, and Other Workingmen undertook the first studies to collect data on labor conditions.

1844 — Massachusetts established the first legislative committee to investigate factory conditions.

Labor Columnist

1866 — In this year, the first labor columnist to write for a commercial newspaper, Thomas Phillips (1833–1916), began his column for the Philadelphia *Public Record.*

Labor Day

September 5, 1882 — The first Labor Day parade was held under the auspices of the Central Labor Union of New York City and Vicinity. Thirty thousand working men and women, accompanied by bands of music, marched down New York's fashionable Fifth Avenue and into Union Square, carrying placards reading: "Eight Hours for Work — Eight Hours for Rest — Eight Hours For What We Will"; Strike with the Ballot"; "Labor Pays All Taxes — Labor Creates All Wealth — To the Workers Should Belong the Wealth"; and "The Laborer Must Receive and Enjoy the Full Fruit of His Labor."

October 7, 1884 — The Federation of Organized Trades and Labor Unions of the United States and Canada became the first national labor federation to adopt a resolution calling for a Labor Day holiday on the first Monday in September. The resolution read: "Resolved, That the first Monday in September of each year be set apart as labor's national holiday, and that we recommend its observance by all wage workers, irrespective of sex, calling or nationality." It was adopted unanimously.

Peter J. McGuire, founder of the Brotherhood of Carpenters and Joiners and one of the founders of the Federation of Organized Trades and Labor Unions, has been called the "Father of Labor Day." However, many believe that Matthew Maguire, secretary of the New York Central Labor Union and member of the Socialist Labor party in New Jersey, is the real "Father of Labor Day."

September 7, 1885 — The first nationwide observance of the first Monday in September as a national holiday — Labor Day — took place. A labor paper reported on the parade in New York City: "Jewish working women, to the number of over two hundred in omnibuses and tally-ho coaches, made a remarkable feature of the procession."

1887 — Oregon became the first state in the United States to make Labor Day official. Similar legislation was passed in Colorado and New York later that year.

June 28, 1894 — A federal law establishing Labor Day as a national legal holiday was passed by Congress and signed by President Grover Cleveland.

Labor Frame-ups

June 21, 1877 — The first labor martyrs were executed. Ten miners who were members of the secret terroristic society the Molly Maguires were hanged after being found guilty of murder on the evidence of labor spy James McParlan. Six of the men were executed in Pottsville, Pennsylvania, and four in Mauch Chunk. Recent studies have concluded that these men were innocent of the charges and were really executed for their militant union activities. Franklin B. Gowen, president of the Reading Railroad Company, was the main force behind the antiunion conspiracy.

June 26, 1893 — The first governor to pardon imprisoned labor leaders on the ground that they were completely innocent was John Peter Altgeld of Illinois. He pardoned Samuel Fielden, Justus Schwab, and Oscar Neebe, who had been imprisoned for their role in the Haymarket Affair. In his pardon message, Altgeld stated that the men were completely innocent, and that they and the four men who had been hanged for their role in the Haymarket Affair were the victims of packed juries and a biased judge. The trade unions distributed fifty thousand copies of the pardon message, and the 1893 AFL convention praised Governor Altgeld.

February 1906 — The first kidnapping of union leaders took place when Charles H. Moyer, William D. Haywood, and George Pettibone were spirited out of Colorado to Idaho, where they were indicted for the murder of ex-Governor Steunenbert. Haywood, the first of the three to be tried for murder, was defended by Clarence Darrow and acquitted. The charges against the other two were dropped.

1912 — Joseph Ettor and Arturo Giovannitti, the IWW organizers of the Lawrence textile strike, were arrested and charged with being accessories to murder. The real aim was to cause the failure of this great strike by removing its leadership. The strike was victorious anyway, but the workers refused to return to work until Ettor and Giovannitti were released. At their trial, the two men were found not guilty. Giovannitti was the first labor poet to face a murder charge. While in prison he wrote a poem called "The Walker."

September 1915 — For the first time, a foreign government intervened in a case of an American labor leader facing execution. The Swedish government instructed its minister in the United States to investigate the case of Joe Hill, a Swedish citizen facing execution for murder in Utah. After reading the record of the case, W.A.F. Ekrengen, the Swedish minister, announced that he firmly believed Hill had not had a fair trial and that the evidence against him should not have resulted in a conviction. Ekrengen appealed to Utah Governor Spry to commute the sentence, but Spry rejected the appeal, and Joe Hill was executed.

December 5, 1916 — The first meeting to protest the sentencing of Thomas J. Mooney to death and Warren K. Billings to life imprisonment was held. Mooney and Billings had been convicted on perjured testimony of having thrown a bomb during the World War I Preparedness Day parade in San Francisco on July 22, 1916. The bomb had killed nine people and wounded forty others. The protest meeting was called by trade unions and socialist locals of New York City.

December 1924 — An AFL convention described Sacco and Vanzetti as "victims of race and national prejudice and class hatred." This, the first AFL resolution pertaining to the case, demanded a new trial for the two men, who were facing death for the supposed murder of two guards in South Braintree, Massachusetts, on April 15, 1920.

August 21, 1927 — The first national strike to protest the pending execution of workers was called by the IWW. The union proposed a two-day national strike to halt the execution of Sacco and Vanzetti. Six thousand out of twelve thousand Colorado miners walked out in sympathy with the IWW strikers. The protest failed, and Sacco and Vanzetti were executed on August 22.

January 7, 1939 — Tom Mooney and Warren K. Billings were freed by Governor Olsen of California after spending twenty-two years in jail for a crime they did not commit.

Labor Holiday

June 13, 1876 — The first "Miners' Day," in honor of the founding of Butte Miners' Union No. 1, was celebrated.

Labor Jury

March 1920 — The first "labor jury" constituted itself when the Pacific Coast labor movement, acting on the initiative of the Seattle Metal Trades, sent representatives to attend the trial of IWW members in Centralia, Washington. On November 11, 1919 — Armistice Day — American Legionnaires had attacked the IWW hall in Centralia, demolishing it and killing IWW members. Eleven IWW members were later tried for murder. The "labor jury" found the defendants innocent and declared that they had not obtained a fair trial. The official jury found seven IWW members guilty of murder — *after* the judge had refused to accept the jury's original verdict, which was that only two of the IWW defendants were guilty, and they only of third-degree manslaughter. The judge ordered the jurors to deliberate further, until they could return a verdict more to his liking.

Labor Lawyers

November 1805 — The first lawyer to defend trade unionists was Caesar A. Rodney, a leading Jeffersonian and later Jefferson's attorney general. He defended Philadelphia shoemakers, members of the Cordwainers' Society, who had been indicted for forming "a combination and conspiracy to raise wages."

January 1912 — Clarence Darrow was the first labor lawyer to be indicted for jury bribery: Darrow was tried twice for bribing jurors in the McNamara case. The first time he was acquitted, and the second trial resulted in a hung jury.

Labor Leaders

1827–1830 — William Heighton (1827–1873) is generally regarded as the first American labor leader. Born in Oundle, Northamptonshire, England, in 1800, he emigrated to the United States as a youth and settled in Philadelphia, where he became a shoemaker and a Ricardian Socialist. Although he had little formal education, Heighton won fame as a speaker and writer. His pamphlets in 1827 helped create the first labor movement in the United States, the Mechanics' Union of Trade Associations of Philadelphia; the first labor paper, the *Mechanics' Free Press,* of which Heighton was the editor; and the first labor party in the United States, the Workingmen's party of Philadelphia (1828), of which he was the principal spokesperson.

January 1845 — The first American woman labor leader, Sarah G. Bagley (c. 1819–1847), was elected president of the Lowell Female Labor Reform Association.

Little is known about Sarah Bagley's life before she obtained employment in 1836 as an operative in the Hamilton Manufacturing Company cotton mill in Lowell, Massachusetts. In late 1844, she began to organize the Lowell Female Labor Reform Association and became its president. Originally a writer for the *Lowell Offering,* she broke with that journal when it refused to publish her articles on the need for the ten-hour day. Bagley became the Female Labor Reform Association's delegate to three conventions of the New England Workingmen's Association, and served as the latter organization's corresponding secretary. She was a frequent contributor to and, for a short time, the chief editor of the *Voice of Industry* after the labor weekly was taken over by the Lowell Female Labor Reform Association. Bagley led the campaign to collect two thousand signatures on a petition to a Massachusetts legislative committee investigating wages, working conditions, and the workers' demand for a ten-hour day, and she appeared as a witness before the committee. A firm believer in the utopian socialist ideas of Charles Fourier, she was elected vice president of the Lowell Union of Associationists. In 1847, she was appointed superintendent of the Lowell Telegraph Office, becoming the country's first female telegraph operator.

1857 —William H. Sylvis, the country's first modern labor leader, joined a molders' local in Philadelphia during a strike.

Sylvis (1828–1869) was born in Armagh, Indiana County, Pennsylvania, on November 26, 1828. He was so poor that he received no formal education at all. At eighteen he was apprenticed to a Pennsylvania founder and became a journeyman molder. He joined the molders' local in 1857, during a strike, and soon became its secretary. In 1859, he was elected treasurer of the National Molders' Union. Sylvis served in the Union Army during the Civil War. After the war, he was elected president of the National Molders' Union. An outstanding labor organizer, Sylvis influenced the entire labor movement during the Civil War and post-Civil War era. He was active in founding the National Labor Union and served as its president until his death in 1869. Sylvis was a strong advocate of independent political action by labor, of powerful, effective unions, of international labor solidarity, of cooperatives, and of women's rights.

1869 —Isaac Myers was elected president of the Colored National Labor Union, the first national organization of black labor in the United States.

Isaac Myers (1835–1891), the first black labor leader, was born a free Negro of poor parents in Baltimore. He grew up in a slave state that afforded no public school education to black children, but managed nonetheless to receive an education in the private day school of Reverend John Fortie. At sixteen, Myers was apprenticed to James Jackson, a prominent black ship caulker. By 1860, he was a skilled caulker, superintending the caulking of clean-line clipper ships. When, after the Civil War, white caulkers insisted that blacks be discharged, Myers led in the forming of a union of black caulkers that sponsored the cooperative company that built the Chesapeake Marine Railway and Dry Dock Company and employed three hundred blacks at an average wage of $3 a day. Representing the Colored Caulkers' Trade Union Society of Baltimore, Myers was one of nine black delegates at the 1869 convention of the National Labor Union. That same year he was elected president of the Colored National Labor Union. Although he stepped down as president in 1871, Myers continued to be active in the organization until its demise in the fall of 1871.

November 1879 — Terence V. Powderly was elected Grand Master Workman of the Knights of Labor.

Terence V. Powderly (1849–1924) joined the Machinists' and Blacksmiths' Union in 1871, and was initiated into the Noble Order of the Knights of Labor in Philadelphia on September 6, 1876. He was elected master workman of the Scranton, Pennsylvania, assembly, and then corresponding secretary of the reorganized district assembly in 1877. In 1878, Powderly was elected on the Greenback Labor party ticket to the first of three two-year terms as mayor of Scranton. He was elected grand master

workman of the Knights of Labor in 1879 to succeed Uriah S. Stephens, and he held the position until he was removed from office in 1893.

November 15, 1881 — Samuel Gompers was elected president of the AFL.

Samuel Gompers (1850–1924) was born in England and apprenticed to a cigar maker. He came to America with his family in 1863; joined the cigar makers' union, and, with Adolph Strasser, reorganized the Cigar Makers' International Union and became president of Local 144. Gompers was active in organizing the Federation of Organized Trades and Labor Unions of the United States and Canada, and the American Federation of Labor. He held the post as president of the AFL from its inception in 1881 until his death in 1924, with the exception of one year.

1895 — The first and only time Samuel Gompers was defeated for reelection (by James McBride) as president of the AFL. Gompers returned as president in 1896 and remained in office until 1924.

December 13, 1924 — William Green was elected president of the AFL to succeed Gompers.

At age sixteen, William Green (1873–1952) followed his father into the coal mines of Ohio. He became a subdistrict president of the United Mine Workers in 1900, and was president of the Ohio District of the union from 1910 to 1913. Green served two terms in the Ohio Senate, where he wrote the state's workmen's compensation act, which was passed in 1911. In 1912, he began a ten-year tenure as international secretary-treasurer of the United Mine Workers. He became a fourth vice president, as well as a member of the Executive Council of the American Federation of Labor, in 1914. Green was president of the AFL from Gompers' death in 1924 until his own death in 1952.

September 5, 1929 —The Trade Union Unity League was born at a convention in Cleveland, with William Z. Foster as leader. The TUUL created the National Miners Union, the National Textile Workers Union, the Needle Trades Workers Industrial Union, and industrial unions of auto workers, steel workers, metal trades workers, and others.

William Zebulon Foster (1881–1961) quit his apprenticeship with an artist in 1894. He was employed for several years as an industrial worker in a variety of occupations. He joined first the Socialist party in 1900, and then the IWW during a free-speech fight in Spokane in 1909. After traveling in Europe for the IWW in 1910, Foster became convinced that the dual unionist policies of the IWW were mistaken. He became an advocate of the English and French radical policy of "boring from within," and sought to advance this program in the AFL and Railroad Brotherhoods through the Syndicalist League of North America, the International Trade Union Educational League,

and the Trade Union Educational League. Foster was instrumental in organizing the packinghouse workers and steel workers in 1917–1919, and led the great steel strike of 1919. In 1921, he joined the Communist party and rose to leadership of the party in 1930 and again in 1945. He retired as party chairman in 1957. Foster was a leader of both the Trade Union Educational League (TUEL) and the Trade Union Unity League (TUUL), and one of the leaders in the fight for militant industrial unionism.

1938 —John L. Lewis was elected president of the Congress of Industrial Organizations (CIO).

John Llewellyn Lewis (1880–1969) started as a coal miner at the age of sixteen and spent ten years in the mines before he was elected an official of the United Mine Workers. He became international president in 1920 and served until his retirement in 1960. Lewis used autocratic methods to beat off all challenges to his leadership by more progressive forces in the union. An advocate of industrial unionism, he was one of the key founders of the Committee for Industrial Organization (CIO), established in 1935 to organize industrial type unions in the unorganized mass-production industries within the AFL. The CIO was expelled by the AFL. In 1938, when it became the Congress of Industrial Organizations, the CIO unions had attained a larger membership than the AFL affiliates.

October 25, 1940 —For the first time, John L. Lewis, president of the CIO, refused to endorse Franklin D. Roosevelt for reelection. Instead he endorsed Wendell Willkie, the Republican candidate. In a nationwide radio speech, Lewis urged CIO members to support Willkie, saying: "It is obvious that President Roosevelt will not be re-elected for the third term unless he has the overwhelming support of the men and women of labor. If he is, therefore, re-elected it will mean that the members of the Congress of Industrial Organizations have rejected my advice and recommendation. I will accept the result as being the equivalent of a vote of no-confidence, and will retire as president of the Congress of Industrial Organizations at its convention in November."

November 22, 1940 —Following Roosevelt's reelection, Lewis resigned as president of the CIO, and Philip Murray was elected to succeed him.

Philip Murray (1886–1952), born the son of a coal miner, in Scotland, emigrated to the United States in 1902 and began working in the mines of western Pennsylvania. He was elected president of a local miners' union, and later became president of the United Mine Workers' District 5, Western Pennsylvania. Murray participated in the establishment of the CIO, and served as president of the Steel Workers Organizing Committee from 1936 to 1942.

May 1946 —Walter Reuther was elected president of the United Automobile Workers (CIO) for the first time.

Walter Philip Reuther (1907–1970) was born in Wheeling, West Virginia, where he became a tool and die maker apprentice at the Wheeling Steel Corporation. He moved to Detroit in 1926 after he was discharged by Wheeling for union activities. In 1931, Reuther was again discharged for union activities — this time by the Ford Motor Company, where he had worked as a tool and die maker. After a three-year world tour with his brother, Victor, that included work in auto plants in the Soviet Union, he returned to Detroit to become a volunteer organizer for the United Automobile, Aircraft, and Agricultural Implement Workers of America (UAW). Reuther became director of the UAW's General Motors Department in 1939, and first vice president of the UAW in 1942. He was elected president of the union in 1946, and that same year was also elected vice president of the CIO. He became president of the CIO in 1951, after the death of Philip Murray.

April 7, 1953 —The first meeting for unity of the AFL and CIO took place under the new presidents of both organizations: George Meany, who had succeeded William Green to the AFL presidency in 1952, and Walter P. Reuther, who had succeeded Philip Murray as president of the CIO in 1951.

George Meany (1894–1980) was born the son of a plumber in New York City on August 16, 1894. He became an apprentice plumber in 1910, a journeyman plumber in 1915, and joined the United Association of Plumbers and Steam Fitters of the United States and Canada. He rose to become business agent of New York Local 463, delegate to the New York City Central Trades and Labor Assembly, and then president of the New York State Federation of Labor. In 1939, Meany was elected secretary-treasurer of the AFL. During World War II, he served as a labor delegate to the National Mediation Defense Board and the National War Labor Board. After the war, Meany became the first director of Labor's League for Political Action in 1948. He was also a member of the executive board of the International Confederation of Free Trade Unions (ICFTU), established to combat the World Federation of Trade Unions (WFTU). After the death of William Green in 1952, Meany was appointed acting president by the AFL Executive Council, and then elected president. He was elected the first president of the merged AFL-CIO in 1955.

1962 — Cesar Chavez, the first Chicano (Mexican-American) labor leader of prominence, formed the National Farm Workers Association in Delano, California.

Cesar Estrada Chavez (1927—   ), was born into a migrant worker family and worked as a field laborer from an early age. He joined the National Agricultural Workers' Union in 1946 and was associated with the Community Service Organization from 1952 to 1962 as

California state organizer (1953—1960), but resigned when it refused to organize the farm *workers*. After forming the National Farm Workers Association, Chavez led the union in strikes at farm labor camps. The strike against the Coachella Valley grape growers gained national prominence when the farm workers employed boycotts, marches, and other methods, to dramatize their struggle. After the strike was won, Chavez became the leader of the United Farm Workers Organizing Committee of the AFL-CIO. The "great grape boycott" of 1967 produced three-year contracts with major grape growers and established a $2 minimum wage and union hiring halls. The AFL-CIO chartered the United Farm Workers' Union, with Chavez as its president, and the union began a struggle to organize all farm workers in California and elsewhere. The effort was fought by the employers, aided by the Teamsters Union. Despite predictions of the demise of the Chavez-led union, it maintained its strength and influence, and in March 1977, the Teamsters Union recognized its jurisdiction over the organization of agricultural workers in the fields.

Labor Legislation

April 1869 — The first mine inspection law was passed in Pennsylvania, but it covered only Schuylkill County mines.

1877 — Massachusetts enacted the first state law requiring factory safeguards.

Labor Lobby

April 1864 — In the first successful lobbying by labor unions during the Civil War era, delegations of trades assemblies of New York City, Brooklyn, and Buffalo defeated a bill against picketing in the New York legislature.

August 24, 1866 — The first labor lobby for Congress and state legislatures was established by the National Labor Union.

1868 — The first permanent labor lobbying committee in Washington was set up by William H. Sylvis, president of the National Labor Union.

Labor's Memorial Day

May 31, 1914 — The first Memorial Day for the martyrs of labor's cause was observed when the Seattle Central Labor Union Council, responding to a suggestion by the Seattle Socialist party, set aside this day of mourning, especially for the recently killed miners, miners' wives, and children in the "Ludlow Massacre" in Colorado. After a parade of all Seattle trade union members, the day was climaxed by an open-air mass meeting on the corner of Third and Blanchard Streets, where Mother Jones was the featured speaker. The committee in charge of Seattle's Labor Memorial Day wrote to Samuel Gompers, president of the American Federation of Labor, to inform him of its success and to suggest that "the custom here be made general" (*Seattle Daily Times,* June 3, 1914).

Labor Novel
(See *Culture*)

Labor Organizations

1648 — The first labor organization was formed when guilds of Boston shoemakers and coopers (barrel makers) obtained a three-year charter. Partially because of the protests of local rural artisans, who considered the guilds a hindrance to free trade, the charters were not renewed.

1662 — The first friendly society was established by porters in New York City. The members' dues went to aid the ill.

1724 — The first labor organization in the building trades appeared in Philadelphia when house carpenters created the Carpenters' Company of the City and County of Philadelphia to establish a "book of prices" for payment for their work "so that a workman should receive the worth of his money." Its "Rules of Work" called for "a price scale bearing a proper proportion to the price of labor with due regard to the increased cost of living." Inconclusive evidence indicates this organization consisted of master carpenters. It was at their meeting house, Carpenters' Hall, that the First Continental Congress met in 1774.

1734 — The first women's labor organization was established by maidservants in New York City to protest the abuses that they suffered at the hands of their mistresses' husbands.

1792 — The first labor organization to maintain a permanent organization was set up by cordwainers in Philadelphia. The organization, whose name is unknown, was formed to maintain or improve wages by collective bargaining. The group lasted less than a year, but it was reestablished in 1794 as the Federal Society of Journeymen Cordwainers, which remained in existence until 1806.

1825 — The first women's labor organization in a trade was formed: the United Tailoresses Society of New York. Later that year, this organization conducted the first strike by a women's labor organization.

1827 — The first federation of labor organizations, the Mechanics Union of Trade Associations, was formed in Philadelphia. This was the first coordinated movement by several trades. Its objectives were "to avert . . . the desolating evils which must inevitably arise from a depreciation of the intrinsic value of human labor; . . . to raise the mechanical and productive classes to

that condition of true independence and equality. . . . " By late 1828, the organization had collapsed.

1834 — The National Trades' Union, the first national labor organization of city federations, was formed in New York City. Its twenty-one thousand members sought "to advance the moral and intellectual condition and pecuniary interests of the laboring classes . . . and to unite and harmonize the effects of all the productive classes of our country." The organization lasted until mid-1837.

1836 — The first national trade asssociation of a single craft was established by the cordwainers, who desired "to form a national compact of the craft." The National Cooperative Association of Journeymen Cordwainers gave financial aid to striking members and cautioned its members against traveling to cities where strikes were occurring. ·The organization disappeared in late 1837.

1850 — The earliest national labor union that still exists was organized: the International Typographical Union.

1867 — The first national women's labor organization was founded: the Daughters of St. Crispin, which consisted of female shoemakers. The union lasted until 1878.

1869 — The Colored National Labor Union became the first national black labor organization.

1881 —The first national organization encompassing several trades was founded. This organization, the Federation of Organized Trades and Labor Unions of United States and Canada, in 1884 became the American Federation of Labor.

Labor Organizers

1830 —Birth of the first great labor orator and organizer: Richard F. Trevellick (d. 1895), ship carpenter and caulker; president of the Ship Carpenters' and Caulkers' International Union (1865); president of the Detroit Trades Assembly; president of the National Labor Union's Labor's Political League (1869, 1871, and 1872).

1830 —Birth of Mary Harris "Mother" Jones (d. 1930), labor organizer and crusader. She toiled mainly among the miners, but she could be found wherever exploitation was fiercest, leading the fight against oppression and cheering the workers on. There is some question as to whether Mother Jones was born in 1830.

1832 —Seth Luther became the first labor organizer to visit more than one state. He was a traveling agent for the *New England Artisan,* a weekly labor paper.

July 25–August 24, 1844 —During this period, S.C. Hewitt, lecturer for *The Mechanic* of Fall River, Massachusetts, became the first organizer to mobilize support for the ten-hour day. He traveled throughout New England, speaking and organizing for the ten-hour day.

1859 —The first paid organizer for the miners' union was hired. John Bates was paid $12 a week and provided with a horse and buggy and traveling expenses.

February 1863 —The first national labor organizer, William H. Sylvis, traveled throughout the country and in parts of Canada, covering over ten thousand miles, to organize for the National Union of Iron Molders.

February 1869 —The first organizing tour in the South was made by William H. Sylvis and Richard F. Trevellick, who were organizing for the National Labor Union.

Labor Pamphlets

1827 —The first labor pamphlets were published by William Heighton, a young Philadelphia cordwainer (shoemaker). Born in Northamptonshire, England, in 1800, Heighton came to the United States as a youth and worked at the shoemakers' trade in Southwork, just below the city line of Philadelphia, where he lived with his wife and daughter. In April he published anonymously *An ADDRESS to the Members of Trade Societies, and to the working classes Generally: Being an Exposition of the Relative Situation, Condition and Future Prospects of Working People in the United States* of America. Together with a Suggestion and Outlines of a PLAN by which They May Gradually and Indefinitely Improve Their Condition. By a Fellow-Labourer. Later that same year, Heighton published a second anonymous pamphlet: An Address, Delivered before the Mechanics and Working Classes Generally, of the city and county of Philadelphia. At the Universal church, in Callowehill Street, on Wednesday Evening, November 21, 1827, by the "UNLETTERED MECHANIC." Heighton financed the publication of the first address himself; the second was paid for by a "Mechanics Delegation." In these pamphlets, Heighton called for the education of the working class through the establishment of a labor press in every city in the United States and a workingmen's library with facilities for reading, lecturing, and debating. He called further for cooperation among the various trade unions in Philadelphia, and the establishment of a workingman's party through which the recently enfranchised workers could make their ballots meaningful. The pamphlets were extremely popular and influential, and led directly to the formation of a Mechanics' Library; the establishment of the Mechanics' Union of Trade Associations of Philadelphia, the first city federation of local trade unions from different crafts in the United States (perhaps in the world); the launching of the Mechanics' Free Press (the first labor paper in the United States), which was edited by Heighton; and the formation of the Workingman's party of Philadelphia, the first labor party in the world.

1832 — The first labor pamphlet published by the labor movement came out: Address to the Workingmen of New England, written by Seth Luther and put out by the New England Association of Farmers, Mechanics, and Other Workingmen (founded in 1831). The pamphlet was a penetrating analysis of the appalling conditions in New England factories, which made a mockery of the Declaration of Independence, and a call to action to restore the ideals of the American Revolution. Luther's Address quickly ran through three editions, and a special edition for European workers was planned.

1845 — The Lowell Female Labor Reform Association, organized by women textile workers in the Lowell mills, published a series of pamphlets called Factory Tracts, which were "to give a true exposition of the Factory system and its effects upon the health and happiness of the operatives." Of these first pamphlets published by working women, only the first number has been preserved (in the Rare Book Room of the Boston Public Library; it is reprinted in its entirety in Philip S. Foner, ed., The Factory Girls [Urbana, Ill., 1977], pp. 130–141).

Labor Papers

1827 — The first American labor paper to be put out was the Journeymen Mechanics' Advocate of Philadelphia. It was edited by a nonworker and died in its first year.

November 10, 1827 — The earliest issue extant of a labor paper is the Philadelphia *Mechanics' Gazette* of this date. This paper, too, was edited by a nonworker.

January 1828 — The first labor paper edited by workingmen and addressed to them was the *Mechanics' Free Press* of Philadelphia. Its editor was William Heighton, a Philadelphia shoemaker. The paper was founded by the Mechanics' Library Company.

During the next few years, other labor papers made their appearance in other cities and states: the *Spirit of the Age* of Tuscaloosa, Alabama; the *Delaware Free Press* of Wilmington, Delaware; the *Farmers' and Mechanics' Advocate* of Charlestown, Indiana; the *Liberalist* of New Orleans, Louisiana; the *New England Farmer and Mechanic* of Gardner, Maine; the *New England Artisan* and the Boston *Working Man's Advocate;* the *Village Chronicle and Farmers' and Mechanics' Advocate* of Newark, New Jersey; the *Mechanics' Press* of Utica, New York; the *Working Men's Advocate* of Albany, New York; the *Independent Politician* of Sandy Hill, Washington County, New York; the *Workingmen's Bulletin* of Buffalo, New York; the *Spirit of the Age* of Rochester, New York; the *Southern Free Press* of Charleston, South Carolina; the *Working Men's Advocate* of Ravenna, Postage County, Ohio; the *Working Man's Advocate,* the *Daily Sentinel,* the *Free Enquirer,* and *The Man,* all of New York City.

February 5, 1830 — The first daily labor paper, the New York *Daily Sentinel,* was published. It was edited by George Henry Evans.

1835 — The first labor paper published for a national audience was the *National Laborer* of Philadelphia.

1845 — The first woman labor editor, Sarah G. Bagley, took over the editorship of the *Voice of Industry,* the leading New England labor paper, for several months. She also edited the "Female Department" of the *Voice of Industry.*

January 1850 — The first German-American labor paper, *Der Republik der Arbeiter* (The Republic of the Working Men), was founded and edited by Wilhelm Weitling in New York City.

July 2, 1863 — On this date, the first truly national labor paper appeared, *Fincher's Trades' Review.* It was published in Philadelphia and edited by Jonathan C. Fincher, a leading figure in the Machinists' and Blacksmiths' Union.

July 1864 — This month saw the inauguration of the first labor paper to last more than ten years, the *Workingman's Advocate* of Chicago, which was edited by Andrew C. Cameron, a union printer.

1880 — The first labor editor to be imprisoned for publishing a letter was J.P. McDonnell. McDonnell, editor of the Paterson *Labor Standard,* was indicted by the grand jury of Passaic, New Jersey, for publishing a letter from a brickmaker that exposed the terrible conditions in the brickyards. He was found guilty and imprisoned.

October 14, 1883 — The first labor paper to be published by a former editor of a commercial paper was *John Swinton's Paper,* put out by John Swinton, formerly editor of the New York *Sun.* It lasted until August 21, 1887, and was considered the best labor paper of the decade.

1884 — The first paper published as part of a boycott was *The Boycotter,* put out by Typographical Union No. 6 of New York City during its dispute with the *New York Tribune.* The paper's name was changed in 1886 to the *Union Printer.* A policy of the paper was to give every *Tribune* subscriber who canceled his subscription a subscription to *The Boycotter.*

June 25, 1886 — The first Jewish labor paper, the *New York Yiddish Volkszeitung,* was published. It lasted until December 20, 1889.

June 1887 — The AFL published its first official journal, *The Union Advocate.* Only a few issues ever appeared.

March 1894 — The first official permanent journal of the AFL appeared. This was *The American Federationist,* edited by Samuel Gompers.

March 18, 1909 — The first issue of the *Industrial Worker,* the IWW's western organ, appeared. It was published in Spokane, Washington, and lasted until September 4, 1913; it was restarted in April 1916.

December 18, 1909 — The first issue of *Solidarity,* the IWW's eastern organ, was published in New Castle, Pennsylvania. The paper lasted until March 18, 1917.

April 1918 — Second-class mailing privileges were withdrawn from a labor paper for the first time. The *Industrial Worker* and other IWW papers were deprived of this privilege under the Federal Espionage Act.

1920 — The first labor paper published by the combined railroad brotherhoods was *Labor.*

November 23, 1933 — The first issue of the *Guild Reporter,* published by the New York Newspaper Guild, appeared.

Labor Parades

July 4, 1788 — The first Grand Labor Parade took place when Philadelphia workers demonstrated in support of the federal Constitution.

February 1860 — The Lynn shoe workers' walkout was the first mass labor parade. Eight hundred women strikers marched for several hours in the snow. At the head of their procession, they carried a banner with the inscription: "American Ladies Will Not Be Slaves. Give Us a Fair Compensation and We Labour Cheerfully."

June 17, 1882 — Glass and steel workers paraded in Pittsburgh in the Grand Labor Parade organized by District Assembly 3 of the Knights of Labor. This was the first labor parade in western Pennsylvania.

November 1883 — The first parade by New Orleans unions in which black and white workers marched together was sponsored by the Central Trades and Labor Assembly. Ten thousand black and white workers participated.

Labor Parties

July 1828 — The first labor party anywhere in the world, the Workingmen's party, was formed in Philadelphia by the Mechanics Union of Trade Associations. The party, whose members included wage earners, craftsmen, and farmers, sought to provide its followers with mutal aid and protection during labor disputes. Some of its demands were for equal public education and an end to monopolies, lotteries, and compulsory military service. The party dissolved after the 1831 election.

1830 — The first statewide labor political organization was created in New York. Three parties titled "Working Men's" parties ran candidates for various local and state offices. The parties pledged to support the following "Working Men's Measures": "Equal Universal Education; Abolishment of Imprisonment for Debt; Abolition of all Licensed Monopolies; An Entire Revision, or Abolition of the Present Militia System; a less Expensive Law System; Equal Taxation on Property; An Effective Lien Law for Laborers on Buildings; A Direct System of Elections; No Legislation on Religion."

1863 — The Workingmen's party of Philadelphia, the first labor party of the Civil War era, was founded.

August 24, 1866 — The first proposal for a national labor party was presented at the 1866 convention of the National Labor Union for the purpose of securing eight-hour laws in Congress and the states. It was adopted by a vote of thirty-five to twenty-four.

1869 — The first post-Civil War labor party to elect candidates to office was the Massachussetts Labor Reform party. It put one candidate in the state senate and two in the lower house.

February 22, 1872 — The first national labor party, the Labor Reform party, was formed at a national convention held in Columbus, Ohio, sponsored by the National Labor Union. The party's presidential candidate was David Davis of Illinois, who declined to campaign, but received one electoral vote in the 1872 presidential election.

August 8, 1877 — The first labor party to be formed after the railroad strikes of 1877 was the Workingmen's party in Louisville, Kentucky. Its platform advocated an eight-hour day, compulsory education, prohibition of labor by children under fourteen years of age, prohibition of prison labor, and a better financial policy. The Workingmen's party elected five of its seven candidates to the state legislature and won 8,850 of the 13,578 votes cast, which placed it ahead of the Democratic party.

August 13, 1877 — The first fusion of labor and greenbackers produced the United Labor party in Pittsburgh.

February 1878 — The first national farmer-labor party, the Greenback-Labor party, was formed at a convention of farmers and trade unionists in Toledo, Ohio. James B. Weaver was its presidential candidate in 1880.

May 1888 — This was the first presidential election in which two labor party candidates ran. The United Labor party nominated Robert H. Cowdrey for president, and the Union Labor party nominated A.J. Streeter as its presidential candidate.

January 13, 1919 — The first labor party to be formed after World War I

was the Independent Labor party of Chicago, which named its own candidates for city offices.

1924 — For the first time, the AFL endorsed a farmer-labor ticket. It supported Robet M. LaFollette, who was the presidential candidate of the Farmer-Labor party. LaFollette was also endorsed by the railroad brotherhoods.

July 16, 1936 — The American Labor party was formed as the New York State affiliate of Labor's Non-Partisan League.

Labor Petitions

1829 — The first petition to the federal government by a labor group complained to the War Department about the low wages received by women making shirts for the army. The petition was rejected.

October 15, 1835 — The first petition to Congress requesting a reduction of hours of labor on public works was presented by the National Trades' Union on behalf of mechanics in Brooklyn and New York for the ten-hour day. It was brought up in Congress by Ely Moore, a labor congressman from New York, and referred to a committee, which buried it.

1884 — Labor presented its first mass petition to Congress, a Knights of Labor petition urging repeal of the contract labor law signed with fifty thousand names. This petition was successful.

November, 1912 — The first petition from a trade union to a U.S. president asking him to intervene in a strike on the ground that the state government was undemocratic was presented by the Brotherhood of Timber Workers (IWW) to President William Howard Taft. The occasion was the timber workers' strike against the American Lumber Company in Merryville, Louisiana. The petition was ignored.

Labor Radio Stations

January 1926 — The secretary of state of Illinois granted incorporation papers enabling the Chicago Federation of Labor to own and operate a radio broadcasting station, the first of its kind in the United States. Secretary Edward N. Nockels of the federation, commenting on the station, said:

> The policies of the labor movement have been so misrepresented in the subsidized press that the public in general has been cruelly deceived as to our purposes and undertakings. On practically all important questions we have been denied a hearing at the bar of public opinion.
>
> We now propose to lay our case before the thoughtful men and women of the country through this broadcasting station which we will own, control and operate ourselves.

Associated with the federation in the undertaking were the Joint Board of the Amalgamated Clothing Workers, the Teamsters' District Council, the Musicians' Union, and several other unions.

Labor's Bill of Grievances

March 21, 1906 — The first labor "Bill of Grievances" was adopted at a conference attended by representatives of 118 national and international unions and members of the AFL Executive Council. The Bill of Grievances complained in general "of the indifferent position which the Congress of the U.S. has manifested toward the just, reasonable, and necessary measures which have been before it these past several years, and which particularly affect the interests of the working people." In particular, the Bill of Grievances called for an anti-injunction law; an effective eight-hour law that would be extended to cover all federal work; a bill to protect workers from the competition of convict labor; a bill to prevent violations of the Chinese Exclusion Act; a bill restricting immigration; a bill to free seamen from involuntary servitude; a bill mandating safety measures for seamen; and a bill to strengthen the antitrust law against monopolies and prevent it from being perverted "so far as the laborers are concerned, so as to invade and violate their personal liberty guaranteed by the constitution." The Bill of Grievances also complained of a Panama amendment to the eight-hour law; called for the restoration of the right of petition for government employees, which had been rescinded by President Theodore Roosevelt; and asked for the reorganization of the House Committe on Labor to make that committee more sympathetic to labor.

March 21, 1906 —For the first time, the AFL was invited to the White House. One hundred representatives of the AFL, headed by President Gompers, met with President Theodore Roosevelt and presented Labor's Bill of Grievances. Roosevelt defended the right of injunction and said he would enjoin labor unions themselves if necessary.

August 15, 1906 —The AFL conducted its first political campaign on behalf of Labor's Bill of Grievances. It was designed to defeat Republican Congressman Charles E. Littlefield of Maine. Though Littlefield was reelected, his plurality was cut from 5,400 votes in 1904 to 1,362 in 1906.

September 1906 —The AFL conducted its first nationwide questioning of candidates for Congress. The issue was the candidates' attitude toward Labor's Bill of Grievances.

Labor Solidarity

1796 —The first appeal for labor solidarity came in a letter signed by the Federal Society of Philadelphia Cabinet Makers that was published in the *New York Argus*. It read:

> From the working Cabinet Makers of Philadelphia to their Mechanical Fellow citizens. We hope and entreat that a union of the respective mechanical branches in this City, and throughout America will immediately take place, in order to repel any attack that has or may be made on societies of this description.
>
> Hasten then, fellow citizens, to declare yourselves ready at any time to assist one another, in a cause which will determine the independence of so useful a body as the working Citizens of America. Signed by order of the Federal Society of Philadelphia Cabinet Makers.

May 6, 1912 —Black and white workers met together in the Deep South for the first time since Reconstruction at the convention of the Brotherhood of Timber Workers in Alexandria, Louisiana. The meeting was called to discuss affiliation with the IWW. When William D. ("Big Bill") Haywood addressed the white timber workers, he asked where the black workers were, and when he was told that they were meeting separately in another hall because it was against the law in Louisiana for black and white workers to meet together, he declared: "You work in the same mills together. Sometimes a black man and a white man chop down the same tree together. You are meeting in convention now to discuss the conditions under which you labor. This can't be done intelligently by passing resolutions here and then sending them out to another room for the black man to act upon. Why not be sensible about this and call the Negroes into this convention? If it is against the law, this is one time when the law should be broken." Haywood's advice was taken, and the blacks were called into the session. The interracial gathering voted to affiliate with the IWW.

November 22, 1919 — This was the first time white trade unionists lost their lives protecting a black trade unionist. L.E. Williams, district president of the AFL and editor of the *Press,* a Bogalusa, Louisiana, labor paper, was killed, along with union carpenters A. Bouchillon and Thomas Gaines, while protecting Sol Dacus, a black trade union organizer for the AFL International Timber Workers Union from an attack by vigilantes in Bogalusa. In December, thirteen policemen were arrested for the murders, but a grand jury refused to return indictments.

September 19, 1981 —The first labor "Solidarity Day" demonstration for jobs, justice, human rights, and social progress, called by the AFL-CIO Council, took place on the National Mall in Washington, D.C. The demonstration protested against "Reaganomics" — the budget cuts, supply side tax cuts, and tight money economic policy of President Ronald Reagan that had increased the burdens of poor people, older citizens, and working people both black and white.

Labor Songs

1794 —The first trade union song, "Address to the Journeymen Cordwainers L.B. of Philadelphia," was written by John McIlvaine to recruit members into the Federal Society of Journeymen Cordwainers of Philadelphia. The first three verses went:

Cordwainers! Arouse! The time has
                        now come!
When our rights should be fully
                        protected;
And every attempt to reduce anyone
    By all should be·nobly rejected.

Fellow-Craftsmen! Arouse! We united
                        should be
    And each man should be hailed as
                        a brother,
Organized we should be in this hallowed
                        cause,
    To love and relieve one another.

Speak not of failure, in our attempt
                        to maintain,
    For our labor a fair compensation;
All that we want is assistance from you,
    To have a permanent organization.

July 21, 1878 —The official eight-hour song, "Eight Hours," was first published in the *Labor Standard.* The words were written by I.G. Blanchard and the music by Reverend Jesse H. Jones. The opening stanza and chorus went:

We mean to make things over, we are
                        tired of toil for naught,
With but bare enough to live upon, and
                        never an hour for thought;
We want to feel the sunshine, and we
                        want to smell the flowers,

We are sure that God has will'd it, and
　　　we mean to have eight hours.

We're summoning our forces from the
　　　shipyard, shop and mill,
Eight hours for work, eight hours for
　　　rest, eight hours for what we will!
Eight hours for work, eight hours for
　　　rest, eight hours for what we will!

June 1885 —This was the date of the
first publication of one of the most
popular songs of the Knights of Labor,
"Storm the Fort ye Knights," sung to
the tune of "Hold the Fort." Its opening
verse and chorus went:

　Toiling millions now are waking,
　　See them marching on;
　All the tyrants now are shaking,
　　Ere their power is gone.

　Storm the fort, ye Knights of Labor,
　　Battle for your cause;
　Equal rights for every neighbor,
　　Down with tyrant laws.

April 4, 1908 —The IWW song,
"Hallelujah on the Bum," a song of the
unemployed, was published in the
Industrial Union Bulletin. The first verse
and chorus went:

　O, why don't you work
　Like other men do?
　How in the hell can I work
　When there's no work to do?

　Hallelujah, I'm a bum,
　Hallelujah, bum again,
　Hallelujah, give us a handout—
　To revive us again.

1909 —The first edition of the IWW's
The Little Red Song Book appeared. In
1956, the twenty-ninth edition was
published.

1911 —Joe Hill, the most famous of the
IWW songwriters, wrote his first song,
"Casey Jones—the Union Scab," to
assist workers on strike on the Southern
Pacific railroad line. The opening and
closing verses went:

　The workers on the S.P. Line
　　To strike sent out a call;
　But Casey Jones the engineer,
　　He wouldn't strike at all

　His boiler it was leaking,
　　And its drivers on the bum,
　And his engine and its bearings,
　　They were all out of plumb.

　　　*　　*　　*

　Casey Jones went to Hell a-flying,
　"Casey Jones," the Devil said, "Oh, fine;
　Casey Jones, get busy shoveling sulphur—
　That's what you get for scabbing on the
　　　　　　S.P. Line."

January 17, 1915 —"Solidarity Forever," written by Ralph Chaplin, was
first sung on this date. This, the most
famous IWW song, was begun during
the Kanawha miners' strike in Hunt-
ington, West Virginia, 1912–1913,
but was not finished until January 17,
1915, in Chicago, on the day of a giant
"Hunger Demonstration." The opening
verse and chorus went:

　When the union's inspiration through
　　　the workers' blood shall run,

There can be no power greater anywhere
                beneath the sun.
Yet what force on earth is weaker than
          the feeble strength of one?
But the union makes us strong.

      Solidarity forever!
      Solidarity forever!
      Solidarity forever!
      For the union makes us strong.

1936 — The first song for sit-down strikers was composed by Maurice Sugar, counsel for the United Automobile Workers:

    When they tie a can to a union man
      Sit down! Sit down!
    When they give him the sack,
             they'll take him back,
    Sit down! Sit down!

    Sit down, just take a seat
    Sit down and rest your feet
    Sit down, you've got 'em beat
    Sit down! Sit down!

Labor Speeches

November 21, 1827 — The first formal speech of the American labor movement, *An Address, Delivered before the Mechanics and Working Classes Generally, of the City and County of Philadelphia. At the Universalist Church, on Wednesday evening, November 21, 1827, by the "UNLETTERED MECHANIC,"* was published by request of the Mechanics' Delegation, and printed at the office of the *Mechanics' Gazette*, No. 2, Carter's Alley. Its author was William Heighton, a Philadelphia shoemaker. (See "Labor Pamphlets.")

May 5, 1836 — In the first speech made in Congress by a labor congressman, Ely Moore defended trade unions. In his maiden speech before the House, he said: "Sir, these associations are intended as counterpoises against capital, whenever it should attempt to exert an unlawful or undue influence. They are a measure of *self-defense* and *self-preservation,* and, therefore, are not *illegal!"*

Labor Spies

October 1875 — In this year, the first widely publicized labor spy, James McParlan, began to operate as a Pinkerton agent in the anthracite mining region, using the name McKenna. He was a leading figure in the "Molly Maguire" frame-up, in which twenty-four union miners were arrested and accused of murder. Twenty were later executed.

May 1913 — For the first time, local officers of a union were exposed as being in the pay of a detective agency. The leaders of IWW's Akron, Ohio, branch of the rubber workers were the hirelings of a Cleveland detective agency.

Labor Standards

1936 — The Public Contracts Act, which set labor standards for government contracts, was passed by Congress.

1938 — The first Fair Labor Standards Act was passed by Congress. It set a minimum wage law of twenty-five cents an hour and outlawed child labor in all businesses under its jurisdiction.

Labor Theater

April 24, 1905 — The first proposal for a "Theater of Labor" was introduced at a meeting of the Central Federated Union of New York City because current drama was composed of "capitalist plays." It was not adopted.

June 7, 1913 — America's first labor play, *Pageant of the Paterson Strike,* was performed by 1,029 striking workers from the Paterson silk mills who were led by the IWW. The plan for the pageant was advanced by John Reed, a graduate of Harvard University, Class of 1910, who had been jailed for four days in Paterson for merely watching the strike. The entire action of the strike was presented in the form of a tableau against a set of a silk mill, before a standing-room-only crowd of more than fifteen thousand in New York City's Madison Square Garden.

November 1937 — The first labor musical opened in New York City: *Pins and Needles,* produced by the Labor Stage of the International Ladies' Garment Workers' Union, with words and music by Harold Rome and union members as performers, was the first big hit of trade union theater and ran for three years.

November 1947 — The first postwar labor musical, *Thursday's Till Nine,* was presented by the New York Department Store Workers Union (CIO), with a cast composed entirely of department store employees. It was written by Norman Franklin and Henry Foner, and the union donated all proceeds to the Disabled American Veterans.

Land Reform

1845 — The slogan "Vote Yourself a Farm" was first used by the National Reform Association, a land reform organization headed by George Henry Evans.

Lincoln

September 1859 — Abraham Lincoln gave his first speech asserting that labor is more important than capital. At the State Fair of the Wisconsin Agricultural Society, he declared "that labor is prior to, and independent of capital; that, in fact, capital is the fruit of labor, and could never have existed if labor had not first existed; that labor can exist without capital, but that capital could never have existed without labor. Hence . . . labor is the superior . . . greatly the superior to capital."

March 6, 1860 — Lincoln became the first presidential candidate to defend labor's right to strike. As the candidate of the Republican party, he declared in a speech in New Haven, Connecticut: "I am glad to see that a system of labor prevails in New England under which laborers can strike when they want to, where they are not obliged to labor whether you pay them or not. I like the system which lets a man quit when he wants to, and wish it might prevail elsewhere. One of the reasons why I am opposed to slavery is just here. . . ." He was referring to the great shoe strike then in progress.

1861 — Abraham Lincoln became the first U.S. president elected to honorary membership in a trade union when he was made an honorary member of the New York City trade unions.

November 1863 — The first White House interview between a president and a delegation representing a trade union occurred when President Lincoln met with a delegation from the National Union of Machinists and Blacksmiths.

July 1864 — In the first appeal by striking workers to a U.S. president to countermand strikebreaking by the U.S. Army, union printers in St. Louis sent a note to President Lincoln presenting their case. Lincoln ordered that servants of the federal government should not interfere with labor's legitimate demands, and the soldiers were withdrawn.

Lockouts

1892 — The first major lockout occurred when Henry C. Frick, manager of the Carnegie steel mill in Homestead, Pennsylvania, locked out members of the Amalgamated Association of Iron, Steel, and Tin Workers and imported three hundred Pinkerton men to smash the union. The company broke the union and eliminated the Amalgamated from its mills.

February 1976 — Major league baseball club owners conducted their first lockout against the Players' Association. Preseason training camps in Florida, Arizona, and California were shut down for seventeen days because of the "reserve clause" decision, until Commissioner Bowie Kuhn ordered the owners to open the camps. On July 12, 1976, owners and players reached agreement on a four-year pact that, for the first time, gave the players freedom of movement by eliminating the so-called reserve system.

Lynching

August 1, 1917 — The first known lynching of a labor organizer happened during World War I, when Frank H. Little, an organizer for the IWW and a member of its General Executive Board, was lynched by vigilantes in Butte, Montana.

Machinery

1828 —The first demand by a working man that workers forced out of work by machinery receive compensation appeared in the September 27, 1828, issue of the *Mechanics Free Press* of Philadelphia:

> If, by the introduction of Labour Saving Machinery, a number of Operatives are thrown out of employment, or in any material degree injured in their trade, such Operatives have as just a claim on the profits which were the result of the improvement, or a remuneration for the losses sustained thereby, as has the land-holder for his lands, which are taken to construct a canal, rail, or turnpike road, or any public work: and it would appear more just to remunerate the Former, as this class of citizens seldom have any thing but their trades to depend on, whereas the land-holder is often remunerated for so much of his land as is necessarily taken, while that which he has remaining increases sometimes two, three, or four fold in value, by the improvement. . . .

1829 —The first demand by a working man that labor appropriate and operate machines was made by Thomas Skidmore, a machinist. He wrote in *Rights of Man to Property:* "If . . . it is seen that the steam engine . . . is likely to greatly impoverish or destroy the poor, what have they do but lay hold of it, and make it their own?"

July 1862 —In the first strike against the introduction of machinery, the Grainmen's Protective Union of New York City walked out when floating grain elevators were introduced.

1867 —The mold was introduced into the cigar trade. It downgraded the status of the skilled cigar maker.

1884 —The first union agreement accepting a machine was signed by the International Typographical Union. The union agreed to the introduction of the Mergenthaler linotype machine, provided that union hand compositors got first claim to the linotype jobs at regular compositors' wages.

Massacres

September 10, 1897 —Sheriff Martin of Luzerne County, Pennsylvania, and about one hundred armed thugs called "deputy sheriffs" ordered a group of striking miners to halt on the public highway where they were marching to the Lattimer Mine to get the men there to come out. The marchers were Austrians, Hungarians, Poles, Italians, and Germans who had been imported by the mine operators as cheap labor, but who had begun to organize and to demand higher wages and better conditions. Suddenly, without warning, the deputies opened fire on the unarmed workers, killing nineteen and wounding thirty-five others. "Most of them were shot in the back," the *Review of Reviews* reported on October 1, 1897, in its story on the "Lattimer Massacre." Not a single "deputy" was found guilty of murder.

April 20, 1914 — During a United Mine Workers' strike, Colorado milita swept a strikers' tent colony near Ludlow with machine-gun fire and then proceeded to burn the tents with people inside them. Thirty-nine men, women, and children were killed. Louis Tikas, the strike leader at Ludlow, and two others were murdered. Crying "Remember Ludlow," enraged miners burned mines and killed guardsmen. Court-martials absolved the soldiers of any responsibility in the Ludlow Massacre.

Today on the site of the Ludlow Massacre, there stands a monument erected by the United Mine Workers. On it is the inscription: "In memory of the men, women, and children who lost their lives in freedom's cause at Ludlow, Colorado, April 20, 1914."

May 30, 1937 — On this Memorial Day, Chicago police opened fire on unarmed steelworkers who were striking against the Republic Steel Company. Ten men were killed, over a hundred were wounded. All the killed were shot in the back. The Memorial Day Massacre increased the determination of the steelworkers to organize their industry, and by 1941, this had been accomplished.

Magazines

1979 — The first magazine to be named after a labor leader, *Mother Jones,* a monthly journal dealing with social reform, appeared. It was named in honor of the militant Mother Mary Harris Jones.

May Day

May 1, 1886 — The first May Day demonstration was held in the United States in response to a resolution adopted at the 1884 convention of the Federation of Organized Trades and Labor Unions of the United States and Canada — precursor of the American Federation of Labor. The resolution asserted that "eight hours shall constitute a legal day's labor from and after May 1, 1886, and that we recommend that labor organizations throughout this district that they so direct their laws as to conform to this resolution." Approximately 340,000 workers throughout the country rallied on May 1, 1886, for an eight-hour day.

Following the May 1, 1886, strikes, employers mounted a counteroffensive that was climaxed by the Haymarket tragedy. Then in December 1888, the American Federation of Labor called for a renewal of the movement for the eight-hour day on May 1, 1890. This date was also selected by the leaders of organized socialist movements of many lands who met in Paris at the founding congress of the Second International on July 14, 1889, the hundredth anniversary of the fall of the Bastille and the beginning of the French Revolution.

Beginning in 1890, May Day demonstrations of workers on an international scale became annual events. However, the AFL, which had originated May Day, later repudiated it as the federation became increasingly conservative.

Mexican-Americans (See also "Agricultural Workers")

1928 — The first important labor organization of Mexican workers in the United States was founded: *Confederación de Uniones Obreros Mexicanos* (Federation of Mexican Workers' Unions). It was organized by a number of local unions in southern California and was patterned after the union movement in Mexico.

December 31, 1964 — Congress passed the first law prohibiting the importation of *braceros* (Mexican agricultural workers).

March 1974 — The Amalgamated Clothing Workers of America signed its first contract with the Farah Manufacturing Company. It came after a successful twenty-one-month strike and boycott. Eighty-five percent of the workers in the Texas and New Mexico plants of Farah were Chicanos.

Militia

October 1898 — Militia was first used to aid strikers when Governor Tanner of Illinois sent soldiers to protect strikers in Pana and Virden against strikebreakers.

Minimum Wage

June 4, 1912 — Massachusetts passed the first minimum wage law. It was scheduled to take effect on July 1, 1913, and established a Minimum Wage Commission of three (one of whom could be a woman), to be appointed by the governor with the advice of the Council.

February 17, 1913 — Oregon became the first state to set up an administrative body to enforce a minimum wage law. It was to be appointed within thirty days after the law was passed, and was to consist of three members, one representing employers, one workers, and one the public.

January 5, 1914 — The first minimum wage for all workers at the Ford Motor Company was instituted: $5 a day for an eight-hour day. Ford probably made this concession to workers to forestall the IWW's organization efforts in the automobile industry.

April 9, 1917 —For the first time, the U.S. Supreme Court upheld a state law fixing minimum wages. It decided that the Oregon law setting a minimum wage for women and maximum hours of work for men was constitutional.

1923 —The first U.S. Supreme Court decision declaring a minimum wage law unconstitutional came in *Adkins v. Children's Hospital,* which involved the minimum wage law of the District of Columbia.

July 1933 —The first code providing for a minimum wage was adopted under the National Industrial Recovery Act. It applied to the textile industry, and stipulated a minimum wage of $13 a week in the North and $11 in the South.

1938 —The Fair Labor Standards Act established the first federal minimum wage law covering all nonagricultural labor. It put a ceiling on hours and a floor under wages, and placed restrictions on the employment of children in industries engaged in interstate commerce.

Motion Pictures

1910 —The first resolution calling upon workers to protest to local theater managements when an antilabor film was shown was adopted by an AFL convention.

September 1911 —The first prolabor film was produced as part of the defense campaign for the McNamara brothers. It was entitled *A Martyr to His Cause*, and subtitled "Incidents in the Life and Abduction of the Secretary-Treasurer of the International Association of Bridge and Structural Iron Workers." The premiere was held at the American Theatre in Cincinnati, where it was seen by an estimated fifty thousand people.

1926 —A seven-reel film —*The Passaic Textile Strike,* dealing with the walkout of textile workers in Passaic, New Jersey —was shown throughout the country to raise funds for strike relief. This was the first movie made of a strike. It began with a prologue enacted by the strikers themselves, dramatizing the life of a striker. Then it showed the strikers braving police clubs and shotguns, fire hoses in zero weather, and gas bombs. Finally, it showed huge mass meetings, with ten thousand workers participating and strike leaders and other speakers addressing the strikers.

1953 —The first film depicting working men and women who had actually been involved in a strike was *Salt of the Earth,* produced by a group of Hollywood professionals, several of whom had been blacklisted during witch-hunts conducted by the House Un-American Activities Committee. The Hollywood group was led by Herbert Biberman, and Oscar-winning screen writers Paul Jarrico and Michael Wilson. Their film was based on the struggle of Local 890 of the Mine, Mill, and Smelter Workers' Union against the Delaware Zinc Company in Silver City, New Mexico. The script was developed in consultation with the men and women of Local 890, and the events and emotions depicted in the film reflected what actually happened in the lives of these people. The actors were Mexicans and Mexican-Americans.

National Guard

1896 —Strikebreakers were sworn in as members of the National Guard for the first time. This happened during the Leadville, Colorado, strike of the Western Federation of Miners when 175 nonunion employees were recruited into militia units.

February 7, 1913 —The first National Guard attack on strikers' living quarters occurred during a Holy Grove, West Virginia, coal strike. Nine hundred strikers' families in tent colonies were attacked by the military and one miner was killed.

April 20, 1914 —The first mass killing of men, women, and children during a strike was the Ludlow Massacre. Thirteen children, two women, and three men were murdered when the National Guard and company-employed gunmen set fire to the strikers' tent colony during a strike by the United Mine Workers against the Rockefeller-dominated Colorado Fuel and Iron Company.

National Labor Federations

April 1796 —The first effort to unite labor on a national scale came when the Federal Society of Philadelphia Cabinet Makers issued an appeal for "a union of the respective mechanical branches in this city, and throughout America. . . ." There was no real response to the appeal.

August 1834 —The first national labor organization of city federations was the National Trades' Union, formed in New York City by labor unions from six eastern cities. Its twenty-one thousand members sought "to advance the moral and intellectual condition and pecuniary interests of the laboring classes . . . and to unite and harmonize the efforts of all the productive classes of our country." The organization lasted until mid-1837.

September 21, 1864 —The first national labor federation of the Civil War era was the International Industrial Assembly of North America, which was founded in Louisville, Kentucky, by delegates from trades' assemblies in eight cities in eight states.

August 20, 1866 — The National Labor Union, organized at a convention in Baltimore by seventy-seven delegates from thirteen states and the District of Columbia, was the first national labor federation of the post-Civil War era.

December 26, 1869 — Uriah S. Stephens organized the first assembly of the Knights of Labor in Philadelphia. It was made up of garment cutters.

January 6, 1870 — The first officers of the Knights of Labor were elected. Uriah S. Stephens was elected master workman.

October 20, 1870 — For the first time, the Knights of Labor admitted workers other than garment cutters. "Sojourners" were permitted to belong.

January 5, 1871 — The first annual report of the Knights of Labor revealed that there were sixty-nine members.

December 25, 1873 — The first District Assembly of the Knights of Labor, District Assembly 1, met in Philadelphia. District Assembly 2, representing Camden, New Jersey, was formed on October 4, 1874; and District Assembly 3, representing Pittsburgh, was formed on August 8, 1875.

January 1878 — The Knights of Labor drew up its first constitution. A Declaration of Principles adopted at the Reading Convention established the Knights on a national basis.

November 15, 1881 — The first convention of the American Federation of Labor took place in Pittsburgh under the name of the "Federation of Organized Trades and Labor Unions of the United States and Canada."

1881 — The Knights of Labor voted to make its name public for the first time.

January 1882 — The Knights of Labor fully abandoned secrecy for the first time.

1883 — The Amalgamated Association of Iron and Steel workers became the first union to withdraw from the AFL. It left because of a resolution adopted by the federation condemning high tariffs.

October 1886 — The first national labor federation to reach a membership of over 500,000 was the Knights of Labor. By this time, its membership was over 750,000.

December 8, 1886 — On this date, the name "American Federation of Labor" was used for the first time. It replaced the name "Federation of Organized Trades and Labor Unions of the United States and Canada." The name change was adopted at a convention in Columbus, Ohio, attended by 25 officers of national unions representing over 300,000 members. Samuel Gompers was elected the first president of the AFL.

1886 — The Knights of Labor became the first federation of labor in the United States to have foreign locals. The Knights established locals in Australia, New Zealand, Belgium, France, England, Ireland, and Canada.

January 2, 1905 — The first meeting leading to the formation of the Industrial Workers of the World (IWW) took place at the Chicago Conference of Industrial Unionists. William D. ("Big Bill") Haywood, secretary-treasurer of the Western Federation of Miners, was elected chairman. The conference adopted an Industrial Union Manifesto that called for a convention in Chicago on June 27, 1905, of all those in labor's ranks who believed that the AFL's craft unionism and other conservative policies were outmoded and that a new labor movement, emphasizing industrial unionism and the class struggle, was needed.

June 27, 1905 — The IWW was founded at a convention of two hundred delegates in Chicago. Haywood opened the convention and declared: "This is the Continental Congress of the working class."

November 14, 1938 — At the first constitutional convention of the Congress of Industrial Organizations (CIO), 34 national and international unions, 8 organizing committees, 23 state councils, 116 city and county councils, and 137 directly affiliated local industrial unions met in Pittsburgh, adopted a constitution designating the new labor federation the "Congress of Industrial Organizations," and elected the following slate of officers: John L. Lewis, president; Philip Murray and Sidney Hillman, vice presidents; and James B. Carey, secretary. An executive board composed of one representative from each affiliated national union, international union, and organizing committee was set up as the governing body between conventions.

December 6, 1945 — For the first time since World War II, negotiations for unity were reopened between the AFL and CIO. The step was taken on the initiative of President Philip Murray of the CIO. It did not succeed.

December 20, 1950 — The AFL for the fist time granted formal recognition to the CIO. A Labor Policy Committee was established, with three representatives each from the AFL and CIO, and three from unaffiliated unions. Its aim was to assist the U.S. government in conducting the Korean war, and it became part of the Office of Defense Mobilization and the Wage Stabilization Board.

October 1954 — The Unity Committee of the AFL and CIO announced its determination to create "a single trade union center . . . which will preserve the integrity of each affiliated national and international union."

May 1955 —The constitution of the newly merged labor organization (which was still nameless) was published. It announced twelve "objects and principles," preceded by a "Preamble," which read:

The establishment of this federation through the merger of the American Federation of Labor and the Congress of Industrial Organizations is an expression of the hopes and aspirations of the working people of America.

We seek the fulfillment of these hopes and aspirations through democratic processes within the framework of our constitutional government and consistent with our institutions and traditions.

At the collective bargaining table, in the community, in the exercise of the rights and responsibilities of citizenship, we shall responsibly serve the interests of all the American people.

We pledge ourselves to the more effective organization of working men and women, to the securing to them of full recognition and enjoyment of the rights to which they are justly entitled; to the achievement of ever higher standards of living and working conditions; to the attainment of security for all the people; to the enjoyment of the leisure which their skills make possible; and to the strengthening and extension of our way of life and the fundamental freedoms which are the basis of our democratic society.

We shall combat resolutely the forces which seek to undermine the democratic institutions of our nation and to enslave the human soul. We shall strive always to win full respect for the dignity of the human individual whom our unions serve.

Its official name was American Federation of Labor–Congress of Industrial Organizations (AFL–CIO).

December 5, 1955 —The merged AFL-CIO, with a membership of fifteen million, held its first convention, making the merger official.

July 1968 —The first new national labor federation to be launched since the CIO in 1938 was the Alliance for Labor Action founded by the UAW (1,600,000) members and the International Brotherhood of Teamsters, Chauffeurs, Warehousemen, and Helpers, the nation's largest non-AFL-CIO union, with two million members. The stated aim of the alliance was to organize the jobless and poor into unions, to achieve cordial relations with young people, and to revive the militant labor spirit. It lasted until mid-1971.

National Trade Unions

November 1835 —The first call for the formation of a national union of printers went out. It was issued by the Franklin Typographical Society of Cincinnati.

March 1, 1836 —The National Cooperative Association of Journeymen Cordwainers became the first national union of a single craft. It gave financial aid to striking members, and warned members against traveling to cities where strikes were occurring. The organization disappeared in late 1837.

October 4, 1836 —The first national union of carpenters was formed at a national convention.

November 7, 1836 —The National Typographical Society, the first national union of printers, was founded at a national convention in Washington, D.C., by delegates from Baltimore, New York City, Washington, Harrisburg, and Philadelphia.

December 1850 —The earliest national union that is still in existence is the International Typographical Union. Originally called the National Typographical Union, it was organized after a national convention of journeymen printers held in New York City, with delegates from New York, New Jersey, Pennsylvania, Maryland, and Kentucky.

May 1852 —At the first convention of the National Typographical Union, delegates representing local unions in New York City, Albany, Philadelphia, Harrisburg, Boston, Richmond, Baltimore, Cincinnati, and Trenton were present. Four years later, at the 1856 convention, delegates came also from Louisville, Memphis, New Orleans, Nashville, Buffalo, and Chicago.

1854 —The Hat Finishers' National Association became the first national union of hat finishers.

1854 —The first national union of plumbers was founded: the Plumbers' National Union.

1854 —The first national union of building trades workers was founded. The National Union of Building Trades included house painters, stonecutters, plasterers, carpenters, bricklayers, plumbers, and masons.

August 1855 —The first national union with locals in both the United States and Canada was the Journeymen Cutters' Association of United States and Canada.

November 1855 —The first union of railroad workers, the National Protective Association (engineers), was formed in Baltimore.

July 1856 —The first national union of lithographers was founded: the Lithographers' National Union.

1856 —The Cigar Makers National Union became the first national union of cigar makers.

June 1857 —The first national union of silver platers was founded: the National Union of Silver Platers.

1858 —The National Cotton Mule Spinners' Association of America became the first national union of textile workers.

April 11, 1859 — The first national union of machinists and blacksmiths was founded when twenty-one delegates from twelve local unions in five cities and three states convened in Philadelphia and established the National Union of Machinists and Blacksmiths. By late 1860, the union had 57 locals and 2,828 members, and in 1862, it launched its own monthly publication, the *Machinists' and Blacksmiths' Review*, edited by Jonathan C. Fincher.

July 5, 1859 — The first national union of iron molders was precipitated by a meeting of thirty-five delegates from twelve local unions in Philadelphia, which led, in 1860, to the formation of the National Union of Iron Molders, with William H. Sylvis as national treasurer. In 1863, it became the largest and most effective trade union of the era.

1859 — The first national union of painters was founded: the Painters' National Union.

1859 — The first national union of shoe workers was formed: the Cordwainers' National Union.

1861 — The American Miners' Association became the first national union of miners.

1862 — The first national union of iron workers to unite more than one craft was the National Forge of the Sons of Vulcan, which joined boilermakers and puddlers.

May 1863 — The first permanent national union of railroad workers was founded: the Brotherhood of the Footboard (engineers), which changed its name in 1864 to the Brotherhood of Locomotive Engineers.

1863 — The first national union of plasterers was formed: the Plasterers' National Union.

1863 — The first national union of curriers was founded: the National Union of Journeymen Curriers.

1863 — The National Union of Ship Carpenters and Caulkers became the first national union of ship carpenters and caulkers.

1865 — The Coach Makers' International Union became the first national union of coach makers.

1865 — The first national union of carpenters was created: the Carpenters' and Joiners' International Union.

January 1866 — The Bricklayers' International Union of the United States of North America became the first national union of bricklayers. By 1899, only one local (the Chicago bricklayers) had refused to join.

1866 —The first national union of hat workers was the National Union of Silk and Fur Hat Finishers.

March 7, 1867 —On this date, the first convention of the Knights of St. Crispin, a secret national union of shoe workers founded in Milwaukee, was held.

1868 —The first national union of railway conductors was formed: the Brotherhood of Railway Conductors.

1868 —The first national union of leather workers was organized: the National Union of Morocco Dressers.

May 1870 —The first national union of coopers was founded: the International Union of Coopers.

1870 —The National Union of Telegraphers became the first national union of telegraph operators.

1871 —The National Union of Painters, the first national union of painters, was founded.

1872 —The first national union in steel was the Brotherhood of Iron and Steel Heaters, Rollers, and Roughers of the United States.

July 1873 —The first national union of furniture workers was created: the Furniture Workers' National Union.

October 14, 1873 —At the first convention of the Miners' National Association, John Siney was elected president.

1873 —The first national union of locomotive firemen was founded: the Brotherhood of Locomotive Firemen.

1874 —The first national union of horseshoers was created: the National Union of Horseshoers.

1883 —The Journeymen Tailors' National Union became the first national union of tailors.

1883 —The first national union of lithographers was formed: the Lithographers' National Union.

August 1886 —The National Union of Brewers of the United States became the first national union of brewers. The union changed its name to the National Union of United Brewery Workmen of the United States in 1887, when it affiliated with the AFL.

1890 —The first national unions of postal employees were formed: the National Association of Letter Carriers and National Association of Post Office Clerks.

April 1891 —The first national union of clothing workers, the United Garment Workers, was formed by forty-seven delegates from the garment unions of Brooklyn, New York, Boston, and Philadelphia. It affiliated with the AFL.

1891 —The Hotel and Restaurant Employees International and Bartenders' International League was formed.

September 2, 1892 —The first national union of street car workers was formed: the Amalgamated Association of Street Railway Employees. It was chartered by the AFL in 1893.

1896 —The first national union of structural iron workers, the International Association of Bridge and Structural Iron Workers, was formed. It had locals in six cities.

January 27, 1897 —The first national union of meat cutters and butchers, the Amalgamated Meat Cutters and Butcher Workmen of North America, was chartered by the AFL.

January 1899 —The first national union of teamsters, the Team Drivers' International Union, was chartered by the AFL. Its name was changed in 1902 to the International Brotherhood of Teamsters.

1900 —The first national union of workers in the women's clothing industry, the International Ladies' Garment Workers' Union, was chartered by the AFL. By 1902, fifty-one locals had affiliated with the international, and its membership had reached 8,865.

1904 —The first national union of fur workers was created: the International

Association of Fur Workers. It did not last long.

1906 —The National Federation of Post Office Clerks became the first post office employees' union to affiliate with the AFL.

1910 —The first national union in the automobile industry was the Carriage, Wagon, and Automobile Workers. It obtained jurisdiction over the automobile industry in its charter from the AFL.

May 1913 —The first national union of actors was formed: Actors Equity Association.

June 16, 1913 —The first national union of fur workers to endure: the International Fur Workers of the United States and Canada, was founded at a convention attended by twenty delegates representing locals in New York, Philadelphia, Washington, Boston, and Toronto. It was chartered by the AFL.

December 26, 1914 —The first convention of the Amalgamated Clothing Workers of America was held. The new union was founded by men's clothing workers, mostly Jewish, who had become disgusted with the United Garment Workers because of its betrayal of their strikes and the indifference of its leaders to workers' needs. The move for an independent union was led by Sidney Hillman and Joseph Schlossberg. The AFL refused to charter the new union.

1916 —The American Federation of Teachers was chartered as a national union by the AFL.

1916 —The first convention of the International Union of Mine, Mill, and Smelter Workers (formerly the Western Federation of Miners) was held.

January 15, 1917 —The first union of baseball players, the Baseball Players' Fraternity, applied for a charter from the AFL. Samuel Gompers declared that the AFL would support the baseball players in a strike if they deemed it necessary. The union presented three demands to the club owners of the major and minor leagues: (1) elimination of contracts permitting the suspension of injured players and the loss of salary during the period of their disability; (2) permission for players to sign new contracts immediately after being notified of their unconditional release; and (3) allowance to players of traveling expenses from their homes to their club headquarters or training camps.

1920 —For the first time, the Amalgamated Clothing Workers surpassed the United Garment Workers in members. It had organized most of the men's clothing markets in the United States and Canada and reached a membership of 177,000.

1920 —The first union to reach a membership of more than half a million was the United Mine Workers of America, which this year had 640,000 members.

December 15, 1933 —The American Newspaper Guild was formed at a convention held at the National Press Club in Washington. Heywood Broun was its first president.

December 27, 1933 —The first national union in the radio industry was the Radio and Allied Trades National Labor Council, with James B. Carey as president.

1933 —The first union of motion picture actors was created: the Screen Actors Guild.

March 21–22, 1936 —The United Electrical and Radio Workers of America (UE) was founded at a convention in Buffalo, with James B. Carey as president and Julius Emspak as secretary-treasurer. It became the United Electrical, Radio, and Machine Workers of America when machinery locals, headed by James J. Matles, joined. In November 1936, the UE joined the CIO.

May 1936 —The Auto Workers Union withdrew from the AFL and shortly afterward affiliated with the CIO as the United Automobile Workers of America.

July 1937 —The first convention of the National Maritime Union was held in New York City. Joseph Curran was elected president, and Ferdinand Smith secretary-treasurer. The NMU voted to affiliate with the CIO. Ferdinand Smith was the first black to hold a top national position in an integrated trade union.

August 11, 1937 — The International Longshoremen and Warehousemen's Union (ILWU) was formed, with Harry Bridges as president. It was chartered by the CIO.

May 19, 1942 — At the first convention of the United Steel Workers of America, Philip Murray was elected president of the union, which had 660,052 members.

Negro Slavery

January 16, 1846 — The first public resolution by a labor organization condemning Negro slavery and supporting the right of slaves to rise up in revolt was adopted by the New England Workingmen's Association convention. The resolution read:

> Whereas, there are at the present time three million of our brethren and sisters groaning in chains on the Southern plantations; and whereas we wish not only to be consistent, but to secure to all others those rights and privileges for which we are contending ourselves; therefore,
>
> Resolved, That while we honor and respect our forefathers for the noble manner in which they resisted British oppression, we, their descendants, will never be guilty of the glaring inconsis-

tency of taking up arms to shoot and to stab those who use the same means to accomplish the same objects.

> Resolved, That while we are willing to pledge ourselves to use all the means in our power, consistent with our principles, to put down wars, insurrections, and mobs, and to protect all men from the evil of the same, we will not take up arms to sustain the Southern slave holder in robbing one-fifth of our countrymen of their labor.
>
> Resolved, That we recommend our brethren to speak out in thunder tones, both as associations and as individuals, and to let it no longer be said that Northern laborers, while they are contending for their rights, are a standing army to keep three millions of their brethren and sisters in bondage at the point of bayonet.

Night Work

1890 — Massachusetts enacted the first law prohibiting night work. It applied to women and minors.

Noise at Work

May 2, 1976 — The first announcement that unions would seek to eliminate excessive noise in factories in their contracts with industry was made.

No-Strike Pledge

April 8, 1917 — Labor made its first pledge that there would be no strikes during a war. Samuel Gompers made the pledge to the Council of National Defense.

December 30, 1941 — The AFL and CIO announced labor's "no strike, no lockout" pledge for the duration of U.S. involvement in World War II against Japan and Nazi Germany.

O

Occupational Diseases

June 10, 1910 —The first National Conference on Industrial Diseases was held in Chicago by the American Association for Labor Legislation.

December 6, 1910 —The first presidential statement on industrial diseases was included in President William Howard Taft's annual message to Congress. It discussed the dangers of phosphorous matches to workers in the industry.

1910 —The first state commission on occupational diseases was the Illinois Commission on Occupational Diseases.

1910 —The first national campaign against occupational disease was launched by the American Association for Labor Legislation.

1911 —The first state law requiring the reporting of injuries due to occupational disease was enacted by California.

1911 —The first state law requiring monthly physical examinations for workers in hazardous industries was enacted by Illinois.

June 1912 —For the first time in its sixty-six years of existence, the American Medical Association placed the problem of occupational diseases on its annual program.

Occupational Safety and Health

1837 —The first report on occupational health hazards was published, B.W. M'Cready's *On the Influence of Trades, Professions and Occupations in the United States in the Production of Diseases.*

1877 —The first law requiring factory safeguards was passed by Massachusetts.

1879 —The first law requiring factory inspections was passed by Massachusetts.

1886 —Massachusetts also enacted the first law requiring the reporting of industrial accidents.

1887 —The first company-financed medical department with a full-time staff was created by the Homestake Mining Company in North Dakota.

1893 —The first baths to be installed in a factory were at the J.H. Wilson Company in Brooklyn, New York.

1903 —C.F.W. Doehring wrote the first federal report on industrial hygiene: *Factory Sanitation and Labor Protection,* which was published by the Bureau of Labor Statistics.

1936 —The Walsh-Healey Act became the first federal legislation setting safety and health standards.

Older Workers

1922 —The first study exposing much of the misery and suffering common to a large segment of America's elderly population was *Facing Old Age* by Abraham Epstein.

1965 —The first federal agency to focus on the needs of older Americans, the Administration on Aging, was established under the Older Americans Act.

1965 —The first national health insurance program for the elderly, called Medicare, was set up by Congress.

1969 —The Age Discrimination in Employment Act prohibited bias against persons aged forty to sixty-five.

"Open Mouth" Sabotage

1912 —The first "open mouth" sabotage was practiced by IWW waitresses and sales clerks, who told workers when food and clothing sold to the working class were adulterated.

Open Shop

July 25, 1901 —The first open-shop attack on unionism was made by the Davis Machine Company and Computing Scale Company in Dayton, Ohio. The company closed down and announced it would "resume operation on or about August 19 as an *open shop.*"

August 20, 1903 —The first presidential order extending the open shop to all branches of the executive department was issued by President Theodore Roosevelt.

October 29, 1903 —The first nationwide open shop organization, the Citizens' Industrial Association was founded, with David M. Parry of the National Association of Manufacturers as chairman.

1918 —The first movement to abolish the "un-American" closed shop was the "American Plan," launched in Buffalo, New York, with an open-shop center.

1921 —The first organization of industrial relations counsellors to spread the open-shop principle was Industrial Relations Counsellors, Inc., founded by John D. Rockefeller, Jr.

1934 —The Mohawk Valley Formula, an antiunion movement organized by the Remington Rand Company, was launched.

Organizing

November 1911 — The "job delegate" system was introduced by the IWW in Local No. 327 on the Canadian Northern Railway in Lytton, British Columbia. Under the system, organizers went into the camps of lumber, construction, and agricultural workers, instead of organizing these workers when they came into the cities and towns during the off-seasons.

1915 — The Amalgamated Clothing Workers initiated an all-out organizational campaign in Chicago. Only one-quarter of Chicago's forty thousand men's clothing workers belonged to the Amalgamated, and nearly all of these worked at the Hart, Schaffner, and Marx establishment. By late September, twenty-five thousand men and women had walked out on strike. The strike ended in defeat.

January 1, 1929 — The first organizing campaign in Gastonia, North Carolina, was conducted by the National Textile Workers Union of the Trade Union Unity League (TUUL).

1932 — For the first time, a fishing club was used as a base for a union organizing drive. The Philrod Fishing Club was organized by workers at the Philco plant in Philadelphia for the ostensible purpose of buying a boat, but its real purpose was to raise money for organizing the plant. Members of the club led a strike at the plant in July 1933, which resulted in the first union contract at Philco.

1932 — The first industry-wide organizational campaign was launched by the Marine Workers Industrial Union of the TUUL among longshoremen on both coasts.

November 9, 1935 — The Committee for Industrial Organization was established when officers from eight AFL unions met in Washington in the United Mine Workers' building and created the CIO. John L. Lewis was elected chairman, John Brophy of the UMW was chosen as director, and Charles P. Howard, president of the Typographers' Union, was made secretary. The other original members of the organization were Sidney Hillman, president of the Amalgamated Clothing Workers; David Dubinsky, president of the ILGWU; Harvey Fremming, president of the Oil Workers' Union; Thomas H. Brown, president of the International Union of Mine, Mill and Smelter Workers; Max Zaritsky, president of the United Hatters, Cap, and Millinery Workers; and Thomas McMahon, president of the United Textile Workers.

The CIO announced that it would operate within the framework of the principles and policies set forth in the minority report at the Atlantic City convention of the AFL, that its functions would be "educational and advisory," and that it would seek to "encourage and promote" the organization of the unorganized and the establishment of collective bargaining in the mass-production industries. Other unions would be asked to join the committee.

June 17, 1936 — The CIO took over the weak and ineffective Amalgamated Association of Iron, Steel, and Tin Workers and established the Steel Workers' Organizing Committee (SWOC), with Philip Murray of the United Mine Workers as its head. Murray announced a campaign to organize the steel industry.

1936 — The Textile Workers' Organizing Committee launched a campaign to organize textile workers in the South. The campaign failed.

May 26, 1937 — The famous "Battle of the Overpass" took place at the Ford River Rouge Plant. Walter Reuther and Richard Frankensteen were beaten by Harry Bennett's Ford Company "service men" when they tried to hand out leaflets to Ford workers urging them to join the UAW.

1963 — The Industrial Union Department of the AFL-CIO launched a drive to organize J.P. Stevens' southern textile mills, jointly with the Textile Workers Union of America (TWUA). The drive failed.

1963 — The first serious effort to organize the unorganized since the formation of the AFL-CIO was launched by the Industrial Union Department. Only 44,244 workers were organized during an eighteen-month period.

June 4, 1968 — The American Federation of State, County and Municipal Employees (AFSCME) began the first national organizing drive to bring state, county, and city employees under union agreements.

October 1968 — The National Organizing Committee of Hospital and Nursing Home Employees was formed by Local 1199 of the Drug and Hospital Employees Union, with Coretta Scott King (Mrs. Martin Luther King, Jr.) as honorary chairperson.

August 1974 — The United Mine Workers, under the leadership of Arnold Miller, reestablished a foothold in Harlan County, Kentucky, after a thirteen-month strike against the "capitive" coal mines of the Duke Power Company. Harlan County had been nonunion during the Boyle administration of the UMW.

November 14, 1976 — In the first move to unionize blind workers, the National Federation of the Blind attempted to organize blind workers employed by the Lighthouse for the Blind in Chicago. Three blind workers were discharged because, according to the federation officials, they were leaders in the move to unionize the workshop.

Outlaw Strikes

April 4, 1920 — The first outlaw strike on the railroads took place. The switchmen began it, and the engineers, firemen, and conductors followed suit. The strike was broken by the Brotherhood leaders, who joined with the federal government in supplying strikebreakers and weeding out the "rebels."

July 1920 — The United Association of Railway Employees became the first union of "outlaw" strikers on the railroads.

July 25, 1920 — The first complete suspension of mining without the formality of declaring a strike occurred when Indiana and Illinois miners who were members of the United Mine Workers walked out in protest against conditions. They continued their informal strike for almost a month, but were unsuccessful.

P

Paid Holidays

1946 — The first paid holidays were achieved at Sylvania, General Cable, and other major electrical manufacturers in contracts negotiated by United Electrical, Radio, and Machine Workers of America (UE). In 1947, the UE won six paid holidays for the first time in its national agreements with General Electric and Westinghouse. At that time there were no paid holidays in the steel, auto, glass, and shipbuilding industries, and very few in the textile industry. Workers in these industries later obtained paid holidays.

Paid Vacations

1929 — Before the Great Depression, paid vacations did not exist in most industries. The few that did have paid vacations usually allowed one week after three years of work and two weeks after ten, with holidays counted as vacation time. Companies, moreover, reserved the right to change or cancel their vacation policies. During the Depression, the companies that did have vacation plans abolished them.

1938 — The first national agreement guaranteeing one week of paid vacation after one year on the job was signed by GE in its contract with the United Electrical, Radio, and Machine Workers of America (UE). In the 1947 agreement with GE, the UE gained three weeks of paid vacation for workers with twenty years of service. Holidays were not counted as part of vacation time.

1941 — Coal and railroad agreements first included paid vacations.

1942 — Major clothing and textile contracts first provided paid vacations late this year. General Motors, until 1942, allowed only one week paid vacation.

Pensions

1636 — The first pension for disabled soldiers was established by the Plymouth Colony.

1776 — The first federal pension was created to assist wounded and disabled Revolutionary War soldiers.

1860 — The Amalgamated Society of Engineers, a union of American and Canadian workers, became the first labor organization to offer a private pension plan.

1875 — The first industrial old-age pension in the United States was established by the American Express Company. This was a noncontributory plan, meaning the employer paid all the costs. The American Express plan was also the first private pension plan offered by any U.S. company.

1880 — The first private pension plan set up entirely by American workers was established by the International Molders' Union of North America.

1902 — The first union pension fund for aged and indigent members was created by the International Typographical Union.

1902 — Victor Berger introduced the first resolution on old-age pensions ever put before an AFL convention. The resolution called for all wage workers who had an average income of less than $1,000 per year to receive an old-age pension of at least $12 a month beginning at age sixty, provided the worker was a citizen and had lived in the United States continuously for at least twenty-one years. It was rejected by the convention.

1907 — The first federal legislation providing for old-age pensions was proposed by Congressman William B. Wilson, Democrat of Pennsylvania.

Wilson became the first secretary of labor in 1913.

1907 — Massachusetts appointed the first state commission to study old-age pensions. No action was taken on the commission's recommendations.

1920 — The U.S. Civil Service Retirement Act was the first law to provide pensions for government employees.

1923 — The first state old-age pension laws that were ruled constitutional were passed by Montana, Nevada, and Pennsylvania. All were weak laws.

1928 — Dr. Francis Townsend first proposed his plan for solving the problems of the aged. Under the Townsend Plan, all persons over the age of sixty, irrespective of their personal means, were to receive $200 per month, provided they retired from employment and agreed to spend all the money every month. Hundreds of clubs supporting the Townsend Plan sprang up around the country during the Great Depression.

December 1929 — An AFL convention endorsed old-age pensions for the first time.

1930 — Massachusetts passed the first state mandatory pension law. The state supplied one-third of the funds, and the localities put up the remainder. The pensionable age was seventy years, and there was a twenty-year state residence requirement.

August 14, 1935 —The first Social Security Act was passed by Congress. It included provisions for unemployment insurance, old-age pensions, aid to dependent children, rehabilitation of the physically handicapped, and the improvement of public health. This was the first time in U.S. history that the federal government enacted a system of insurance payments to cushion workers against the loss of jobs. Social Security was to be financed by contributions of both employers and workers.

1940 —The first beneficiary to receive a retirement check under the Social Security Act was Miss Ida Fuller of Ludlow, Vermont.

April 1972 —The first baseball players' strike was called by the Players' Association over the pension plan. The issue was resolved and the strike was called off.

Picketing

1806 —The first picket line was set up by Philadelphia cordwainers demonstrating in front of shops of employers against whom a strike had been called.

January 13, 1874 —The first mounted picket line took place on this date. Black sugar workers of Louisiana, who were striking for wages of $15 per month,

mounted on horseback and rode from plantation to plantation to persuade other workers to join the strike.

July 20, 1907 —The first "silent demonstration" during a strike was conducted by the IWW. At a strike against the American Tube and Stamping Company in Bridgeport, Connecticut, strikers picketed the plant without uttering a word in order not to violate a local ordinance.

January 1912 —The "moving picket line," a chain of pickets around plants twenty-four hours a day, was first used in the IWW strike in Lawrence, Massachusetts. Twenty thousand workers formed an endless picket line.

April 1912 —The first "thousand-mile picket line" was set up in the IWW strike of the Canadian Northern Railway. Strikers and their sympathizers picketed employment offices from Vancouver to San Francisco to keep out scabs.

February 1922 —The first "iron battalions" were organized during a New England textile strike against wage cuts. Pickets with drums and bugles in the early hours of morning laid siege to textile mills that were to be struck, and remained until the strike was accomplished.

February 24, 1934 —The "cruising picket squad" was introduced during a strike by Local 574 of the International

Brotherhood of Teamsters in Minneapolis. "Flying squadrons" on picket duty kept scabs out, and the strike was won after five weeks.

April 12, 1934 —For the first time, the unemployed picketed to help striking workers. The American Workers party and its Toledo affiliate, the Lucas County Unemployed League, joined the picket set up by striking workers of Local 18384 against the Electric Auto-Lite Company of Toledo. The strike, which was marked by violence by police, sheriffs, and National Guardsmen against the strikers, ended on June 4 with union recognition, a minimum wage of 35 cents an hour, and the rehiring of the local's members.

May 28, 1976 —The first union of pickets, the Independent Order of Pickets, was organized to provide pickets for any strike. It intended to promote decent conditions for pickets.

July 29, 1976 —Members of the American Federation of Teachers picketed their own union headquarters for the first time. Two hundred para-professional teachers charged that the union had shown no interest in the demise of the Para-professional Teacher Education Program at the City University of New York.

Political Action

1734 —The first political party to enjoy considerable labor support and leadership was the Popular party in New York City, whose leader was John Peter Zenger, a printer. After the party had won several seats on the Common Council (one by John Fred, a laborer), the infuriated governor of New York charged Zenger with libel. However, Zenger was acquitted in a trial that set a precedent for freedom of the press.

1768 —For the first time, the mechanics of Charleston, South Carolina, elected their own representatives to the General Assembly.

1784 —The first labor organization to nominate its own political candidate was the Mechanics Union. The union ran a candidate for the New York State Assembly.

May 1834 —The Democratic Working Men's General Committee of New York City became the first organization to present labor's viewpoint to the Democratic party.

October 29, 1835 —The first labor candidates to be nominated by candlelight were from New York City. After the Tammany organization turned off the gas at a meeting, the workers lit candles with "loco-foco" matches and nominated their candidates for office. It was called the "Loco-Foco" ticket.

March 1837 — The first labor protest against the use of troops to prevent a labor meeting was organized by the Equal Rights party of New York City.

1885 — The first electoral victories of the Knights of Labor assemblies came when labor candidates were elected to office in Michigan, Illinois, Connecticut, Massachusetts, New York, and Virginia.

1902 — The Missouri State Federation of Labor was the first AFL body to question candidates for office on how they stood on labor issues.

September 1904 — The AFL first questioned candidates for Congress and state legislatures on specific labor issues.

October 1906 — The AFL established the Labor Representation Committee to elect congressmen and state legislators friendly to labor.

April 2, 1936 — Labor's Non-Partisan League, the political arm of the CIO, was formed.

July 7, 1943 — The Political Action Committee was formed by the CIO Executive Board, with Sidney Hillman as chairman.

March 1944 — The first issue of the *Political Action News* appeared. It was published by the Political Action Committee (PAC) of the CIO, and the paper's purpose was to register voters

and mobilize them for the presidential and congressional elections.

Presidents of the United States

1834 — President Andrew Jackson became the first president to use the army to break a strike when he ordered regulars into Maryland to end a strike by Irish workers on the Chesapeake & Ohio Canal.

July 1877 — Rutherford B. Hayes was the first president to use the regular army to break a strike on a national scale. He ordered troops into strike areas from West Virginia to Chicago to San Francisco. One hundred workers were killed and the great labor uprising of 1877 was smashed.

October 3, 1902 — President Theodore Roosevelt became the first president to mediate during a strike when he called a conference in the White House to settle the 1902 coal strike. The meeting between John Mitchell, who was representing the United Mine Workers, and coal company and government officials failed to settle the strike.

1903 — The first presidential order prohibiting government employees from seeking wage increases by attempting to influence legislation in Congress was issued by President Theodore Roosevelt.

1903 — For the first time, a president of the United States reinstated an employee to government service after he was dropped by his union for antiunion activity. William A. Miller was reinstated by President Theodore Roosevelt to the bindery of the Government Printing Office after having been expelled from the Bookbinders' Union.

May 1907 — The first president of the United States to condemn union men awaiting trial was Theodore Roosevelt. He called Moyer and Haywood, who were awaiting trial for murder in Idaho, "undesirable citizens." His comment aroused widespread condemnation in labor circles.

November 17, 1908 — The first "labor legislation" dinner was held at the White House. President-elect William Howard Taft met with labor leaders to discuss labor's legislative demands.

November 17, 1915 — For the first time, a president of the United States appealed for reconsideration of the case of a labor leader facing execution. After worldwide protests, and a charge by the AFL convention that Joe Hill, "a workingman of the State of Utah, and active in the cause of labor," had not had "a fair and impartial trial," President Woodrow Wilson telegraphed Governor Spry of Utah, "urging justice and a thorough reconsideration of the case of Joseph Hillstrom [Joe Hill]." This was actually President Wilson's second appeal in the Hill case. In the first, he had

asked for a stay of execution, which was granted. The president's second appeal was rejected, and Joe Hill was executed by firing squad on the morning of November 19, 1915. His last words were: "Don't mourn, organize."

July 4, 1916 — Woodrow Wilson became the first president to lay the cornerstone for a labor headquarters. It was at the new AFL building in Washington, D.C.

May 8, 1920 — Eugene V. Debs became the first imprisoned labor leader to be nominated for president of the United States. Debs, who was incarcerated in a federal prison in Atlanta for violating the Espionage Act by making an antiwar speech in Canton, Ohio, was nominated for president by the Socialist party. He polled close to one million votes.

January 11, 1944 — Franklin D. Roosevelt became the first president to issue an "Economic Bill of Rights." In his State of the Union message, he said:

> In our day, these economic truths have become accepted as self-evident. We have accepted, so to speak, a second Bill of Rights under which a new basis of security and prosperity can be established for all — regardless of station, race, or creed.
>
> Among these are:
>
> The right to a useful and remunerative job in the industries, or shops or farms or mines of the Nation;

The right to earn enough to provide adequate food and clothing and recreation;

The right of every farmer to raise and sell his products at a return which will give him and his family a decent living;

The right of every businessman, large and small, to trade in an atmosphere of freedom from unfair competition and domination by monopolies at home or abroad;

The right of every family to a decent home;

The right to adequate medical care and the opportunity to achieve and enjoy good health;

The right to adequate protection from the economic fears of old age, sickness, accident, and unemployment;

The right to a good education.

All of these rights spell security. And after the war is won, we must be prepared to move forward, in the implementation of these rights, to new goals of human happiness and well-being.

America's own rightful place in the world depends in large part upon how fully these and similar rights have been carried into practice for our citizens. For unless there is security here at home, there cannot be lasting peace in the world.

Roosevelt's "Economic Bill of Rights" was distributed in hundreds of thousands of leaflets and posters by the National Political Action Committee (PAC) of the CIO.

January 20, 1981 —The first trade union president to become president of the United States was Ronald Reagan, formerly president of Screen Actors' Guild. He was inaugurated fortieth president of the United States.

August 1981 —The first president to destroy a union and discharge its members from government employment, Ronald Reagan, fired 17,500 air traffic controllers because their union — the Professional Air Traffic Controllers Organization (PATCO), AFL-CIO — called a strike. Using the excuse that no one has the right to strike against the government, Reagan had the courts decertify the union, which eventually ceased to exist. Ironically, PATCO was one of the few unions to endorse Reagan in the 1980 presidential campaign.

Profit-Sharing

1794 —The first profit-sharing plan was introduced by Albert Gallatin at his New Geneva, Pennsylvania glassworks. Gallatin was later secretary of the treasury under Jefferson and Madison.

January 20, 1890 —The first post-Civil War profit-sharing plan was set up by Rogers, Peet, and Company of New York City. In addition to wages, the company began paying a dividend to all workers based on profits.

Protocol of Peace

July 1910 —Sixty thousand cloak-makers, of whom six thousand were women, walked off their jobs in what was called "The Great Revolt." The strike of the New York cloakmakers lasted seven weeks and ended in the Protocol of Peace. A Committee on Grievances would henceforth consider minor disagreements between manufacturers and employees, while a Board of Arbitration, composed of representatives from the manufacturers, the union, and the public, would handle important disputes. The establishment of these permanent boards and the inclusion of a representative of the general public provided a model for future strike settlements in the apparel trades.

The Protocol of Peace inaugurated in the cloak, suit, and shirt industries of Greater New York established the first nongovernmental factory inspection institution, and marked the first time in American industry that an employers' association and a union endeavored to establish and enforce healthful working conditions in an industry through a joint "board of health."

R

Raiding

December 1949 — The CIO chartered the International Union of Electrical, Radio, and Machine Workers (IUE), with James B. Carey as president, in an attempt to destroy the UE by raids against its members.

June 1953 — The first concrete step toward unity was taken by the AFL and CIO. A subcommittee of the AFL and CIO proposed a "no-raiding" agreement by the two organizations, and it was approved by both organizations and became effective in July 1954.

Railroad Labor Board

July 1920 — In its first ruling, the Railroad Labor Board ordered a general wage increase for railroad workers.

Rank and File

February 1874 — In the first successful rank-and-file revolt against a union leader, Charles I. Wilson was removed as grand chief engineer of the Brotherhood of Locomotive Engineers by the nearly unanimous vote of delegates to a special convention. Wilson was ousted because of his conservative policies, and because he had attacked striking engineers of the East Tennessee, Virginia, and Georgia Railroad, and the engineers on the Pennsylvania Railroad. The Pittsburgh engineers published an eight-page monthly, the *Locomotive Engineers' Advocate* (probably the first trade union rank-and-file paper), which sharply attacked Wilson's policies. Peter M. Arthur, who was elected as a "reform candidate" in the rank-and-file revolt, turned out to be even more conservative than Wilson during the next quarter of a century.

1920 — The Trade Union Educational League (TUEL) was founded, with William Z. Foster as its leader. This was not a dual union, nor did it propose to organize dual unions. It did, however, recommend the organization of rank-and-file unionists, urging them to replace the "moribund" AFL leadership with young, dedicated men and women who would organize the unorganized.

January 1934 — The first issue of the *AFL Rank and File Federationist* appeared with demands for (1) a Workers Unemployment Insurance Bill; (2) industrial unions with rank-and-file control; (3) trade union democracy; (4) a policy of militant struggle; (5) genuine social insurance; (6) the right to belong to any political party; (7) an end to racketeering and gangsterism; (8) an end to discrimination aimed at Negro workers, including equal rights to jobs and to treatment within the union; (9) unity of all labor. The Workers Unemployment Insurance Bill, sponsored by the AFL Committee for Unemployment Insurance, called for the immediate establishment by an act of Congress of "a system of federal government unemployment insurance . . . guaranteeing the average wages in the respective industries and territories in the United States. The unemployment insurance shall not be less than $10 weekly for adult workers, $3 for each dependent, to all workers wholly unemployed through no fault of their own, for the entire period of unemployment. . . ." No worker was to be deprived of unemployment insurance because of race, color, sex, age, or political opinion.

The *AFL Rank and File Federationist* was edited by Louis Weinstock of the AFL Painters' Union, a leading communist trade unionist.

1964 — The first union to be born of rebellion against the policies of existing unions, the Association of Western Pulp and Paper Workers, organized the rank and file against AFL-CIO paper industry international unions. After winning an NLRB election, the young "rebel union"

adopted a highly democratic constitution.

1969 — Three different rank-and-file movements were established in the United Mine Workers: The Black Lung Association, Miners for Democracy, and the Disabled Miners and Widows of Southern West Virginia. The Black Lung Association was formed shortly after seventy-eight men were killed in the methane and coal-dust explosion at Consol No. 9 in Mannington, West Virginia, in November 1968, and following a successful West Virginia Lung Strike in early 1969. Miners for Democracy was formed to back Joseph "Jock" Yablonski's challenge to W.A. "Tony" Boyle, who had been president of the UMW since 1963. This challenge to the Boyle machine cost Yablonski, his wife, and his daughter their lives. Boyle was convicted or organizing their murders and sentenced to life imprisonment.

May 25–28, 1972 — The first convention of Miners for Democracy nominated Arnold R. Miller and a nine-man slate to challenge President "Tony" Boyle and his slate.

December 15, 1972 — In the first major rank-and-file victory over an entrenched union machine since World War II, Arnold R. Miller and his slate were elected to office on the Miners for Democracy ticket. On December 18, W.A. "Tony" Boyle resigned the UMW presidency.

Recall

May 1874 — The first labor proposal for recall of public officials was made by the Junior Sons of '76.

June 10, 1912 — The first mayor to be recalled from office for associating with organized labor was Reverend H. Ferguson, mayor of Hoquiam, Washington. Ferguson had supported the IWW in a strike against the Hoquiam sawmills.

Regional Organizations

February 1832 — The first labor body to combine skilled and unskilled workers was the New England Association of Farmers, Mechanics, and Other Workingmen. This was also the first regional labor organization and the first major labor organization to include factory workers.

Reparations for Discrimination

March 1976 — The U.S. Supreme Court ruled that persons who had been denied employment or promotions because of race or sex were entitled to such employment or promotion from the date they had first applied for the job. The court said that the employer must "make whole" the injured parties, meaning that the employees must get the jobs requested, full back pay for all monies lost, full restoration of seniority as though they had been properly hired in the first place, and full benefits they would have received if they had been treated equally originally.

Reserve Clause

December 1975 — The first decision marking the end of the "reserve clause" was handed down. The clause bound every baseball player irrevocably to the club holding his contract, thereby fixing his place of employment and ensuring that his salary would ultimately be determined solely by the club owner. A three-man arbitration panel ruled that two players — Andy Messersmith of the Los Angeles Dodgers and Dave McNally of the Montreal Expos — were released from affiliation with their clubs because they had played out their existing contracts, plus an additional year, and were therefore free agents entitled to sign up with whatever club they wished, at any pay they could command.

Restriction of Production

1870 — The Workingmen's Benevolent Association became the first union to control chronic overproduction when it restricted the tonnage of coal a union member could mine daily.

Retired Members' Homes

1905 — The first home for retired union members was established: the Union Printers' Home.

Right to Belong to a Union

November 28, 1805 — The Philadelphia Cordwainers' Society made the first appeal to the public to support the right of workers to join a union and determine their wages in an advertisement in the *Philadelphia Aurora.*

May 15, 1894 — New Jersey became the first state to prohibit an employer from discriminating in employment against members of trade unions. Entitled "An Act in Relation to the Employment of Labor by Corporations," the law stated that violators would be subject to a fine not to exceed $500 or three months' imprisonment.

1912 — The first law granting federal employees the right to lobby on their own behalf and to affiliate with organized labor was the Lloyd-LaFollette Act. It was not enforced in the Post Office for several years.

1914 — Congress enacted and President Woodrow Wilson signed the Clayton Anti-Trust Act, the first law to assert that labor organizations are not to be considered as illegal combinations or conspiracies in restraint of trade under the federal antitrust law. Section 6 read: "That the labor of a human being is not a commodity or article of commerce. Nothing contained in the anti-trust laws shall be construed to forbid the existence and operation of labor, agricultural, or horticultural organizations, instituted for the purpose of mutual help, and not having capital stock or conducted for profit, or to forbid or restrain individual members of such organizations from lawfully carrying on the legitimate objects thereof; nor shall such organizations, or the members thereof be held or construed to be illegal combinations or conspiracies in restraint of trade under the antitrust laws."

Section 20 provided that "no restraining order or injunction shall be granted by any court of the United States . . . in any case between an employer and employees, or between employers and employees, or between employees, or between persons employed and persons seeking employment, involving, or growing out of a dispute concerning terms or conditions of employment, unless necessary to prevent irreparable injury to property, or to a property right, of the party making the application, for which injury there is no adequate remedy at law. . . ."

Samuel Gompers hailed the law as "Labor's Magna Charta," but the "irreparable injury to property" exception enabled the courts to seriously undermine the law's intent.

June 24, 1915 — The first federal government report blaming the power of capital and economic conditions for the discontent in working-class circles, and upholding the right of workers to organize and bargain collectively, was published. The *Final Report* of the U.S. Commission on Industrial Relations concluded, after months of investigation: (1) American workers had not received a fair share of their nation's wealth and a great portion of America's industrial population lived in dire poverty. Between one-fourth and one-third of the families employed in manufacturing earned "less than enough to support themselves in anything like a comfortable decent condition." In the rural areas, tenant farmers were "badly-housed, ill-nourished, uneducated and hopeless." (2) Corporations dominated the state of industrial relations. An individual worker was in no position to bargain with a huge corporation. (3) "Unjust distribution of wealth and income" was a major cause of industrial discord. Only 2 percent of the nation's population owned 60 percent of its wealth; 65 percent of the people controlled only 5 percent. (4) "As a prime cause of a burning resentment and a rising feeling of unrest among the workers, unemployment and the denial of an opportunity to earn a living is on a parity with the unjust distribution of wealth." Most laborers in basic industries suffered joblessness for 20 percent of any twelve-month period: "At all times during any normal year there is an army of men who can be numbered only by hundreds of thousands, who are unable to find work." (5) "No testimony presented to the Commission has left a deeper impression than the evidence that there exists among the workers an almost universal conviction that they, both as individuals and as a class, are denied justice." (6) "No group of workers can become free except by combined action," so the commission called for constitutional amendments and laws to protect and guarantee the right of laborers to organize and bargain collectively.

April 1918 — The federal government first recognized the right of workers to organize into trade unions and to bargain collectively through representatives of their own choice. This recognition was granted by the War Labor Board, which was composed of five employer representatives, five members nominated by the AFL, and two representatives of the public — one selected by the employers (William Howard Taft), and one by the unions (Frank P. Walsh). The board's function was to settle disputes arising between employers and workers in any field of production necessary for the effective conduct of the war. The board adopted the principle that there should be no strikes or lockouts during the war, and that disputes should be settled through mediation and conciliation. In addition to recognizing the right of workers to organize into trade unions, the board declared that workers were not to be discharged for membership in trade unions or for legitimate trade union activities. On the other hand, workers were forbidden to use coercive tactics to induce other workers to join unions, or to compel employers to deal with them.

June 16, 1933 — President Franklin D. Roosevelt signed the National Industrial Recovery Act. Section 7(a) of the act included the first federal provision for the establishment of codes of hours, wages, and working conditions, and the right of workers to join unions. The section read:

> Every code of fair competition, agreement, and license approved, prescribed, or issued under this title shall contain the following conditions: (1) That employees shall have the right to organize and bargain collectively through representatives of their own choosing, and shall be free from the interference, restraint, or coercion of employers of labor, or their agents, in the designation of such representatives or in self-organization or in other concerted activities for the purpose of collective bargaining or other mutual aid or protection; (2) That no employee and no one seeking employment shall be required as a condition of employment to join any company union or to refrain from joining, organizing, or assisting a labor organization of his own choosing; and (3) That employers shall comply with the maximum hours of labor, minimum hours of pay, and other conditions of employment, approved or prescribed by the President.

May 1935 — The U.S. Supreme Court declared the National Industrial Recovery Act unconstitutional, including Section 7(a), which gave workers the right to organize into unions of their own choosing.

July 5, 1935 — The first National Labor Relations Act (Wagner Act) was passed. It declared that workers "shall have the right to self-organization to form, join or assist labor organizations, to bargain collectively by representatives of their own choosing, and to engage in concerted activities for the purpose of collective bargaining or other mutual aid or protection." It created a National Labor Relations Board (NLRB) with the power to enforce the act, including the prohibition of certain unfair labor practices by employers against unions. The board's first chairman was Joseph Warren Madden.

"Right to Know" Laws

January 22, 1981 — The Philadelphia City Council passed amendments to the City Air Management and Fire Codes that vastly expanded the right of workers and the community to know what toxic substances were being used, manufactured, or stored in Philadelphia plants, and emitted into the community environment.

No other city in the United States had heretofore enacted similar "right to know" legislation, and only four states — New York, Maine, Michigan, and Connecticut — had made any legal provision for giving workers the right to know when they were working with hazardous materials.

A campaign initiated by a coalition of unions and environmental, minority, women's, and health organizations — including the Philadelphia Area Project on Occupational Safety and Health (PHILAPOSH) — scored the Philadelphia "right to know" victory.

"Right-to-Work"

January 1914 — The first "right-to-work" bill was proposed. In contrast to present misuse of the term, this bill, proposed by the IWW to the California legislature, embodied a genuine "right-to-work" concept because it demanded legislation giving the unemployed the

right to work on jobs furnished by the state. The bill failed to pass.

1946 — The first "right-to-work" laws were passed in Florida and Arkansas. The Florida amendment to the state constitution provided that "the right of persons to work shall not be denied or abridged on account of membership or non-membership in any labor union."

"Rustling Card"

May 1899 — The "rustling card," which required that an applicant for employment affirm that a union was a criminal conspiracy and that he would never join one, was first used in the Coeur d'Alene strike. Its use was fully developed in 1912 by the Anaconda Copper Company.

Scabs
(See also
"Strikebreaking")

November 1803 —The first union to appeal to workers in a trade throughout the nation not to come and scab during a strike was the Journeymen Curriers' Society of Philadelphia. It did so in an advertisement in the *Philadelphia Aurora* addressed "To the Journeymen Curriers of all parts of the Union."

1806 —The first public mention of the word "scab" was made during a conspiracy trial to describe nonunion men. Definition: "A scab is a shelter for lice."

November 20, 1816 —The first known use of the word "rat" to describe a workman who refused to abide by union rules was in a letter from the Albany printers' union to New York City printers.

1832 —The first international action against strikebreaking was taken by the Typographical Association of New York when it sent a delegate to visit the Journeymen Printers' Union of Great Britain to urge members not to come to the United States to act as scabs.

1882 —The first scabs to reject their strikebreaking role and form a union were the Jewish workers who had been hired as scabs during a freight handlers' strike in New York City. Once they found out there was a strike, they formed a Jewish branch of the Central Freight Handlers Union, and on July 14, 1882, five hundred Jews were among those who marched from the Battery up Broadway to the union headquarters on the Bowery.

1902 —President Charles W. Eliot of Harvard University, in a speech before the Boston Economic Club, said: "A strikebreaker is a good type of the American hero." This was the first public praise of the scab uttered by a college president.

May 1907 —The first international agreement to prevent strikebreaking was achieved by the IWW. It established relations with the Rumanian Syndicalist General Commission in Bucharest to keep Rumanian workers from coming to the United States as strikebreakers.

January 24, 1910 —The first women's antiscab battalion was formed by wives of strikers at the Standard Steel Car Company in Hammond, Indiana.

"Armed with brooms, clubs, stove pokers, rolling pins and other kitchen utensils, hundreds of women from the foreign settlement surrounding the Standard Steel Works today joined the ranks of their striking husbands as pickets and brought about the worst clash that the authorities have yet encountered since the strike began. The women stood with their husbands against the weight of the policemen who tried to open a way to the gate for the workmen going to work. . . . A number of the special police were targets for the broomhandles and irons, one of them being severely injured with a long poker that an amazon had measured across his back. The women held a mass meeting this afternoon and promised to do picket duty again tomorrow morning" (Lake County [Indiana] *Times*, January 25, 1910). The strike was led by the IWW and was successful.

"Scientific Management"

May 1898 — Frederick W. Taylor introduced "scientific management" with a reorganization of the Bethlehem Steel works in South Bethlehem, Pennsylvania, to increase production.

1903 — Taylor fully outlined his principles for the first time, including his notion of how to speed up work, in a paper entitled "Shop Management," which he delivered at a meeting of the American Society of Mechanical Engineers.

1910 — The first strike against the introduction of Taylor's "scientific management" methods took place at the Bethlehem Steel Company. The strikers lost.

Seamen

1862 — The first union of seamen, the American Seamen's Protective Association, was formed by black seamen in New York City.

1895 — The first law abolishing imprisonment as a penalty for desertion from coastwise vessels, the Maguire Law, was passed by Congress, but declared unconstitutional by the Supreme Court in the *Arago* case in 1897.

October 1901 — In its first agreement with employers, the Sailors' Union of the Pacific obtained wage increases and a reduction in hours. In return, the union promised not to engage in sympathy strikes.

November 4, 1915 — The first federal law to provide protection for seamen was LaFollette's Seamen's Act. It abolished imprisonment for desertion in a safe harbor and limited the penalty to the forfeiture of personal effects left on board; granted seamen the right to demand half of their wages earned and unpaid in ports of loading and discharging cargo; raised the standard of living and food allowance for sailors and established a nine-hour day while in port.

Self-Defense for Workers

1875 — The first workingmen's military organization for self-defense against police and militia, the Lehr und Wehr Verein, was formed by Chicago German socialists.

July 10, 1892 — The first organization to give union members military training, Our Own Club, was formed in Boston to prepare workers to defend themselves against Pinkertons and other "hired assassins and mercenary desperadoes" employers used to destroy unions.

Sit-Down Strikes

1842 — The first sit-down strike occurred when Pittsburgh iron puddlers and boilermakers seized a mill during a strike.

1896 — The first sit-down strike of the post-Civil War era took place when New York City laundresses sat down and refused to work. They took this action in support of the garment workers' strike.

December 10, 1906 — The first sit-down strike of the twentieth century

involved three thousand IWW members of the General Electric Industrial Workers' Union, who struck when the company refused to reinstate three discharged union draftsmen. The strikers remained in the plant and stopped production for about sixty-five hours, while receiving food and drink from the outside.

November 13, 1933 — The first sit-down strike during the New Deal period occurred at the George A. Hormel and Company packing plant in Austin, Minnesota. Strikers sat down in the plant for thirty days. The strike was settled as a result of mediation hearings.

November 17, 1936 — The first sit-down strike by auto workers took place at the South Bend (Indiana) plant of the Bendix Products Corporation, 24 percent of whose stock was owned by General Motors. The strike was caused by the company's refusal to grant a closed shop or to designate the United Auto Workers' local in the plant as the exclusive bargaining agent for the company's forty-three hundred workers. It lasted until November 23, making it the longest sit-down strike in American history up to that time. While the union did not achieve its objective, the strike gave it great prestige and strength at the plant.

November 27, 1936 — At the first sit-down strike in Detroit, twelve hundred workers at the Midland Steel Products Company, which made steel body frames for Chrysler and Ford, sat down to demand wage increases, reduced work hours, and the abolition of piecework. The strike was settled on December 4 with a complete victory for the workers, and gave added prestige to the United Auto Workers.

December 30, 1936 — A historic sit-down strike began at Fisher Body No. 2 plant in Flint, Michigan, with fifty workers. The strike lasted forty-four days and became the greatest sit-down strike in American history and one of the turning points in American labor history. It produced a song associated with sit-down strikes forever after. Written by Maurice Sugar, one of the UAW attorneys, the song's opening verse and chorus went:

> When they tie the can to a Union man,
> Sit down! Sit down!
> When they give 'im the sack, they'll take
> 'im back.
> Sit down! Sit down!
>
>> Sit down, just take a seat
>> Sit down, and rest your feet
>> Sit down, you've got 'em beat —
>> Sit down! Sit down!

The Flint sit-down touched off a wave of sit-down strikes across the nation. Between September 1936 and May 1937, 485,000 workers engaged in sit-down strikes.

February 11, 1937 — In the first major breakthrough against antiunionism in the automobile industry, the Flint sit-down strike ended with an agreement with General Motors. The UAW agreed to evacuate the plant and GM, in turn, agreed to recognize the union as the spokesman for its members, and not to discriminate against union members, as well as to rehire all strikers and withdraw injunction and contempt proceedings against them. When General Motors and the UAW opened negotiations on February 16 for a collective bargaining agreement, the company announced a 5-cent-per-hour wage increase. The sit-down strikers ratified the agreement amid wild cheering.

April 9, 1937 — The first anti-sit-down strike legislation was enacted in Vermont. It provided penalties of two years' imprisonment and a fine of $1,000 for anyone found guilty of acting "unlawfully to occupy, hold and possess certain buildings against the will and without the consent of the lessee thereof."

March 13, 1941 — The first sit-down strike at the Ford Motor Company took place when thirty thousand Ford workers sat down to protest the firing of eight union men. The men were rehired, making this the first strike victory in Ford history.

Slogans

1835 — The first labor slogan, a ten-hour slogan, appeared: "From 6 to 6 with 2 hours off for meals."

January 1912 — The first use of the slogan "We Want Bread and Roses, Too" was by women strikers in the IWW strike in Lawrence, Massachusetts. The slogan led to the writing of a song by James Oppenheim, the opening and closing verses of which went:

As we come marching, marching in the
beauty of day,
A million darkened kitchens, a thousand
mill lofts gray,
Are touched with all the radiance that a
sudden sun discloses,
For the people hear us singing: "Bread and
roses! Bread and roses!"

As we come marching, marching, we
bring the greater days.
The rising of the women means the rising
of the race.
No more the drudge and idler — ten that
toil where one reposes,
But sharing of life's glories: Bread and
roses! Bread and roses!

March 1921 — The first slogan of the unemployed, "Fight, Don't Starve," was adopted at a post-World War I conference of the unemployed in New York City.

Smith Act

December 8, 1941 — The first Smith Act trial took place. Members and leaders of the Minneapolis General Drivers Local 544 (CIO) and of the Socialist Workers party were tried under the Smith Act of 1940, which made it a crime to conspire to overthrow the government by force and violence. Eighteen defendants were convicted, ten were acquitted. Those found guilty were sentenced to federal prison for from one year to sixteen months.

Socialism

February 25–March 7, 1825 — The first socialist speech in the United States was given by Robert Owen, the British Utopian Socialist. He addressed both houses of Congress.

1825 — Robert Owen established the first socialist colony in the United States: New Harmony, Indiana. It failed.

March 1, 1842 — The first article on Fourier's system of socialism to appear in the United States was written by Albert Brisbane, an American disciple of Fourier, and published in the *New York Tribune*. It called for the establishment of phalanxes on a cooperative basis.

January 17, 1843 — The first Fourier colony was established in the United States at Sylvania in western Pennsylvania by a group of New York workingmen. It failed.

1851 — The first Marxist labor organization established in the United States was Proletarierbund, founded in New York City by Joseph Weydemeyer.

January 1852 —The first Marxist paper to appear in the United States, *Die Revolution,* was published in New York City and edited by Joseph Weydemeyer.

October 25, 1857 —The first communist organization in the United States was the Communist Club of New York City, founded by German-Americans with F. Kamm as chairman.

July 19, 1876 —The Workingmen's party of the United States, the first Marxist party formed in this country, was founded at a convention in Philadelphia by Lassalleans (followers of Ferdinand Lassalle) and Internationalists (former leaders of the First International) who were Marxists. In December 1877, the party changed its name to the Socialist Labor party.

March 20, 1883 —The first meeting of socialist, nonsocialist, and anarchist groups was a memorial meeting in honor of Karl Marx, who had died six days earlier. It was sponsored by the Central Labor Union of New York City and Vicinity and was attended by thousands at the Cooper Institute.

April 6, 1888 —*Di Nu Yorker-Idishe Folkszeitung* published the first Yiddish translation of a work by Karl Marx in the United States. The translation of Marx's forty-year-old pamphlet, *Wage-Labor and Capital,* appeared in issues running from April 6 to June 8. The articles were later reissued as a pamphlet.

1892 —The first presidential candidate of the Socialist Labor party was Simon Wing of Massachusetts. He received 21,000 votes.

August 31, 1895 —The first issue of *Appeal to Reason,* which was the earliest socialist paper with a mass circulation, was published by J. A. Wayland in Girard, Kansas.

June 1897 —The first convention of Social Democracy in America (formerly the American Railway Union) was led by Eugene V. Debs, who had been converted to socialism by Victor Berger while in the Woodstock County (Illinois) jail.

July 1901 —The first convention of the Socialist party of America was held in Indianapolis, with delegates representing all socialist groups in the country except the followers of Daniel De Leon.

July 14, 1906 —William D. ("Big Bill") Haywood was the first union official to be nominated for political office while in prison. Haywood was nominated for governor of Colorado on the Socialist party ticket.

1910 —The first Socialist administration was elected in Milwaukee. It cleaned up corruption and instituted planning and efficient service in a "City Beautiful" that became a national model for excellence in government.

1911 —Victor L. Berger of Wisconsin became the first Socialist to be elected to the U.S. Congress.

May 6, 1933 —The first Continental Congress of Workers and Farmers was called by the Socialist party. It established a National Committee of Correspondence and Action "to explore the best methods of economic and independent political action by the producing classes for the achievement of a cooperative commonwealth."

South

1810 —The first trade union in the South was organized by printers in New Orleans.

February 1898 —The Southern Confederacy of Labor, the first attempt to form an independent federation of southern white workers, was established with headquarters in Atlanta, Georgia. The attempt failed.

January 1899 —The first Southern Organizing Campaign was launched by the AFL. It was successful in Alabama and Louisiana.

August 4, 1897 —The first strike of southern white women against the employment of black women took place when two hundred women and girls at the Fulton Bag and Cotton Mills in Atlanta, Georgia, members of the Textile Workers' Union, walked out

when twenty-five black women were put to work in the folding department. Four hundred men were also called out by the union "in sympathy with the striking female operatives," and the factory was closed down.

1900 —The Joint Labor Legislative Board of Texas, the first influential state legislative labor organization in the South, was organized by the Railroad Brotherhoods and the Texas State Federation of Labor. In 1902, it formed an alliance with the Farmers' Union. The Joint Labor Legislative Board secured the passage of such legislation as a 1901 law outlawing the use of company checks, tickets, or symbols of any kind that were redeemable only in merchandise at company stores; a child labor law in 1903; two laws in 1907, one giving railroad telegraphers an eight-hour day, and the other establishing antiblacklisting and mine safety codes; a 1909 law providing workmen's compensation for railroad workers, which was extended in 1911 to industrial workers; the establishment of a bureau of labor statistics in 1909; the abolition of the convict lease system in 1910; and the passage of legislation in 1911 giving an eight-hour day to state employees and establishing a nine-hour day and a fifty-four hour week for women in manufacturing.

1912 —One hundred and eighty-eight delegates from twelve southern states met in Atlanta and launched the Southern Labor Congress to "unite the farmer, railroad and working man to bring about certain reforms so sadly needed in the South."

December 1927 — The Southern Industrial Conference was formed to propagandize against low wages and poor working conditions. Bishop James A. Conner was chairman of the executive committee.

1927 — The first Southern Summer School for Women Workers in Industry was sponsored by the North Carolina Federation of Labor.

March 12, 1929 — The first of the great textile strikes in the South was called by the National Textile Workers Union in Elizabethton, Tennessee.

September 14, 1929 — Ella May Wiggins, a twenty-five-year-old songwriter and leader of the National Textile Workers Union strike in Gastonia, North Carolina, was murdered by vigilantes. This was the first murder of a strike leader during the southern textile strikes.

September 29, 1930 — The first strike of the AFL southern organizing campaign occurred when four thousand members of Local 1685 of the United Textile Workers of America at the Dan River and Riverside Cotton Mills in Danville, Virginia, walked out for union recognition. The strike failed, partly because the AFL refused to provide financial assistance to the strikers, and partly because the company used black workers, who were ineligible for membership in the union, as strikebreakers. The failure of the strike was a devastating blow to the AFL's southern organizing campaign.

1932 — The Southern Tenant Farmers' Union of black and white sharecroppers was organized in Tyronza, Arkansas.

May–July 1946 — Operation Dixie, the first post-World War II southern organizing campaign by the AFL and CIO, was launched and failed.

August 1974 — The Textile Workers Union achieved its first victory in the decade-long fight to unionize the southern plants of J.P. Stevens and Company. The struggle was marked by a dozen Labor Board decisions ordering the company to "cease and desist" from unfair labor practices and three U.S. Supreme Court decisions against the company. The union won an election in the seven-plant Stevens complex in North Carolina, and its victory was viewed as marking "a new day in Dixie — first J.P. Stevens, then the textile industry, and then the whole South." Finally, in October 1980, after years of negotiations, J.P. Stevens signed its first union contract with the Amalgamated Clothing and Textile Workers Union.

Strike Benefits

May 31, 1786 — The first union strike benefit was authorized when twenty-six members of the Typographical Society of Philadelphia agreed "that we will support such of our brethren as shall be thrown out of employment on account of their refusing to work for less than $6 per week." After the society's demand for $1 a day was met, the fund was abandoned.

1827 — The first provision for assistance to an individual union by a city central labor body during a strike was made in the constitution of the Mechanics' Union of Trade Associations. It stipulated that if two-thirds of the delegates approved a proposed strike by a union, the union would become eligible for assistance from the association. During the strike, single men would be given travel expenses of from $3 to $6, provided they left the Philadelphia area for its duration. Married men were to receive $2, with additional sums for each member of their family, and were not expected to leave the city.

Strikebreaking
(See also *"Scabs"*)

July 21, 1828 — The first use of the militia to break a strike in the post-Revolutionary War period was in Paterson, New Jersey. Factory workers struck to protest the changing of their dinner hour, and eventually demanded a ten-hour day. The militia quelled the strikers, but the workers were successful in preventing the change of their dinner hour.

July 6, 1892 — The first pitched battle between strikers and Pinkerton strikebreakers took place during a strike against the Carnegie Steel Company in Homestead, Pennsylvania. The battle raged from 4 o'clock in the morning until 5 o'clock that afternoon. Nine workers were killed, along with three Pinkertons. The Pinkertons finally surrendered.

An 8-foot shaft stands today at a street intersection in Homestead and carries this inscription: "Erected by the members of the Steel Workers Organizing Committee Local Unions, in memory of the Iron and Steel workers who were killed in Homestead, Pa., on July 6, 1892, while striking against the Carnegie Steel Company in defense of their American rights."

1892 — Colorado was the first state to refuse to appropriate funds for the National Guard because of its role in breaking strikes. The Populist legislature declined to make the appropriation after the National Guard was used in the 1892 Coeur d'Alene strike.

May 1913 — The American flag was first used as a strikebreaking device. Paterson, New Jersey, stores displayed flags during the silk strike, with the inscription: "We live under this flag; we fight for this flag; and we will work under this flag." The strikers substituted the inscription: "We wove the flag. We dyed the flag. We won't scab under the flag." However, the strike was lost due to a combination of terrorism and hunger.

December 3, 1946 — The first county-wide strike was called by the Central Labor and Building Trades Councils of Alameda County, California, because the city of Oakland had used police to protect strikebreakers in two department stores. The strike tied up the entire county and ended with Oakland authorities agreeing not to use the police to protect strikebreakers in the future.

Strikes

1619 — The first dispute that may properly be called a strike happened in Jamestown, Virginia. Polish glass factory workers stopped working to protest being denied the right to vote. In response to their action, the Council of London yielded. The *Records of the Virginia Company of London* stated that "they shall be enfranchised and made as free as any inhabitant there."

1636 — The first labor action taken because of economic problems occurred when fishermen on Richmond Island, off the coast of Maine, went on strike to protest the withholding of a year's worth of wages.

1659 — A protest by New York City bakers against the low prices they were receiving for their goods constituted the first strike by master craftsmen.

1677 — The first criminal prosecution of strikers took place after a strike of cartmen in New York City.

1741 — New York bakers refused to work unless they received higher pay in what some consider the first American strike. However, others regard this and similar actions by labor in the Colonial period as strikes of masters against city governments rather than of wage earners against employers.

October 28, 1763 — The first strike by black workers occurred when Negro chimney sweepers in Charleston, South Carolina, struck for higher wages.

March 31, 1768 — Twenty journeymen tailors in New York City announced that they would only work at "three shillings and six pence per day" with "Diet." This was the first strike by journeymen.

1779 — In the first seamen's strike, sailors in Philadelphia demanded higher wages to offset rising prices due to inflation. The strike was put down by the militia.

1786 — The first strike in which participants were assisted by a strike fund was the journeymen printers' strike in Philadelphia for $1 a day's pay. The fund was abandoned after their demand was adopted.

1791 — In the first strike in the building trades, journeymen carpenters in Philadelphia struck against master carpenters for a working day that began at six in the morning and ended at six in the evening, with two hours off for meals. This was the first American strike for the ten-hour day. After the journeymen failed to win their demands for a ten-hour day and overtime pay, they set up a cooperative society that advertised rates that undersold the master carpenters.

1792 — The first strike by a permanent union was conducted by an organization of Philadelphia journeymen cordwainers who were protesting a reduction in wages.

1799 — The first sympathy strike occurred in Philadelphia. When the Federal Society of Journeymen Cordwainers walked out to protest a reduction in wages, the Philadelphia bootmakers walked out with them. A compromise settlement was reached, making this the first organized strike that utilized collective bargaining.

1799 — The first person paid to check that strikers did not report to work was hired by the Philadelphia cordwainers.

1805 — New York City cordwainers established the first permanent strike fund.

1809 — The Journeymen Cordwainers Society of Baltimore organized the first local industrywide strike. They were seeking a closed shop.

1824 — The first strike in which women participated took place in Pawtucket, Rhode Island.

1825 — The first large-scale strike for a ten-hour day was called by six hundred journeymen carpenters in Boston. The strike failed.

1825 — The United Tailoresses Society of New York called the first strike by a women's labor organization.

June 1828 — The first strike to last longer than a month occurred when six hundred Philadelphia journeymen house carpenters struck against dawn-to-dusk summer working hours. The strike lasted for almost two seasons. This was also the first mass strike. The house carpenters failed to achieve their demand.

1828 — The first use of the militia after the Revolutionary War to break up a strike was in Paterson, New Jersey, where factory workers were protesting the changing of their dinner hour and also demanding a ten-hour day. The militia broke the strike, but the workers were successful in preventing the change of their dinner hour.

June 29, 1831 —The first railroad strike occurred when laborers on the Baltimore and Ohio refused to work after a contractor on the third division absconded with their wages. The military were called out and put down the strike.

1834 —Federal troops were first used during a strike by President Andrew Jackson. At the request of the Maryland legislature, he dispatched troops to end a strike of Irish workers on the Chesapeake and Ohio Canal.

1835 —Boston ship carpenters went on the first strike for a two-hour lunch period. The strike failed.

1835 —The first general strike in American history took place in Philadelphia. Workers went out for the ten-hour day, and were victorious.

1835 —The first strike of federal government workers took place at the navy yard in Washington, D.C. Workers sought a "change of hours and a general redress of grievances."

1842 —In the first sit-down strike, Pittsburgh steel puddlers and boilermakers seized a mill.

1845 —In the first invasion of a factory during a strike to oust strikebreakers, Pittsburgh factory girls tore down a fence and broke into the mills to drive out the strikebreakers. The strike was for the ten-hour day.

1847 —Workers at the Tredegar Iron Works in Richmond, Virginia, were the first white workers in the South to strike against the use of slaves for factory work. The strike leaders were tried, found guilty, and sent to prison.

April 1849 —The first strike organized in the anthracite coal region was called by Bates' Union for higher wages and the abolition of the store-order system.

February 22, 1860 —The first regional strike in American history was the shoemakers' strike, which began in Lynn, Massachusetts, and spread throughout New England. By the end of February, Mechanics' Associations of shoe workers were organized in at least twenty-five towns. Close to twenty thousand shoe workers, including women, went on strike. Most of the strikers gained wage increases.

1863 —Illinois and Minnesota passed the first legislation providing for fines and imprisonment of strikers who prevented other persons from working.

October 1865 —The first united strike of black and white workers in the South was the successful strike by New Orleans screwmen for higher wages.

November 1865 —Ballet dancers met in New York City "to discuss the feasibility of a strike" and resolved to demand a raise in pay from $5 to $9 a week. When management turned them down, they organized the first strike by ballet dancers and succeeded in winning their demand.

November 1868 — The New York Cigar Makers' Union organized the first "rolling strike" — closing a few shops at a time, while workers in other establishments gave financial support to the strikers.

January 29, 1869 — The first strike of sailors against land "sharks" took place in New York City.

April 16, 1869 — The first strike of horse car workers was called by the Second Avenue Car Drivers in New York City.

June 2, 1869 — The first strike for the eight-hour day was called by New York City tailors.

April 5, 1873 — A strike by the New York Gasmen's Protective Association for the eight-hour day was the first strike to plunge large sections of a city into darkness. "The Reign of Darkness" was the heading of a *New York Times* editorial, which observed that because of the strike, the "streets of the City below Grand-street had become dangerous by the absence of light." The strike was lost.

January–June 1875 — In the first "long strike" by coal miners, the Workingmen's Benevolent Association struck against wage cuts in the anthracite mines. The strike lasted six months and ended in defeat and the crushing of the union.

August–September 27, 1875 — The first strike called a "Great Vacation" took place in Fall River, Massachusetts. Textile workers struck against wage cuts, and on September 27, 1875, the strikers marched to the City Hall to demand bread for their starving children. They were met by three companies of militia and a cordon of police, who prevented them from presenting their demands. Late in October, the strike ended in defeat. For many years thereafter, September 27 was marked in Fall River by mass meetings to commemorate the "Great Vacation."

July 16–30, 1877 — The great railroad strike of 1877 was the first national strike in American history. It stretched from the Atlantic to the Pacific, and became a general strike in St. Louis. The strike was triggered by a 10 percent wage cut imposed by all railroads. For many railroad workers, this was the third 10 percent cut since the beginning of the economic crisis of 1873. Over a hundred workers were killed when the strike was broken by the U.S. Army and state militias.

October 1877 — The cigar makers went on the first general strike to abolish the tenement house system. After 107 days of strike in New York City, the battle was called off.

1880 — The first strike of western metalliferous miners was staged in Leadville, Colorado. Three thousand miners went on strike and won.

1882 — The Dress and Cloakmakers' Union of New York City called the first strike of Jewish needle trades workers. Demands were for the ten-hour day and a piece rate that would allow a $15 weekly wage. This walkout, called the first "immigrant strike," was successful.

August 10, 1883 — American District Telegraph Messenger Boys in New York City called the first strike of telegraph messenger boys.

August 12, 1883 — In the first strike by newsboys, several hundred New York City newsboys took to the streets when they were told they must pay more for the *Evening Sun* and the *Evening World.* The strike spread to Brooklyn. *The New York Times* reported on April 13, 1883: "Newsboys on Strike. . . . Some of the delivery wagons on the up-town routes had a serious time of it. All the way up on Broadway and on the west side they were followed by a howling mob of half-grown men and boys. . . ."

1883 — The first strike by telegraph workers was called by the Knights of Labor against Western Union. The strike was lost.

March 1885 — The first strike on a railroad owned by Jay Gould was called by the Knights of Labor on the

Southwest Railroad. The strike was won and played an important role in the spectacular rise of the Knights.

July 1885 — The Saginaw Valley lumber strike, led by the Knights of Labor, was the first strike in which strikers forced mills to shut down by turning off steam and banking fires. The strike was for a ten-hour day "with present wages," and lasted from July 6 to September 1. It ended with the ten-hour day established without any reduction in pay. Most of the strikers were Polish workers.

March 1, 1886 — The first strike in which strikers took over and occupied property was the second Gould strike. Strikers took possession of the railroad property, but they lost the strike.

March 17, 1886 — In the first strike of schoolchildren, pupils at St. Anne's Parochial School in Brooklyn, New York, struck for the removal of a 10 cents per week fee, and picketed the school. *The New York Times* reported on March 18, 1886: "The most remarkable strike that has yet grown out of difference of opinion between the person or persons fixing wages or making rules and those for whom wages are fixed or rules made occurred in Brooklyn. . . . Upon approaching the school building . . . three boys, who had been appointed a committee by the strikers, were discovered on picket duty. Perceiving that an attempt was about to be made by a pupil to enter the school building in defiance of the strikers, two of the committeemen ran forward to assault the 'scab.'" The *Times* headline read: "A Burlesque on Strikes. Pupils of a Parochial School in Brooklyn Catch the Contagion."

On April 12, 1886, schoolboys went on strike in Greenpoint, Brooklyn, and in Troy, New York, and on April 19, sixty pupils of the South Boston Public School struck for shorter hours.

May 1, 1886 — In the first national general strike, and first designated "May Day" strike, approximately 340,000 workers demonstrated in several cities for the eight-hour day.

June 5, 1886 — The first general strike of all horse street car lines in a city took place when the Empire Protective Association called out all conductors and drivers in New York City, Brooklyn, and Long Island City in response to the refusal of the Third-Avenue Railroad Company to recognize the union and grant its conductors and drivers higher wages and shorter hours. The general walkout lasted for one day and resulted in a victory for the workers.

June 28, 1886 — In the first strike by salesmen, Singer Manufacturing Company salesmen struck for higher commissions and won.

September 16, 1890 — On this date, the boys' choir at St. George's Church in New York City refused "to work for ice cream and demanded wages. . . . So the immature Knights went on their strike, at least, all but three who were derisively called 'scabs'" ("Choristers on Strike," *New York Times,* September 17, 1890). This was the first strike by a boys' choir.

July 1892 — The first strike that featured an armed battle between strikers and Pinkerton strikebreakers occurred in Homestead, Pennsylvania, where iron and steel workers were striking against the Carnegie Company. On the morning of July 6, the Pinkertons marched toward the plant, and in the resulting pitched battle, seven strikers and three Pinkertons were killed and many were wounded.

December 17, 1893 — In the first strike by members of a symphony orchestra, the New York Symphony Orchestra, conducted by Walter Damrosch, went out on strike against the employment of Anton Hegner as cellist because he was not a member of the Musical Mutual Protective Union. The strike was settled on December 22 when the union permitted Hegner to play, but only as a soloist.

April 1894 — The first strike by the American Railway Union was called against the Great Northern Railroad. All trains except mail trains were stopped when all nine thousand employees of the railroad struck. After eighteen days, the strike ended in complete victory for the union.

May 11, 1894 —Workers struck the Pullman Company for the first time in Illinois. This action later led to the strike against the Pullman Company by the American Railway Union, which resulted in the crushing of the union.

November 15, 1895 —The first strike of cab drivers took place in New York City.

October 30, 1897 —In the first strike by foreign workers visiting the United States, members of the Banda Rossa band, who had been brought to the United States from Italy, went on strike because of inadequate wages. The strike ended when the Italians won a new contract with higher wages.

July 1900 —The first great strike of Italian laborers took place on Croton Dam, New York. The strikers were arrested and imprisoned.

September 12, 1900 —The United Mine Workers led the first complete strike of the entire anthracite coal region. The union entered the strike with eight thousand members in good standing, and emerged from it victoriously with 100,000 members.

September 19, 1900 —The first strike of the Hebrew Actors' Union was conducted with the support of the United Hebrew Trades, with which the actors' organization was affiliated.

February 21, 1901 —Members of the White Rats' Association struck against the Association of Vaudeville Managers of the United States over the commissions charged by the managers. This was the first strike by a vaudeville union. It ended on March 6 with an agreement that no commissions would be charged in the future.

August 1901 —In the first general strike against the U.S. Steel Corporation, the Amalgamated Association of Iron and Steel Workers led over sixty-two thousand workers. The strike was lost.

June 2, 1902 —The first United Mine Workers strike in West Virginia took place when sixteen thousand miners in Kanawah, New River, Norfolk, and the western districts walked out under the leadership of the UMW. The strike lasted until July 1903. Though the union failed to organize West Virginia, it did win an agreement with the Kanawah Valley coal operators, covering seven thousand miners.

August 20, 1902 —George F. Baer, president of the Philadelphia and Reading Railway, was the first capitalist to publicly assert that his class had a divine right to control wealth and rule the working class. He said that "the rights and interests of the laboring man will be protected and cared for, not by the labor agitator, but by the Christian men to whom God has given control of the property rights of the country." Baer made this statement during the 1902 coal strike, which tied up the entire industry.

September–October   1902 — J.P. Morgan became involved for the first time in settling a strike against one of his companies. He met with Secretary of State Elihu Root aboard his yacht, *Corsair,* during the 1902 coal strike.

June 21, 1904 — The first general strike in shops of the New York Clothing Manufacturers' Association (men's clothing industry) began. Twenty-five thousand workers were on strike by July 1, and the strike spread to Chicago and St. Louis, but it was lost.

July 12, 1904 — The first general strike in the meat-packing industry was called by the Amalgamated Meat Cutters and Butcher Workmen of North America. Fifty thousand packinghouse workers in nine cities went out on this strike, which lasted until September 8 and ended in defeat for the union.

January 1, 1906 — In the first general strike in the printing industry, members of the International Typographical Union struck for the eight-hour day in book and job printing establishments in sixty-nine cities. The strike lasted four months and brought the eight-hour day to sixteen thousand printers in the two trades.

December 1906 — The AFL's International Union of Machinists called the first strike in the automobile industry against the Pope Motor Company in Toledo, the largest manufacturer of automobiles. The strike was lost.

March 7, 1907 — The IWW first employed the strategy of presenting demands to employers *after* a strike had begun during a strike by Portland (Oregon) sawmill workers.

July 1909 — For the first time, a strategy used in European strikes was employed in an American strike: an "Unknown Committee" to manage the strike was established in a strike against the Pressed Steel Car Company at McKees Rocks, Pennsylvania.

September 1909 — The IWW attained the first victory in a strike by unskilled steel workers in the Pressed Steel Car Company strike at McKees Rocks, Pennsylvania.

November 22, 1909 — The first general strike in the women's clothing industry took place. Dress and waist makers assembled at a mass meeting in Cooper Union in New York City to hear a report on the importance of calling a general strike of all dress and waist makers. The meeting was dominated by the moderate Samuel Gompers, who urged the workers not to act hastily. Thereupon, Clara Lemlich, a young girl who was a member of the executive board of Local 25, asked for the floor, and said: "I have listened to all the speakers. I would not have further patience for talk as I am one who feels and suffers from the things pictured. I move we go on a general strike." Her speech was greeted with a roaring endorsement and the chairman asked the workers if they would take the old Jewish oath. With hands raised, they vowed: "If I turn traitor to the cause I now pledge, may this hand wither from the arm I now raise." A committee left Cooper Union to carry the message to Beethoven Hall and the other halls, where groups cheered the decision to strike just as wildly. Thus began the most significant struggle of women for unionism in the nation's history. Within a few days, fifteen thousand women had walked off their jobs.

On December 20, the strike spread to Philadelphia, where the demands were for union recognition, a nine-hour work day, a fifty-hour week, and uniform wage scales.

The strike ended on February 15, 1910, with agreements providing for a fifty-two-hour week, a wage raise, abolition of subcontracting, limited night work, and paid legal holidays. The general strike had lasted thirteen weeks.

July 7, 1910 — In the first general strike of cloakmakers in the entire women's clothing industry of New York City, fifty thousand cloakmakers walked out under the leadership of the ILGWU. The strike was won.

October 26, 1910 — The first general strike of forty thousand men's clothing workers took place in Chicago. The strike was called off by leaders of the United Garment Workers without the consent of the workers, who continued their strike until it was once again called off by heads of the union without consulting the strikers. The strike lasted 133 days.

August 1911 — The IWW conducted its first strike in Lawrence, Massachusetts, when the cotton weavers struck the Atlantic Mill. The action failed.

September 30, 1911 — The first strike of the Harriman System Federation involved forty thousand workers. A simultaneous strike occurred on the Illinois Central Railroad. The strikes were lost.

January 1912 — The first "singing strike" was the IWW strike in Lawrence, Massachusetts. "This movement at Lawrence was strangely a singing movement," wrote journalist Ray Stannard Baker.

May 18, 1912 — When Ty Cobb of the Detroit Tigers was suspended by Ban Johnson, president of the American League, for going into the stands and attacking a New York Yankee fan who had been riding him, Tiger players refused to play against the Philadelphia Athletics. Thus began the first strike in baseball history. Strikebreakers were recruited to play for the Tigers at $10 each. The strike lasted only one day. It ended when Cobb urged his teammates to resume play after Johnson warned that unless they reported for their following game on May 21 in Washington, he would "drive every one of you out of baseball." Johnson fined nearly every player on the Tigers $100. Cobb received a $50 fine and a ten-day suspension.

June 20, 1912 — The first general strike in the fur industry began when nine thousand fur workers in New York City struck for recognition of their union, a closed shop, the nine-hour day (fifty-four hours a week), paid legal holidays, no homework, no contracting, sanitary conditions, a union wage scale, and overtime limited to the three months of the busy season, and then at time-and-one-half. The first collective agreement in the industry was signed on September 8, 1912, after twelve weeks of general strike. Except for the closed shop and abolition of contracting, the strikers won all of their demands.

September 30, 1912 — A mass protest strike in Lawrence, Massachusetts, involving twelve thousand workers in the textile plants was the first industry strike conducted for the purpose of obtaining the release of labor prisoners. The prisoners in question were Ettor and Giovannitti, two IWW leaders. They were found not guilty by a jury on November 25.

December 30, 1912 — The first general strike in the men's clothing industry began in New York City: By the end of the first week, 110,000 workers were on

strike. The strike was conducted by members of the United Garment Workers, but a rift developed between the strikers and the union leadership when President T.A. Rickert, without consulting the local leaders, ended the strike. The strike continued until March 12, 1913, when the workers gained terms more favorable than those Rickert had accepted for them. The strike caused a deep division between the rank and file and union leadership.

January 17, 1913 — The first strike by reporters on Jewish-language newspapers began in New York City and lasted until March 15, 1913. The strike was won.

February 10, 1913 — The first strike of rubber workers was the result of an announcement by the Firestone Tire Company in Akron, Ohio, that there would be a 35 percent reduction in piecework rates paid to finishers in the automobile tire department. The Firestone strikers, who were members of the IWW, were joined by the Goodyear and Goodrich workers, but the strike failed.

March 19, 1913 — For the first time, a strike meeting was held in a town other than that in which the strike took place. When Paterson, New Jersey, silk strikers were forbidden to meet in Paterson, they assembled in the nearby town of Haledon, whose mayor was a socialist.

March–April 1913 — For the first time, thousands of strikers were arrested during a strike. Forty-eight hundred strikers were arrested in the course of the Paterson silk strike, and thirteen hundred of them were sent to jail.

May 13, 1913 — The first IWW local to win recognition and the right to bargain collectively was Marine Transport Local 3 of Philadelphia, composed of black and white longshoremen and headed by Ben Fletcher, prominent black IWW leader.

June 17, 1913 — The first strike in the Detroit auto industry took place at Plant No. 1 of the Studebaker factory. It was led by ʳhe IWW. The strike was lost.

April 23, 1914 — The first strike of convicts began when 180 men working in the knitting department of New York's Sing Sing prison struck because Governor Glynn vetoed a bill permitting a prisoner to apply for parole after one year in jail.

July 20, 1914 — The Baseball Players' Fraternity called its first strike. It was called off on July 21.

September 1915 — The Amalgamated Clothing Workers encountered its first test when it attempted to extend union control to the entire Chicago men's clothing industry. The union called a general strike on September 27 for the closed shop; a forty-eight-hour week; no work on legal holidays with no reduction in pay; overtime at the rate of time-and-one-half; a 25 percent increase in all wages; abolition of the system of fines and of arbitrary discharge; a minimum wage; and suitable arbitration machinery. When the strike was called off on December 12, 1915, Amalgamated had achieved some concessions but no recognition of the union itself.

1915 — The first strike at a Standard Oil Company refinery took place at the Bayonne refinery of Jersey Standard. The strike was lost.

August 1916 — For the first time, a vote was taken by railroad workers on calling a strike against all railroads. The vote to strike for the eight-hour day carried, with 98.7 percent in favor.

February 6–11, 1919 — In the first general strike on the West Coast, sixty thousand workers in Seattle, Washington, walked off their jobs. The strike was lost.

February 1919 — New England telephone operators in twenty-six cities and towns went on strike, the first strike by telephone operators. The telegraph lines were controlled by the U.S. Post Office, and the strike led to an agreement for wage increases between the assistant postmaster general and the telephone operators' unions.

August 8, 1919 — In the first general strike by actors, Actors Equity Association in New York City struck against the

Producing Managers' Association for recognition and better conditions. The strike was won.

September 9, 1919 — The first policemen's strike took place in Boston, whose police voted to strike for higher wages by 1,134 to 2. The strike was broken by Massachusetts Governor Calvin Coolidge, and none of the strikers was reinstated.

September 22, 1919 — In the first general strike in the history of the steel industry, 343,100 steel workers struck. Every steel-producing region was affected, and almost every mill was either wholly or partially shut down. The strikers' demands included: the right of collective bargaining; reinstatement of all men discharged for union activities, with pay for time lost; the eight-hour day; one day's rest in seven; abolition of the twenty-four-hour shift; an "American living wage"; double pay for overtime; dues checkoff and seniority; and the abolition of company unions and of physical examinations. The strike, led by William Z. Foster, secretary of the National Committee for the Organizing of the Iron and Steel Industry, was called off on January 8, 1920, and ended in failure. Eighteen strikers were killed as a result of unprecedented police and militia brutality. On June 17, 1920, the National Committee was disbanded.

1919–1920 — In the first "vacationist movement," New York printers and pressmen struck for a forty-four-hour week. They won their demand.

May 1, 1921 — The first East Coast general strike in the American shipping industry involved all ships from Maine to Texas. The strike lasted fifty-two days and ended in defeat for the International Seamen's Union.

April 1922 — For the first time, miners in the anthracite and bituminous coal fields went on strike together. The United Mine Workers' contracts expired simultaneously in both fields, and 300,000 miners walked out of the mines. When the strike was settled in September 1923, the union was granted recognition and an eight-hour day.

April 1923 — The first nationwide strike for political prisoners was called by the IWW to gain the release of Wobblies still imprisoned under the Espionage Act.

April 1926 — The sheriff of Passaic, New Jersey, cited the Civil War Riot Act in prohibiting all meetings and picketing during the Passaic textile strike called by the Trade Union Educational League. This was the first time the Civil War law had been used in a strike.

November 1931 — Theodore Dreiser, the noted American novelist, visited Harlan County, Kentucky, to study at first hand the repressive measures taken against the strikers there, who were led by the National Miners' Union. As chairman of the National Committee for the Defense of Political Prisoners, Dreiser invited other Americans to look at the situation in Harlan, and a group of leading writers responded. The product of their visit was a book called *Harlan Miners Speak.*

August 16, 1933 — In the first general strike in the dress industry, workers in virtually all shops — union and non-union — walked out in both New York City and out-of-town shops. The sixty thousand strikers in New York made it the largest strike ever called by the ILGWU. The strike lasted for four days, and was won by the union. The employers accepted the closed shop and agreed to raise wages.

September 21, 1933 — The open shop was abolished in the automobile industry after tool and dye makers, members of the Mechanics Education Society, which was organized in February 1933, struck the General Motors plant in Flint, Michigan. Within the next few days, every auto plant in the Detroit-Pontiac-Flint area (except Ford and Graham-Paige) was closed by the first general strike in the auto industry by tool and dye makers. The walkout ended on November 6 with union recognition, an increase in wages, and reinstatement of the strikers without reprisals.

February 23, 1934 — The first strike by a newly organized federal labor union of the AFL took place when Toledo Auto-Lite workers rejected an agreement reached by their AFL leaders. By May 23, more than ten thousand workers were on strike.

September 1, 1934 — The first national textile strike was led by the United Textile Workers of the AFL and involved 400,000 textile workers. This was the first Labor Day weekend mass strike and extended from Maine to Alabama. The strike failed.

November 17, 1934 — The first major strike by the Newspaper Guild was called after eight Guildsmen were fired from the *Newark Ledger.* After nineteen weeks of strike, the *Ledger* recognized the Newark Guild and the discharged men were reinstated.

1934 — This was the first year in American history that over one million workers were on strike. There were 1,856 work stoppages involving 1,470,000 workers.

February 14, 1936 — The "first CIO strike" was the Goodyear rubber strike in Akron, Ohio. The strike, which began spontaneously on February 14, was preceded by a three-day sit-down at the Firestone Tire and Rubber Company and very brief sit-downs at the Goodyear and Goodrich plants. On February 14, workers on three of the four shifts in Goodyear's Plant 2 sat down to protest the layoff of seventy workers on the fourth shift without the customary three-day notice. The United Rubber Workers agreed to support the strike, and on February 17, the union established an "endless human chain" of pickets around Plant 2. The next day, five hundred tire builders sat down in Plant 1 for twenty hours, and after they emerged, pickets also closed this unit. By February 19, production at Goodyear had been paralyzed and fifteen thousand workers were out. The CIO sent in organizers and funds to help the strikers, and Adolph Germer came to help direct their efforts. In the course of the strike, which lasted until March 21, the longest picket line in the history of strikes in the United States up to that time was established. The settlement was viewed as a victory for the workers, even though it did not eliminate the company union in the plant or result in the designation of the United Rubber Workers as the exclusive bargaining agent for the Goodrich workers. However, the settlement did give the United Rubber Workers and the CIO great prestige.

Although the sit-down aspect of the strike was brief, the Goodyear rubber strike was the first in this country to focus public attention on the sit-down as a labor tactic.

July 23, 1936 — The UE conducted its first strike, against the Radio Corporation of America (RCA) in Camden, New Jersey. The strike was won.

March 8, 1937 — The first UAW strike against Chrysler began. It ended on April 6 with an agreement similar to that obtained from General Motors: the corporation recognized the UAW as the

bargaining agent for its members, and pledged that it would not "aid, promote, or finance" a rival organization "for the purpose of undermining the union."

February 1938 — For the first time, a mayor of New York City would not permit the police to interfere with strikers. Mayor Fiorello H. LaGuardia ordered the police not to attack fur strikers and not to allow employers to use hired thugs against the strikers. The strike was won on May 26, when the workers gained seasonal job security (guaranteed work for eight consecutive months), wage increases, and other concessions.

1940 — The U.S. Supreme Court ruled for the first time that a strike, even a sit-down strike, was not a combination in restraint of trade under the Sherman Anti-Trust Act. The case was *Apex Hosiery Co. v. Leader.*

February 26, 1941 — The first union victory in the fifty-year history of the Bethlehem Steel Corporation was won by thirteen thousand steel workers in the Lackawanna, New York, plant. The company signed a contract recognizing the CIO steel workers' union.

April 1, 1941 — The first strike of Ford workers was called by the UAW. It ended on April 11 when Ford agreed to recognize the CIO union.

May 1, 1942 — The government seized mines for the first time during a strike.

After every soft coal mine under contract with the United Mine Workers was closed down by a national strike, President Franklin D. Roosevelt ordered government troops to seize the struck mines.

June 17, 1943 — The first successful strike of tobacco workers took place at the R.J. Reynolds Tobacco Company in Winston-Salem, North Carolina. Eleven thousand tobacco workers, black and white, won their strike and the recognition of their union — Local 22 of the Food, Tobacco, Agricultural, and Allied Workers Union (CIO). Women played a decisive role in the strike, including such leaders as Moranda Smith, Velma Hopkins, and Viola Brown.

January 21, 1946 — For the first time, the entire U.S. Steel Corporation was closed down and U.S. Steel yielded to a strike. In the largest single strike the United States had ever seen, 800,000 steel workers in the entire basic steel-fabricating industry walked off their jobs. The strike ended on the twenty-sixth day when U.S. Steel capitulated and granted the United Steel Workers (CIO) an 18½-cents-per-hour across-the-board wage increase.

1946 — For the first time, more that five million workers were engaged in strikes in one year.

April 8, 1952 — Six hundred thousand steel workers walked off their jobs for wage increases and other improvements, but the strike ended when President Harry S Truman seized the steel mills.

June 2, 1952 — The U.S. Supreme Court, by a six-to-three decision, denied President Truman had the authority to seize the steel industry, whereupon the steel workers went on strike again, this time for fifty-three days. An agreement was reached on August 2.

1953 — The first strike of *braceros* (Mexican workers imported as agricultural laborers) took place in the lettuce fields of Salinas, California.

May 8, 1959 — Local 1199 called the first strike in the voluntary hospitals of New York City. After an election victory at Montefiore Hospital in the Bronx, six thousand workers were brought into the union during a three-month organizing drive. The union demanded elections at seven hospitals, and when the trustees refused, thirty-five hundred workers walked off their jobs and stayed out for forty-six days in a strike that was supported by the New York City Central Labor Council, the AFL-CIO, Dr. Martin Luther King, Jr., A. Philip Randolph, and other black leaders. The strike was victorious, even though the workers did not win the right to organize under New York State law until 1963, following a fifty-six-day strike in 1962.

November 7, 1960 — The United Federation of Teachers conducted its first strike in New York City. The one-day strike did not bring a union contract, but a contract with the city was signed after another one-day strike on April 11, 1962.

October 1962–March 31, 1963 — The Typographical Union struck for the first time in its sixty-five years of existence. The strike against the Publishers Association of New York was over the issue of automation. It lasted 114 days and ended with the employers accepting the workers' basic demands and instituting the thirty-five-hour week.

January 1965 — Municipal employees in New York City went on their first major strike, in spite of a state law prohibiting such strikes. New York City Welfare Department workers struck in the face of the Condon-Wadlin law, which banned strikes by public employees in New York State. No worker was fired.

January 1966 — The Transport Workers' Union of New York struck for the first time. During the twelve-day walkout, President Michael Quill and five other union officers were arrested. The strikers won a pay raise, and municipal authorities abandoned their attempt to fine the union $322,000 for every day of the strike, and to imprison the union leaders.

July 1966 — The first strike by firemen took place in Kansas City. The demand was for a shorter work week.

March 23, 1967 — The first strike in the thirty-year history of the American Federation of Television and Radio Artists (AFTRA) began. The strike, for pay increases and payment for overtime, ended in victory on April 10.

May 2, 1968 — The first wildcat strike at the Dodge main plant in Detroit was called by DRUM (Dodge Revolutionary Union Movement) against a speedup and discrimination against black auto workers.

March 28, 1968 — Martin Luther King, Jr., led the first parade in Memphis, Tennessee, in support of a strike by black sanitation workers called by Local 1773 of the American Federation of State, County, and Municipal Employees (AFSCME). On April 4, King was assassinated in Memphis while preparing to participate in a second parade in support of the sanitation strikers.

June 27, 1969 — Local 1199 of the Hospital Workers Union in the South achieved its first victory after a 113-day strike of workers, mainly black, at Medical College Hospital in Charleston, South Carolina. Local 1199B, the first local formed by the National Union of Hospital and Nursing Home Employees, led the strike. Victory was achieved through the unity of the workers and the Southern Christian Leadership Conference (SCLC) under the slogan, "Union Power Plus Soul Power Equals Victory." Reverend Ralph Abernathy, who had become head of the SCLC after the assassination of Martin Luther King, Jr., was jailed for supporting the strikers on the picket line. He was released after the victory.

December 1969 — General Electric workers struck for the first time. The issue was "Boulwarism," a plan introduced by Lemuel Boulware to eliminate unionism as an effective force at the company. Under it, the company would present to the various unions a set of contract proposals, permitting only minor adjustments, while waging a nationwide struggle to discourage and demoralize the workers. After 150,000 workers conducted a fourteen-week strike, GE was compelled to sign a single collective agreement.

April 1970 — Postal workers went out on strike for the first time in the 196-year history of the U.S. Postal Service. The issue for 160,000 post office employees in two hundred cities was wage increases. President Richard M. Nixon declared a national state of emergency — the first since World War II — and U.S. Army troops and National Guardsmen were sent in to carry mail. The strike ended when the workers obtained increases.

July 1974 — Members of the United Steel Workers struck for the first time since their president, I. W. Abel, had negotiated a no-strike agreement. The strike involved eighteen locals of taconite and iron-ore miners in the Mesabi Range of Minnesota and extended into Michigan. The locals were not covered by the no-strike agreement, and their victory demonstrated the importance of not giving up the right to strike.

August 1974 — The United Mine Workers, under the leadership of Arnold Miller, reestablished a foothold in Harlan County, Kentucky, after a thirteen-month strike against the "captive" coal mines of the Duke Power Company. Harlan County had been non-union during the Boyle administration.

July 12, 1976 — For the first time, striking workers sought help for their cause from delegates to a national presidential convention. Thousands of striking hospital workers, members of District 1199 of the National Union of Hospital and Health Care Employees, rallied outside the Democratic National Convention at Madison Square Garden in New York City. The strikers carried signs declaring "We Can't Work for Peanuts," a reference to the commodity raised by Democratic presidential candidate Jimmy Carter in his home state of Georgia. The strike, the largest hospital strike in U.S. history, ended on July 17 when the hospitals agreed to submit the union's demand for cost-of-living wage increases to binding arbitration.

October 6, 1976 — The first strike by doctors occurred when members of the Committee of Internes and Residents struck against three private nonprofit hospitals in New York City. The committee, representing three thousand members in twenty-one hospitals, called the strike to compel the hospitals to recognize internes and residents as employees, and not merely as students.

August 1977 —United Automobile Workers members walked out of several Chrysler plants during a heat wave in which temperatures reached over 100° F. in the plants. This was the first strike over the issue of unbearable heat in the workplace. The union declared that it would make factory heat a key demand in local contract talks.

March 17, 1981 —The first strike by doctors for the purpose of improving patient care began. Two thousand physi'ians-in-training struck six municipal and two private voluntary hospitals in New York City to demand guaranteed minimum staffing levels for nurses, aides, technicians, and other support personnel, and an end to what they called chronic shortages of lifesaving medical equipment. "The issue is not money," strike leader Dr. Jonathan House declared, "but the need to enforce standards of patient care in our contracts." The strike ended in failure.

Strike Ban

1974 —The first industrywide peacetime strike ban was agreed to when top officers of the United Steel Workers of America signed the Experimental Negotiating Agreement (ENA) with the steel industry. The agreement was to last until 1977, at which time it could be renewed until 1980. ENA became a leading issue in the rank-and-file movement to elect Edward Sadlowski president of the union in 1977. Sadlowski promised to abandon the ENA on the ground that it had weakened the steel workers' bargaining position.

Strike Fund

June 1786 —The first provision for strike benefits in the United States was made by twenty-six compositors and pressmen, who resolved that they would "support such of our brethren as shall be out of employment on account of their refusing to work for less than six dollars per week." The strike had been called by Philadelphia printers to resist a wage cut.

1805 —The New York cordwainers set up the first permanent strike fund. It was to be used for no other purpose but the support of strikes.

March 1884–April 1885 —The first union to spend over $100,000 in strike benefits was the Cigar Makers' International Union. In combating a lockout in Cincinnati, the union distributed $140,000 in strike benefits. The strike was lost nonetheless.

Strike Relief

June 10, 1901 — The International Machinists' Association became the first union to extend financial aid to nonunion men who went out on strike with the union strikers.

January 1932 — A committee of New York writers, including Waldo Frank, Edmund Wilson, Malcolm Cowley, and Mary Heaton Vorse, together with delegations of clergymen and students, visited Harlan County, Kentucky, with truckloads of food and clothing for the strikers there.

October 1933 — The first laborers of any kind to receive food from a federal agency during a strike were Mexican workers in California. In a strike led by the Cannery and Agricultural Workers' Industrial Union, Governor James Rolph, acting on federal advice, ordered the California Emergency Relief Administration to provide the Mexican agricultural workers with relief. The striking cotton pickers were demanding $1 per hundredweight.

Suffrage

1776 — Pennsylvania adopted a constitution that made it one of the few states without property qualifications for voting.

1790 — Pennsylvania extended the franchise to all who paid any kind of tax.

1791 — Vermont became the first state to provide universal manhood suffrage without tax qualification.

1831 — The first labor demand for woman suffrage came from the Association for the Working People of New Castle, Delaware. It demanded suffrage for women, asking: "Wherefore should they be denied the immunities of free men? Does anyone deem that their interference in public affairs would be prejudicial to the general interest?"

June 17, 1865 — The first labor demand for Negro suffrage was made by the *Boston Daily Evening Voice,* the official organ of the Boston central labor union. It declared Negroes should have the right to vote, both in the North and South. It also called for suffrage for Asiatics and women: "In popular government every class and every individual is entitled in some form or other to an adequate representation. You may exclude incompetents, idiots, criminals, etc.; but upon some ground of equal and universal principle. If ignorance be the ground of exclusion, or any other test be adopted, let it be impartial in its application — not applied to one class while another is exempted."

November 1891 — An AFL convention first endorsed woman suffrage.

Sunday Work

1821 — The first mass meeting of workers to end Sunday work was initiated by New York City bakers.

Supreme Court

November 2, 1887 — The U.S. Supreme Court made its first ruling affirming the death sentence of labor men found guilty by a jury in the Haymarket case (*Spies et al. v. The People*).

1898 — The U.S. Supreme Court handed down its first decision in the field of labor legislation. By a vote of seven-to-two, the court upheld a law passed by the state of Utah limiting the hours men could work in the mines to eight per day (*Holden v. Hardy*).

May 7, 1930 — For the first time in thirty-six years, a presidential appointment to the Supreme Court was rejected by the Senate. The AFL and the National Association for the Advancement of Colored People (NAACP) joined forces to defeat the Senate confirmation of Judge John J. Parker of North Carolina as associate justice of the Supreme Court because of his record as a racist and an "injunction judge." In 1927, Parker had handed down the Red Jacket decision, which enjoined the United Mine Workers from "trespassing upon the properties" of 316 coal companies in southern West Virginia or from inciting the forty-thousand employees of these companies "to break their contract of employment." This was probably the most hated labor injunction of the decade.

April 12, 1937 — The U.S. Supreme Court upheld the constitutionality of the National Labor Relations (Wagner) Act.

"Sweating System"

1883 — New York passed the first law prohibiting the manufacture of cigars or tobacco in any form in tenement houses. It was declared unconstitutional by the state Supreme Court in 1885.

August–September 1891 — The first investigation of a sweatshop industry was conducted by the Illinois Women's Alliance and the Chicago Trades Assembly.

March 1892 — Congress undertook its first investigation of the "sweating system."

1892 — Illinois became the first state to enact a law providing for inspection and tagging of all garments manufactured outside the state prior to sale to make certain they were produced under healthful conditions and not in sweatshops.

T

Taft-Hartley Act

June 23, 1947 —The first major revision of the Wagner Labor Act, the Labor-Management Relations Act (commonly known as the Taft-Hartley Act), was passed by Congress over President Harry S Truman's veto. Taft-Hartley, which was based largely on suggestions made by the antiunion National Association of Manufacturers, forbade unions from engaging in certain specific practices, including: (1) the closed shop; (2) inducing an employer to discriminate against an employee who had been expelled from a union for any reason other than the failure to pay dues; (3) restraint or coercion of employees in their right to organize into trade unions; (4) refusal to bargain collectively with any employer; (5) inducing a strike or boycott with the purpose of forcing an employer to institute a closed shop or to recognize a union not certified by the NLRB, or to force management to recognize a union when another union had been certified by the board, or to force management to assign work to members of a certain union or craft when the employer was already complying with an NLRB certification order; (6) charging excessive initiation fees when a union shop was in existence; and

(7) attempting to cause an employer to pay for work not actually performed.

Each union desiring to use the NLRB had to file reports with the secretary of labor showing the union's internal structure and finances. The union also had to provide financial information to its own members annually. In addition, for the first time in American history, each union official of a national or international union desiring to use the NLRB was required to file an affidavit assuring the government that he was not affiliated with communism or the Communist party. Failure to comply would cause the union to lose the protection and privileges of the law.

Under the Taft-Hartley Act, the NLRB was authorized to conduct elections to determine the certification of unions to act as bargaining agents for employees, and to hold runoff elections whenever an election was inconclusive. Management was permitted to discuss with its employees, and to publicize, its views on trade unions, provided it did not coerce or threaten individuals who planned to become or were union members. Unions could be sued in district courts for breaches of contract, illegal boycotts, and strikes. In case of a strike affecting the welfare of the entire nation, the attorney general was authorized to secure an injunction prohibiting the strike for eighty days. At the end of that period, the NLRB was to conduct a poll of the employees on the employer's last offer. If employees voted to accept, the strike would be called off. If they voted to reject the offer, the strike could occur. The act prohibited strikes by federal employees and contributions and expenditures by unions in elections, including primary elections that were national in scope. Section 14(a) of the act gave federal sanction to state "right-to-work" laws that forbade the union shop. The act's provision prohibiting the so-called secondary boycott seriously weakened labor solidarity during strikes.

December 5, 1947 — The AFL organized Labor's Educational and Political League to fight for the repeal of the Taft-Hartley Act.

January 1948 — Organized labor announced a campaign for repeal of the Taft-Hartley Act, under the slogan "Repeal the Taft-Hartley Slave Labor Act." The campaign reached its height during the presidential election of 1948, when nearly one hundred union members were elected in primaries as delegates to the Republican and Democratic national conventions. The Republican convention rejected a demand for repeal of the Taft-Hartley Act, but the Democratic convention endorsed labor's program. Labor's political campaign against the Taft-Hartley Act played an important part in President Harry S

Truman's reelection over the highly favored Republican candidate, Thomas E. Dewey. However, a coalition of Republicans and southern Democrats in Congress rendered the entire campaign fruitless, and despite President Truman's message to Congress urging outright repeal of the act, the hated law remained on the statute books.

Trade Agreements

1799 — The first trade agreement was signed. It was between Philadelphia cordwainers and their employers.

1866 — Iron puddlers and their employers concluded the first national trade agreement.

1869 — The first trade agreement in the coal industry was drawn up between the Miners and Laborers Benevolent Association and the coal operators.

March 25, 1891 — The first national trade agreement between the Stove Molders' Union and the employers' association was signed.

1898 — The first collective trade agreement between employers and a group of unions in an industry was the "Syracuse Agreement, signed by United Typothae (the employers' association) and three unions in the industry: the International Typographical Union, the International Pressmen and Assistants' Union, and the International Brotherhood of Bookbinders. It provided for a gradual reduction of hours from ten to nine.

February 1907 — For the first time, conductors and trainmen negotiated as a body with western railroads. A committee representing forty-two railroads negotiated an agreement with unions representing both labor groups relating to a reduction of working hours and an increase in wages.

Trade Unions

1825 — The Nailers' Union and the Weavers' Union of New York City were the first labor organizations to use the word "union" in their name.

September 1835 — The first union with both men and women members was the United Men and Women's Trading Society of Baltimore.

October 1844 — The first labor federation to include a union of women workers was the New England Workingmen's Association. Article 9 of its constitution read: "Female Labor Reform Associations shall be entitled to all the rights, privileges and obligations secured by this Constitution."

February 1849 — The first miners' union in the United States was Bates' Union, named after John Bates, the English miner who was its founder.

1850 — The Upholsterers' Union of New York City became the first multinational union. It had German-American, Irish-American, French-Canadian, English, and native American sections.

1851 — The first effective southern union, the Screwmen's Benevolent Association of New Orleans, gained wage increases by simply threatening to strike.

March 21, 1853 — The first labor organization to unite all of labor, regardless of skill or national origin, the American Labor Union, was founded in New York City by Germans and Americans. Joseph Weydemeyer, the first American Marxist, was one of its chief organizers.

1858 — The first union of iron workers, the Sons of Vulcan, was formed in Pittsburgh. It was a union of puddlers.

1862 — The first seamen's union, the American Seamen's Protective Association, was organized in New York City by William P. Powell, head of the Colored Seamen's Home. Its purpose was to improve the conditions of black seamen.

1863 — New York City letter carriers formed the first union of federal employees.

August 1879 —The Cigar Makers' International Union became the first American union to openly model itself after British trade unions. It was led by Adolph Strasser and Samuel Gompers.

August 1879 —The Cigar Makers' International Union became the first union to adopt the principle of "equalization of funds," under which international officers had the power to order financially stable locals to transfer some of their funds to locals in financial distress.

1879 —The first union of western metalliferous miners was formed in Leadville, Colorado.

1880 —The first citywide ethnic labor organization, the United German Trades, was formed by German-American workers in New York City, Chicago, Milwaukee, and St. Louis.

February 14, 1883 —New Jersey enacted the first state legislation legalizing trade unions. The act, entitled "An Act Relative to Persons Combining and Encouraging Other Persons to Combine," provided that combinations organized to persuade workers to enter or leave employment were not unlawful.

April 8, 1884 —The first law to officially recognize that a trade union exists for the "well-being" of its members in "their everyday life, and for mutual assistance in securing the most

favorable conditions for the labor of its members" was passed by New Jersey.

1888 —The International Typographical Union established the first permanent union headquarters of a national union.

1891 —The first union of newspaper men was formed when the International Typographical Union issued a charter to a newswriters' local in Pittsburgh. By 1900, about a dozen more locals had been chartered.

1892 —The first union planned in prison was the Western Federation of Miners. It was projected during discussions among the prisoners of the U.S. Army who had been incarcerated in the Ada County jail for contempt of court in defying an injunction issued during the Coeur d'Alene strike. The discussions were led by Ed Boyce, future president of the Western Federation of Miners.

November 5, 1893 —The first union of "brain workers" was founded. The Brain Workers' Union, Limited, applied for a charter from the Central Labor Federation of New York City. It was composed of "men of all races and creeds who work with their brains."

October 29, 1912 —The first association organized by baseball players to improve their working conditions was the Players' Fraternity, formed by David L. Fultz, a former college and major league pitcher and lawyer in New York City. The organization began with 288 players.

November 28, 1912 —The first union of rag pickers was formed in New York City.

August 1, 1919 —For the first time, a union of policemen voted to affiliate with the AFL. The Boston Social Club, formed in 1896, received a charter from the AFL on August 15.

September 17, 1933 —A meeting of three hundred reporters, rewrite men, and copy readers led to the formation of the New York Guild of Newspapermen and Women, with Allen Raymond as president.

Traveling Cards

1826 —The printers' societies were the first to make use of "traveling cards." The cards enabled a union member to work in cities other than the one in which he lived.

Unemployed and Unemployment Insurance

1817 —The first union organization to provide for its unemployed members was the Philadelphia Typographical Society. It announced it would "take all just and honorable methods of procuring situations" for unemployed members.

1856 —The Typographical Union of New York City was the first union to establish permanent relief funds to support members during periods of unemployment.

November 5, 1857 —At the first mass meeting of the unemployed, fifteen thousand workers rallied in Tompkins Square in New York City to demand public works to relieve unemployment.

November 1857 —The first organization to mobilize support for aid to the unemployed was the Central Workingmen's Committee of Philadelphia. It was started by German-Americans, who were later joined by other nationalities.

1857 —Mayor Fernando Wood of New York City was the first public official to call for public works to relieve the distress of the unemployed. He sent a message to the City Council recommending issuance of public construction funds to alleviate the sufferings of unemployed workers. Persons accepted for employment in these works were to be paid one-quarter in cash and the rest in cornmeal and potatoes.

April 1868 —San Francisco set up the first public labor exchange to assist people in finding employment.

February 21, 1874 —For the first time, a demonstration of the unemployed was broken up by a police attack, with serious injuries to the demonstrators. At the Tompkins Square Riot in New York City, police attacked unarmed workers, including women and children, who had met to demand relief for the unemployed. The incident led to a protest meeting at Cooper Union on March 26, 1874.

September 10, 1893 —The first Trade Union Conference for the Relief of the Unemployed was composed of AFL unions and sponsored mass meetings of the unemployed in New York City.

May 1, 1894 —The first national march of the unemployed on Washington, Armies of the Commonweal, was led by Jacob Sechler Coxey. "Coxey's Army" demanded public works for the unemployed. Coxey himself was arrested for stepping on the grass when his army arrived in Washington, and the marchers then disbanded without obtaining any action from the federal government.

1894 —The first unemployment compensation plan financed jointly by employers and unions was established in the wallpaper industry.

January 1908 —At the first IWW demonstration for unemployed workers, St. Louis IWW leaders led six hundred marchers to City Hall to demand work from the city government for the unemployed.

August 25, 1911 —The first national organization of the unemployed, the Brotherhood Welfare Association, was founded. It advocated that Congress set up a free national employment bureau.

January 1914 —In the first arrest of IWW members for leading a demonstration of the unemployed, Frank Tannenbaum, a member of the Waiters' Industrial Union, and 190 unemployed men were taken into custody by police for participating in an unlawful assembly. They had invaded churches in New York City to demand food and shelter. Tannenbaum was sentenced to one year in jail and fined $500. He later became a

professor at Columbia University and a labor historian.

February 27, 1914 —The first national unemployment conference, called by the American Association for Labor Legislation (AALL), met. It grew out of the Paris Conference on Unemployment, held in 1910, which resulted in the formation of the International Association on Unemployed. An American section was organized and affiliated with the International Association. At the 1914 conference, the chief recommendation was for a system of "public works and emergency public relief, at the usual hours and wage rates. . . ."

1914 —New York became the first state to publish employment figures obtained directly from employers.

May 1915 —Idaho enacted the first state law providing public work for all who met a residency requirement. This law gave every person who had resided in the state for six months the right to ninety days' public work a year at 90 percent of the customary wage if married with dependents; otherwise, at 75 percent.

1915 —The American Association for Labor Legislation, in a pamphlet entitled *A Practical Program for the Prevention of Unemployment in America,* made the first proposal for unemployment insurance in which employers, workers, and the states would be joint contributors.

1916 —The first bill to come before a state legislature providing for unemployment compensation was introduced in Massachusetts. It failed to pass.

1916 —The Dennison Manufacturing Company of Framingham, Massachusetts, established the first employer-financed unemployment benefit plan for employees.

1918 —The first congressional proposal for unemployment insurance was introduced by Meyer London, a Socialist congressman. It was attacked by AFL President Samuel Gompers.

March 1921 —The first postwar unemployment conference was held in New York City. It was sponsored by the Communist party and attended by representatives of thirty-four AFL and independent unions. The conference formulated a program for jobs, unemployment insurance, and relief, and established the Unemployed Council of Greater New York. Israel Amter, a leading Communist, was elected secretary, and the slogan "Fight — Don't Starve" was adopted.

September 1921 —The first federal conference on unemployment was called by President Warren G. Harding. The conference termed unemployment a by-product of the functioning of the entire economic system and recommended a system of unemployment insurance, financed by employers, workers, and the government.

1923 —The first unemployment insurance system was introduced into shops by the Amalgamated Clothing Workers in Chicago.

1927 —The first huge layoffs took place at the Ford Motor Company. Ford laid off sixty thousand men for more than a year while changing over from the Model "T" to the Model "A" car.

March 6, 1930 —The first nationwide demonstrations of the unemployed were held in some thirty cities and towns. They had been called by the Communist party. The New York demonstration, in Union Square, was attacked by the police.

July 4, 1930 —The National Unemployed Council, created at a convention in Chicago attended by 1,320 delegates, was the first national organization of the unemployed during the Great Depression. Its aim was to create subsidiary councils, organize the jobless, especially black unemployed workers, stage demonstrations against evictions for nonpayment of rent, and campaign for unemployment insurance. The council's program called for a system of federal relief to be administered by representatives of the unemployed, with all federal expenditures allocated from funds already appropriated for the military.

December 21, 1930 —The first model unemployment insurance plan was presented by the American Association for Labor Legislation. It was called "An

American Plan for an Unemployment Reserve Fund" and provided that employers would contribute 1.5 percent of their payrolls to an industry reserve fund. Strikers were not to be eligible for unemployment insurance.

1930 — The first AFL state federation to urge the national AFL to back a state-supervised unemployment insurance system to which employers, workers, and the public would contribute was the California Federation of Labor. Its proposal was backed by a unanimous vote.

February 10, 1931 — The first federal agency to arrange for construction of public works in order to alleviate unemployment was the U.S. Employment Stabilization Board. However, it did very little.

October 1931 — In the first serious campaign at an AFL convention for unemployment insurance, the California Federation of Labor, Seattle Central Labor Council, Teachers' Union, and Flint Glass Workers' Union introduced resolutions in favor of unemployment insurance. They were all defeated.

December 1931 — The first National Hunger March on Washington took place. Marchers demanded: (1) immediate unemployment insurance; (2) other forms of social insurance; (3) appropriation by Congress of an amount sufficient to pay each unemployed worker $150 in cash, with $50 for each dependent, for immediate winter relief; (4) immediate undertaking of extensive public works, particularly the construction of new homes, schools, and hospitals, in working-class neighborhoods, with work to be paid for at union wages; (5) immediate distribution of wheat and cotton stocks held by the Farm Board, to be transformed into bread and clothing for unemployed workers; (6) no eviction of the unemployed from their homes, and the provision of free rent, gas, light, water, etc., to all unemployed workers, and reduced rates and rents for part-time workers; (7) a seven-hour day, with no reduction in wages, for most workers, and a six-hour day for miners, railroad workers, and young workers; (8) payment by employers of full wages for all part-time and "stagger plan" workers; (9) prohibition of all forced labor and coercion of any kind in connection with insurance relief for the unemployed, and no discrimination against blacks or the foreign-born as to jobs, relief, or insurance; (10) full and immediate payment of the balance of the bonus due to ex-servicemen.

The program and hunger march were organized by the Communist party, the Unemployed Councils, and the Trade Union Unity League (TUUL).

January 1932 — Ten thousand persons in one thousand automobiles, led by James R. Cox, participated in a demonstration for unemployment relief. This was the first demonstration by the unemployed in the automobile industry.

January 1932 —For the first time, the United Mine Workers endorsed unemployment insurance.

January 1932 —Wisconsin passed the first state unemployment compensation act.

March 7, 1932 —In its first action to alleviate the needs of the unemployed, Congress directed that forty million bushels of wheat and five hundred million bales of cotton be given to the Red Cross for distribution to the needy. Four and a half million families were assisted.

March 7, 1932 —The first fatalities in a demonstration of the unemployed occurred when four workers, black and white, were killed by Dearborn and Ford Service Company police during a demonstration for jobs at the Ford Motor Company plant led by the Trade Union Unity League's Auto Workers Union, the Unemployed Councils, and the Communist party. The demonstrators demanded jobs, the right to organize, a reduction of the speedup, abolition of labor spies, elimination of graft in the hiring process, two fifteen-minute rest periods daily, the six-hour day without any reduction in pay, an unemployment bonus for every laid-off worker, and free medical treatment for Ford workers and their families.

July 21, 1932 —The first Emergency Relief and Construction Act (RFC) was passed. It provided $300,000,000 for loans to the states "to be used in furnishing relief and work relief to needy and distressed people and in relieving the hardship resulting from unemployment," and made $322,234,000 available from the U.S. Treasury for public works.

July 22, 1932 —For the first time in its history, the AFL Executive Council endorsed unemployment insurance. On July 23, 1932, *The New York Times* reported: "Unable to withstand the rapidly mounting tide of sentiment for compulsory unemployment insurance, evidenced by a flood of communications from local unions, city central labor bodies and State Federations of Labor, the executive council of the American Federation of Labor abandoned today its traditional opposition to the proposal, which has been denounced by labor leaders since the days of Samuel Gompers as 'the dole.'" At the time of the endorsement, it was estimated that more than sixteen million workers were unemployed.

July 28, 1932 —The first U.S. Army attack on unemployed veterans was the Battle of Anacostia Heights. In the spring and summer of 1932, about twenty-five thousand impoverished veterans and their families converged on Washington —the so-called Bonus Army —to demand the immediate payment of a bonus —amounting to from $50 to $100 —rather than in 1945, as provided in the original legislation for World War I Veterans.

Congress adjourned on July 17 without taking any action. President Herbert Hoover ordered the army, under General Douglas MacArthur, to drive all the veterans out of their tent colony in Anacostia Heights. In a massive assault upon their shacks, containing women and children, scores were severely injured and one infant was killed. The army won the Battle of Anacostia Heights.

July 1932 —The Democratic party became the first major political party to support unemployment insurance. Its national platform endorsed unemployment insurance under state laws, a position that was approved by its presidential candidate, Franklin D. Roosevelt.

August 26, 1932 —The first national conference to propose sharing-the-work as a solution to the unemployment problem was called by President Herbert Hoover. It established the Share-the-Work Committee, with Walter C. Teagle, president of the Jersey Standard Oil Company, as chairman.

November 1932 —The first trade union to win unemployment insurance paid for exclusively by employers was the Fur Department of the Needle Trades Workers Industrial Union of the Trade Union Unity League, under the leadership of Ben Gold. The agreement, the first of its kind in American labor history, provided that each company would contribute 1 percent of its payroll

to the fund, and that if unemployment continued to be severe by July 1933, the employers would contribute an additional 0.5 percent to the fund. The fund was to be administered solely by the workers.

December 1, 1932 —The first National Hunger March to demand relief and unemployment insurance to be broken up by the police was organized by the Trade Union Unity League, the Unemployed Councils, and the Communist party. During the march, Ben Gold, leader of the delegation representing the Needle Trades Workers Industrial Union, was arrested by the Wilmington, Delaware, police, along with twenty-two other marchers. Gold was found guilty of "assault" and served forty days in a Delaware prison.

December 1932 —For the first time, an AFL convention went on record in favor of state unemployment compensation legislation to be financed by employers under government supervision.

July 4, 1933 —The first National Unemployed Leagues were established at a convention in Columbus, Ohio. It was called by the Conference on Progressive Labor Action, headed by Reverend A.J. Muste, which had already organized a large number of unemployed leagues in several states.

1933 —The first organization to organize the unemployed in order to prevent them from taking work from strikers was the American Workers party, which had itself been organized by the Conference on Progressive Labor Action.

1933 — Wisconsin passed the nation's first unemployment insurance law.

February 1934 — Women delegates to a convention of the unemployed made the first presentation of special demands by unemployed women to the Department of Labor. Their demands included decent and permanent shelters for women; an unemployment insurance bill with equal compensation for women; the right to organize; the establishment of nursery schools with free food, clothing, and care for children of working women; free medical and maternity care for working women; and free food, clothing, and medical care for children in schools.

February 1–10, 1935 — A subcommittee of the House Labor Committee held hearings on the Lundeen Unemployment Insurance Bill. The hearings revealed a list of the organizational endorsers of the bill that included more than three score city councils, five international unions, six state federations of labor, twenty-nine central labor bodies, more than three thousand local unions, and more than two score independent unions. The House Committee reported favorably on the bill.

August 1936 — The first unemployment insurance check ever issued to an American worker was a check for $15 paid by the Wisconsin Industrial Commission to Neil D. Ruud of Madison. The check was drawn on the state unemployment fund, which had been established by the Wisconsin Unemployment Compensation Law, enacted in February 1932.

Union Cemetery

1902 — The first union cemetery was established at Mount Olive, Illinois, midway between Springfield and St. Louis, on land purchased by Local 728 of the United Mine Workers of America. A wooden arch with "Union Miners Cemetery" painted on it was erected over the gateway. In the cemetery, miners killed fighting for the union and others active in union struggles are buried. The most famous grave is that of Mother Mary Harris Jones, who was buried with her "boys" at her request. On October 11, 1936, a monument dedicated to her was unveiled at this, the only union-owned cemetery.

Union Contracts

1870 — The first comprehensive written union contract of the post-Civil War era was one between the Workingmen's Benevolent Association and the Schuylkill County Anthracite Board of Trade. It covered wages and conditions under which miners could be discharged, and set up grievance machinery. It lasted for one year.

1871 —The first union contract in the shoe industry covering all branches of the trade was signed by the Knights of St. Crispin and the Lynn, Massachusetts, shoe manufacturers.

1898 —The United Mine Workers and operators in the central competitive field concluded the first national agreement in any important industry.

March 1903 —The first union contract won by street car employees was signed by the Amalgamated Association of Street Car Employees and the Manhattan Elevated Company of New York City.

1903 —The first recognition of the United Textile Workers by employers came after a six-month strike of twenty-six thousand textile workers in Fall River, Massachusetts.

April 1907 —Butte Miners' Union No. 1 was the first affiliate of the Western Federation of Miners to sign a contract. The five-year contract, which provided for an eight-hour day and a sliding scale of wages, was repudiated by the federation, whose leaders did not believe in contracts at that time.

1912 —The first IWW local to sign a contract with an employer was the local in Great Falls, Montana. Its charter was revoked by the IWW General Executive Board because it violated the IWW principle of "no contracts."

October 1917 —The Actors Equity Association won its first standard contract, with the United Manager Protective Association. It provided for free transportation to and from New York City, limited rehearsal time, two weeks' notice before dismissal, compensation for actors dismissed without pay after more than one week's rehearsal, limitation of extra performances without pay, and full pay for all weeks worked.

1928 —Josephine A. Roche, head of the Rocky Mountain Fuel Company, signed a union recognition agreement with the United Mine Workers, thus ending the era of company unionism instituted by John D. Rockefeller, Jr., after the defeat of the union in the Colorado strike of 1914.

July 15, 1933 —The first union agreement in the electrical industry was signed by Philco with its strikers. The agreement provided for an eight-hour day, a forty-hour week, time-and-one-half for overtime, abolition of penalties for poor work, payment for waiting time between jobs, a shop committee to handle grievances, and minimum wages of 45 cents an hour for men and 36 cents an hour for women. The company agreed to recognize the union, which was chartered by the AFL as Radio and Television Workers Federal Labor Union No. 18368 on August 3.

September 21, 1933 —The first Appalachian agreement in the soft coal industry was concluded. It covered

Pennsylvania, Ohio, West Virginia, eastern Kentucky, and Tennessee, and United Mine Workers Districts 2, 3, 4, 5, 6, 17, 19, 30, and 31. The UMW won the checkoff of union dues (but not the union shop); no payment in scrip; no requirement that miners purchase supplies at the company store or live in company houses; and no employment of any boy under seventeen in a mine or in a hazardous occupation in the vicinity of a mine. The agreement, which included the eight-hour day and the forty-hour week, also established base rates.

October 30, 1933 — The first agreement covering captive coal mines owned by the steel companies was signed. It provided for the checkoff of union dues and initiation fees.

April 3, 1934 — The Cannery and Agricultural Workers Industrial Union won its first contract. It was with Seabrook Farms, Inc., in New Jersey.

April 7, 1934 — The Philadelphia-Camden Guild signed a contract with J. David Stern's *Philadelphia Record,* providing for a union shop, a forty-hour week, and minimum salaries. This was the first contract signed by the Newspaper Guild.

March 3, 1937 — The United States Steel Corporation, once the stronghold of the "open shop" in the industry, came to terms with the Steel Workers' Organizing Committee without a strike. The agreement, negotiated between

Board Chairman Myron C. Taylor and John L. Lewis, made the CIO union the exclusive bargaining agent for "Big Steel" workers. Two weeks later, wages were raised 10 percent and the company agreed to the eight-hour day, the forty-hour week, and time-and-one-half for overtime.

March 5, 1937 — Carnegie-Illinois, the largest U.S. Steel subsidiary, signed its first contract with the Steel Workers' Organizing Committee. The agreement recognized the CIO union as the bargaining agent for its members and granted a 10 percent wage increase, the forty-hour week, time-and-one-half for overtime, vacations with pay, and seniority rights. Within a week, thirty steel companies agreed to collective bargaining.

February 1938 — The United Electrical, Radio and Machine Workers (UE) won its first major agreement with General Electric. It covered Schenectady, New York, Lynn, Massachusetts, Bridgeport, Connecticut, New Kensington, Pennsylvania, and Cleveland, Ohio.

May 26, 1938 — The contract ending the general strike of New York fur workers was the first union contract in the needle trades industry to cover young, unskilled workers. The Fur Floor and Shipping Clerks, Local 125, won a closed shop, a minimum wage of $18 a week, a forty-hour week, nine paid holidays, an automatic July increase, and eight months' equal division of work, with no discharge. The last provision meant that the work would be divided so that no one would be fired.

May 26, 1938 — The first union contract to include a clause permitting workers to boycott goods from Nazi Germany was signed to settle the general strike of New York fur workers. Under the clause, workers could refuse to work on skins imported from Nazi Germany.

March 25, 1941 — Nineteen thousand of twenty-one thousand steel workers at the Bethlehem Steel Company plants in Bethlehem, Pennsylvania, walked off their jobs. Bethlehem's status as an open-shop city ended when the strikers won a union contract.

March 1941 — Westinghouse signed its first written agreement with the UE, covering nineteen unionized plants.

May 22, 1941 — The UAW-CIO won an NLRB election at the Ford Motor Company. Within a month, the company signed the first union shop agreement in the automobile industry. Ford agreed to recognize the UAW as the bargaining representative within its jurisdiction at all Ford plants in the United States. The company also agreed to grant the union shop, to require membership in good standing as a condition of employment, and to check off UAW dues. Ford cars would henceforth carry the union label. The hated Ford Service Department, headed

by Harry Bennett, was to be disbanded.

1948 — The UAW won the first union contract to include an "escalator clause," meaning workers would receive pay increases tied to the U.S. Bureau of Labor Statistics' cost-of-living index. The UAW contract was signed with the General Motors Corporation.

March 6, 1950 — John L. Lewis signed the historic National Bituminous Coal Wage Agreement. This was the first industrywide contract and ended seventeen years of intense struggle in the coal fields. Between 1933 and 1950, there had been thirty-four major work stoppages, including eleven industrywide strikes, and the federal government had taken over the mines on five different occasions. During this period also, the United Mine Workers had been victimized by the two largest fines ever imposed on any union up to that time: one for $710,000 and the other for $1,420,000.

October 1980 — J. P. Stevens and Company signed its first union contract with the Amalgamated Clothing and Textile Workers Union (ACTWU). The union contracts, covering thirty-five hundred workers at Roanoke Rapids, North Carolina, were the first Stevens had agreed to since it moved South after World War II. During a seventeen-year campaign to organize one of the most stubbornly antiunion firms in America, the union and the AFL-CIO's Industrial Union Department spent at least $30 million, by far the largest amount ever expended on a campaign directed at a single employer.

Union Label

1874 — The union label was initiated by the Cigar Makers' International Union and first adopted in San Francisco to combat Chinese labor. The label was furnished free to all manufacturers who used native labor.

July 24, 1888 — The Cigar Makers' International Union brought the first trade union suit to prevent use of a counterfeit union label by employers against J. R. Williams.

August 1894 — The first Allied Printing Trades Council to control the union label and other matters of joint interest to printers' unions was established in New York City.

1909 — The first Union Label Department was established by the AFL.

Union Liability

February 3, 1908 — For the first time, the U.S. Supreme Court held that under the Sherman Anti-Trust Act a company could sue a union for damages suffered by reason of the Union's boycott. In *Lowe V. Lawler,* the court ruled that the company could sue the United Hatters' Union for three times the amount of damage it had sustained as a result of the boycott. The decision led to the payment of $234,000 in fines in 1915.

February 9, 1909 — The first court to rule that unions must pay for damages incurred by a manufacturer during a strike was the New York State Supreme Court, in *Jones Speedometer v. International Machinists Association.*

December 18, 1911 — The U.S. Supreme Court upheld for the first time the constitutionality of a state (Illinois) statute calling for indemnification of owners of property damaged by strike "mobs" or "riots."

1922 — The U.S. Supreme Court ruled for the first time that an unincorporated labor union was financially liable for its acts. In the *Coronado* case, the Court ordered District 21 of the United Mine Workers to pay $2,200,000 to eight coal companies in western Arkansas that had gone bankrupt during a strike. After a second Supreme Court decision, District 21 settled in 1927 for $27,500, with each side to pay its own costs.

Union-Management Cooperation

1900 — The first national organization combining capitalists, union leaders, and public representatives for the purpose of achieving industrial peace was the National Civic Foundation, founded by Ralph Easley, with Mark

Hanna as chairman and Samuel Gompers as vice chairman.

January 15, 1910 — The American Railroad Employees and Investors Association, the first organization uniting the railroad corporations and Railroad Brotherhoods in joint action against congressional legislation regulating railroads, was formed.

1921 — For the first time, union and management cooperated in railroad shops on the Baltimore and Ohio Railroad. This led to the Baltimore and Ohio Plan of Welfare Capitalism, a union-management cooperative program.

1923 — The first union-management cooperation plan was introduced in the Glenwood shop of the Baltimore and Ohio Railroad by Otto S. Beyer, Jr.

1924 — The AFL Railway Employees' Department for the first time endorsed union-management cooperation plans.

Union Membership

1817 — The first labor body to expel employers from membership in a union was the New York Typographical Society.

1886 — For the first time in American labor history, union membership reached the one million figure.

1900 — AFL membership exceeded half a million for the first time. It was at 548,000.

1904 — The membership of a national labor federation passed the one million mark for the first time. AFL membership reached 1,676,000.

1920 — For the first time, union membership passed the five million mark. It reached 5,047,800.

December 1929 — The first major decline in union membership over a ten-year period was reported. It went from 5,047,800 in 1920 to 3,442,600 at the end of 1929.

September 1937 — For the first time, CIO membership exceeded three million. It reached 3,700,000.

1941 — For the first time, union membership increased by more than five million in less than a decade. It went from 2,805,000 in 1933 to 8,410,000 at the end of 1941.

Union Officers

October 1902 — The International Association of Bridge and Structural Iron Workers established the first full-time salaried positions for men holding the offices of president and secretary-treasurer of a union.

1902 — The first union official to be elected for life was Martin B. ("Skinny") Madden. He was elected president, treasurer, and business agent of the Steamfitters' Helpers' Union of Chicago. In 1943, Joseph P. Ryan was elected international president of the International Longshoremen's Association for life.

Union Registration

1943 — The Texas legislature passed the first law requiring registration of unions. The Manford Act stipulated that all union organizers must register and obtain identification cards from the Texas secretary of state.

Union Shop

1794 — Philadelphia shoemakers compelled employers to hire union members only.

1913 — The first preferential union shop in the men's clothing industry was established at Hart, Schaffner, and Marx in Chicago.

August 17, 1933 — Philco of Philadelphia signed an agreement granting the local union in its plant a union shop. This was the first union shop in the radio industry. All new employees were obliged to become union members within two weeks of being hired. With this agreement, the organization of the largest radio plant in the United States was complete.

Union Soup Line

May 4, 1982 — Laid-off steel workers in Homestead, Pennsylvania, lined up for free bread, milk, and canned goods when their union, the United Steelworkers of America, opened a food bank. Nearly a third of the seven thousand workers at U.S. Steel's Homestead Works had lost their jobs. The food was given to union members whose unemployment benefits had expired, and to heads of households who were out of work. The food giveaway was financed by a benefit rock concert, raffles, and donations at mill gates. Retired union members volunteered to hand out the grocery bags.

U.S. Government and Labor

October 1915 — The Department of Justice conducted the first federal investigation of the IWW. Its purpose was to discover evidence of an interstate conspiracy that could be used as a basis for prosecuting the IWW leaders. The investigation, which had been demanded by the hop growers, failed to produce any evidence to justify prosecution.

May 1917 —For the first time, the AFL participated in a government mission to a foreign country. James Duncan, first vice president of the AFL, was a member of the mission sent by President Woodrow Wilson to Russia under the chairmanship of Elihu Root to dissuade the Russian government from concluding a separate peace treaty in World War I. The mission failed.

June 15, 1917 —For the first time, a union was represented on a committee established by the Council of National Defense for an industry. Seven members of the United Mine Workers were appointed to the coal committee after the union lodged a protest.

June 19, 1917 —The federal government made its first use of the prevailing wage through the Cantonment Adjustment Commission, which was established by a wartime agreement between the War Department and the AFL. The commission set up boards to deal with labor relations problems during the war, marking the first time the federal government used government contracts to promote social change. This, the first agreement between organized labor and the U.S. government, was signed by Secretary of War Newton D. Baker and Samuel Gompers. It provided that union-scale wages, hours, and working conditions as of June 1, 1917, would be adopted as the basic standards in the construction of cantonments. However, the agreement did not include provision for the closed shop.

September 5, 1917 —The Espionage Act, passed during World War I, was used for the first time to attack labor. The Department of Justice made simultaneous raids on IWW headquarters in Pittsburgh, New York City, Boston, Baltimore, Detroit, San Francisco, Milwaukee, Los Angeles, Spokane, Seattle, Portland (Oregon), Omaha, Minneapolis, and Lincoln (Nebraska).

October 1917 —In the first government indictment of the entire leadership of a labor federation, 166 members of the IWW were indicted for violating the Federal Espionage Act. They included General Secretary-Treasurer William D. ("Big Bill") Haywood, all members of the General Executive Board, the secretaries of the industrial unions, the editors of the English and foreign-language papers, and all active organizers.

January 1918 —In the first mass arrests of union members, two thousand IWW members were seized by the federal and state governments and charged with violating the Espionage Act and state criminal syndicalist laws.

Wage Legislation

1621 —The first fixed wage rates were set by the governor of Virginia and the council of the London Company.

March 22, 1630 —The first wage legislation setting maximum wages was passed by the Massachusetts Bay Colony. Workers in the building trades were limited to 2 shillings per day. However, six months later, the regulations were abolished by an order that stated: "Wages of carpenters, joyners, and other artificers and workmen . . . shall be lefte att libertie as men shall reasonably agree."

1879 —Massachusetts enacted the first wage payment law. It required that "cities shall, at intervals not exceeding seven days, pay all laborers who are employed by them . . . if such payment is demanded."

July 14, 1880 —The first state law providing for payment of wages in cash was enacted by Pennsylvania.

1891 —Kansas passed the first prevailing wage law.

1912 —Massachusetts became the first state to pass a minimum wage law for women and children. Eight other states passed similar legislation in 1913. In 1923, the Supreme Court declared all such laws unconstitutional.

May 25, 1914 —For the first time, the U.S. Supreme Court upheld a statute ordering semimonthly cash payments to railroad employees.

1919 —The first states to enact equal pay legislation for women were Michigan and Montana.

1931 —The first federal legislation regulating wages, the Davis-Bacon Act, was passed. It required the payment of the prevailing wage for workers employed under government contracts.

1936 —The first federal legislation setting minimum wages for workers employed on government contracts was the Walsh-Healey Public Contracts Act. It not only set minimum wages but also called for overtime compensation for covered employees who worked more than eight hours in a day or forty hours in a week. It also contained convict labor provisions and health and safety requirements.

1938 —The Fair Labor Standards Act, the first federal minimum wage law covering all nonagricultural labor, was passed by Congress. It set the minimum wage at 25 cents per hour.

Wage Scales

1800 —The first complete wage scale was presented to employers by the Franklin Typographical Society of New York City.

1802 —The Philadelphia Typographical Society designated the first known committee to visit individual employers with a wage list.

1815 —The first debate over the need to create a uniform wage scale in the printing trade throughout the country was conducted by the New York Society of Printers.

1825 —New York stonecutters conducted the first strike for a uniform wage scale.

1865 —Pittsburgh iron puddlers, members of the Sons of Vulcan, won the first contract arbitration and use of a sliding wage scale.

May 8, 1917 —The first agreement between the U.S. Shipping Board, the Atlantic Coast Steamship Owners, and the International Seamen's Union was concluded. The union was granted a wage scale for all classes under its jurisdiction, in addition to a bonus of 50 percent to seamen employed in vessels passing through the war zone and $100 compensation for loss of personal effects caused by war accidents. In return, the union agreed to relax its apprenticeship regulations.

Wages

1741 —The first announcement by labor that it would accept payment for work only in lawful money was made by the journeymen caulkers of Boston.

May 1887 —The Chicago Bricklayers' Union presented the first labor demand for payment of wages at the end of each week and on Saturday.

September 8, 1900 —The first Arbeiter Secretariat, or Labor Correspondence Bureau, was formed by German trade unions in the United States. The principal duty of the organization was to proceed in the courts against dishonest employers who failed to pay workers their wages on pay day. The secretariat employed a lawyer to look after all such claims free of cost to the claimant. About five thousand German workers in New York City were represented in the organization.

June 1, 1916 —The first wage conference representing every railroad division in the United States, with delegates from the four Brotherhoods, was called to discuss the eight-hour day. The conference broke up without an agreement.

July 1918 —The War Labor Board was responsible for the first assertion by the federal government that all workers, including common laborers, were entitled to a living wage.

April 8, 1942 —In the first "wage-freeze" order, President Franklin D. Roosevelt issued a "hold-the-line" executive decree placing wages under severe controls.

July 15, 1942 —The War Labor Board announced the "Little Steel Formula," denying the United Steel Workers' demand for a $1-a-day wage increase. It stated: "For the period from January 1, 1941 to May, 1942 . . . the cost of living increased about 15%. If any group of workers averaged less than a 15% increase in hourly wage rates during or immediately preceding or following this period, their established peacetime standards have been broken. If any group averaged a 15% increase or more, their established peacetime standards have been preserved." The award gave steel workers an increase of 44 cents a day.

June 14, 1945 —Labor called its first conference to discuss postwar action to make up for wages lost during World War II.

August 14, 1945 (V-J Day) —President Harry S Truman issued Executive Order 9599, abolishing wage controls.

Wagner Act

December 16, 1935 —The first election under the Wagner Act resulted in victory for a union. A majority of the nine hundred workers in the Wayne Knitting Mills (now defunct) in Fort Wayne, Indiana, voted for representation by the American Federation of Hosiery Workers.

War Labor Board

June 1918 —The National War Labor Board employee representation plan was first applied at the General Electric plant in Pittsfield, Massachusetts. It provided for election of committees for workers to deal with management.

Western Labor

May 10, 1898 —The first western labor movement was begun by the Western Labor Union (which later changed its name to the American Labor Union). It was formed by western labor unions that considered the policies of the AFL leadership too conservative.

1902 —The first western association of railroad workers, the Western Association, was formed by conductors and trainmen. It had jurisdiction over all railroads west of a line drawn from Chicago to Duluth, and southwest from Chicago along the branch of the Illinois Central Railway. The Western Association was intended for joint action in case of strikes.

Women

1926 — The first woman to head a state industrial commission was Frances Perkins of New York. In 1929, she became the first woman state industrial commissioner, having been appointed to the post by Governor Franklin D. Roosevelt.

March 4, 1933 — The first woman secretary of labor and the first woman Cabinet officer in U.S. history was Frances Perkins. She was appointed by President Franklin D. Roosevelt on this day and served until June 30, 1945. Thus she was the only Cabinet member to serve through all of President Roosevelt's administrations.

Women's Auxiliary

1765 — The first women's auxiliary, the Daughters of Liberty, was formed to assist the Sons of Liberty in opposition to British rule.

May 1844 — The first union women's auxiliary was the Ladies Mechanics' Association of Fall River, Massachusetts.

Women Workers

January 28, 1734 — In the first organized effort by women workers to improve their conditions, maidservants announced in an advertisement in the *New York Weekly Journal* that they would no longer work for families where the husband beat them.

1824 — The first women to participate in a strike were the female weavers in Pawtucket, Rhode Island, who accompanied male strikers in resisting wage cuts and increased hours.

1825 — The first women's labor organization in a trade was the United Tailoresses Society of New York City. Later that year, this organization conducted the first strike by a women's labor organization.

1828 — The first strike by women factory operatives took place at the Dover Manufacturing Company in Dover, New Hampshire. Four hundred women struck against a wage reduction and for the ten-hour day.

July 1829 — The first speech by a woman to a labor audience, "Address to the People of Philadelphia," was delivered in the Walnut Street Theatre by Frances Wright at the invitation of Philadelphia trade unions.

February 1834 — The first union of women factory workers was the Lowell Factory Girls' Association.

February 1834 — For the first time, working women demanded women's rights. The leader of the Lowell Factory Girls' strike against a 15 percent wage cut made a "flaming Mary Wollstonecraft speech on the rights of women and the iniquities of the monied aristocracy." Mary Wollstonecraft was the pioneer British women's rights advocate and author of the 1792 *Vindication of the Rights of Woman.*

June 1834 — In the first show of support by men for women trade unionists, the Lynn Cordwainers' Union supported the trike of the Ladies' Shoe Binders of Lynn for higher wages.

1844 — Massachusetts conducted the first government investigation into women's working conditions. The resulting report stated that the conditions did not warrant legislation since women workers' health was not being impaired, and that reduced working hours would affect wages and hurt competition. The committee ignored the testimony of women workers in factories who stated they needed a ten-hour day for health reasons.

January 1845 — The first permanent union of women workers, the Lowell Female Labor Reform Association, was organized by women textile workers in the Lowell (Massachusetts) mills.

March 1845 — The first industrial union of women workers, the Female Industrial Association of New York City, was founded.

May 1845 — Sarah G. Bagley became the first woman delegate to a labor federation convention. She was the Lowell Female Labor Reform Association delegate to the New England Workingmen's Association convention in Boston.

May 1845 — The first woman officer of a general labor organization was Sarah G. Bagley, who became corresponding secretary of the New England Workingmen's Association.

August 1845 — Sarah G. Bagley achieved another first for women when she became the first woman labor editor. The paper was *Voice of Industry,* a labor weekly in Lowell, Massachusetts.

September 15, 1845 — The first mass strike of women workers for the ten-hour day took place when five thousand women in the textile mills of Allegheny City and Pittsburgh, Pennsylvania, walked off their jobs. The strike was unsuccessful.

September 16, 1845 — Male trade unionists of Allegheny City and Pittsburgh, Pennsylvania, became the first male auxiliary when they protected women strikers from police attacks.

September 23, 1845 — The first regular section of a labor paper published by women workers was the "Female Department" of *Voice of Industry*. It was furnished by the Lowell Female Labor Reform Association.

November 1846 — Women achieved their first defeat of a candidate for office, even though they could not vote. William Schouler lost his bid for reelection to the Massachusetts legislature after the Lowell Female Labor Reform Association appealed to male voters to vote against him.

July 1848 — In the first imprisonment of women strikers, Pittsburgh women factory workers were jailed for destroying property while trying to prevent scabs from working.

April 1850 — The first union to write a constitution prohibiting women from working in any shops controlled by the union (except members' wives and daughters) was the Journeymen Cordwainers' Union of New York City.

March 29, 1852 — Ohio enacted the first law regulating working hours of women. It set "the hours of manual labor of children under eighteen, and women" at no more than ten hours per day. The law lasted until 1887, when it was replaced by a new code dealing with women and children.

November 1863 — The first placement bureau, training center, and center for legal protection of women workers was the Working Women's Protective Union in New York City.

August 24, 1866 — The first national demand by labor for equal pay for equal work for men and women alike was a resolution adopted by the National Labor Union convention. In this respect, the American labor movement was further advanced than the European labor movement.

1867 — The first national women's labor organization was formed: the Daughters of St. Crispin, which consisted of female shoemakers. The union lasted until 1878.

1867 — The Cigar Makers' International Union became the first national union to alter its constitution to admit women to membership.

September 1868 — The first women delegates to attend a convention of the National Labor Union were Susan B. Anthony and Mary Kellogg Putnam, representing the New York Working Women's Protective Association, and Mary McDonald, representing the Women's Protective Labor Union of Mount Vernon, New York.

September 1868 — The first resolution adopted by labor asserting the "right of workingmen and working women of this nation to strike, when all other just and equitable concessions are refused" was introduced by Mary McDonald at the 1868 convention of the National Labor Union. It was adopted unanimously.

1868 — The first national union to recognize a women's local and accept its credentials was the Typographical Union. The local was Women's Typographical Union No. 1 of New York City.

1868 — The first woman was appointed an officer of a national labor federation. Kate Mullaney, chief directrix of the Collar Laundry Workingwomen's Association of Troy, New York, was made assistant secretary of the National Labor Union by President William H. Sylvis. Her job was to organize women and bring them into the NLU.

September 1869 — The first woman to be ejected from a labor convention was Susan B. Anthony. By a vote of sixty-three to twenty-eight, the 1869 convention of the National Labor Union voted to remove her because she had provided women strikebreakers during a strike by the printers' union. Her defense was that this was the only way women could get work in the printing trade.

1869 — The first woman to serve as an officer of a national union was Gussie Lewis of New York. She was elected corresponding secretary of the National Typographical Union.

1870 — For the first time, a woman was elected a leading officer of a national labor federation. Mrs. Willard of the Sewing Girls Union of Chicago became second vice president of the National Labor Union.

April 14, 1871 — The Daughters of St. Crispin in Baltimore staged the first strike by women shoe workers. The strike, for higher wages and shorter hours, was won.

March 22, 1872 — Illinois passed the first state equal employment legislation. The act, which went into effect on July 1, 1872, provided that "no person shall be precluded or debarred from any occupation or employment (except military) on account of sex; provided that this act shall not be construed to affect the eligibility of any person to an elective office. Nothing in this act shall be construed as requiring any female to work on streets or roads, or serve on juries. All laws inconsistent with this act are hereby repealed." This was the first law prohibiting discrimination against women in the United States.

August 1876 — The first strike by women department store workers took place in St. Louis. The strike, which was for the right to sit down during the day, was lost.

May 28, 1879 — Illinois passed the first law prohibiting the employment of women in a specific industry. The law, entitled "An Act Providing for the Health and Safety of Persons Employed in the Coal Mines," banned the use of women in Illinois mines. It took effect on July 1, 1879.

1879 — The first resolution introduced in the Knights of Labor General

Assembly that would permit women to become members and to organize assemblies was tabled.

1880 — The Knights of Labor General Assembly adopted a resolution that for the first time allowed women to form assemblies of their own. Grand Master Workman Terence V. Powderly named a committee to amend the male-oriented initiation ritual so that women could participate. The General Assembly of 1882 changed the ritual.

November 18, 1881 — The New York City cigar packers staged the first strike by male workers against the employment of women.

1881 — The first exclusively female local of the Knights of Labor, Garfield Local Assembly No. 1684 in Philadelphia, was organized by Harry J. Skeffington. The second female local was established in Chicago in 1882 by Lizzie Swank and Elizabeth Rogers. By 1887, the Knights' female locals numbered in the hundreds.

1882 — The AFL first appealed to women's organizations to join the federation.

July 1883 — In the first strike by women garment workers in New York City, over 750 strikers, half of whom were women, walked off their jobs to demand a daily wage of $2.50 for a ten-hour day. Other workers joined the strike, and on August 1, it ended in victory.

1883 — The first law regulating the hours of labor for women workers in stores was enacted in New York. It lasted for only one year.

1883 — The first woman delegate to a national convention of the Knights of Labor was Mary Sterling. A Philadelphia shoe worker, she represented Garfield Local Assembly No. 1684.

1883 — The first scientific study of working women, *The Working Girls of Boston* by Carroll Wright and staff, was published. More than 1,000 female employees in the Boston area were interviewed, in addition to 170 prostitutes in brothels known to the Boston police. The study reported that *"the average weekly earnings* of the working girls of Boston for a whole year are $4.91."

1884 — Mrs. Elizabeth Rogers became the first woman to hold the position of master workman of the Knights of Labor. She was a master workman of District Assembly 24 in Chicago, which was composed of both men and women.

1884 — The first Working Girls' Club was established in New York City by a group of young working women. Grace Dodge, who came from an extremely wealthy family, became the prime mover of the club. The idea of Working Girls'

Clubs caught on, and by 1885, there were branches in several states. The stated objective of the clubs was to provide busy young women with additional opportunities "for social intercourse and the development of higher and nobler aims." Girls fourteen and older were eligible to join the clubs. Unfortunately, the clubs did not deal with the real problems of working women.

1885 — Leonora M. Barry, a worker in a hosiery mill, undertook a national organizing drive among women workers for the Knights of Labor. She was the first woman national labor organizer.

1885 — The first Committee on Women's Work was created by the Knights of Labor. It sent out a questionnaire on working conditions of women and discovered that ten hours constituted the average work day and that women workers earned an average of $5 per week.

May 15, 1886 — In the first strike by women members of the Knights of Labor, the "Joan of Arc" Assembly of Troy, New York, was locked out. Both the strike and the lockout were called off.

1886 — The first Department of Women's Work was created by the Knights of Labor. It established the office of general investigator, who was to inquire into "the abuses to which our sex is subjected by unscrupulous employers." She would also "agitate for the principles which our Order teaches, of equal pay for equal work and the abolition of child labor." The assembly elected Leonora Barry to fill this post.

June 1888 — The first union of women workers to be chartered by the AFL was Ladies' Federal Labor Union No. 2703 of Chicago, under the leadership of Mary Kenney.

1890 — "Mother" Mary Harris Jones became the first paid woman organizer. She was hired by the newly formed United Mine Workers of America.

1891 — The first women to address an AFL convention were Eva McDonald Valesh, a Milwaukee journalist interested in the labor movement, and Ida M. Van Etten, a member of the New York Working Women's Society.

April 1892 — The first woman general organizer commissioned by the AFL was Mary E. Kenney, leader of the Chicago Bindery Workers' Union and Ladies' Federal Labor Union No. 2703.

August 1894 — Ballet girls at the Eldorado Theatre in New York City formed the first union of ballet dancers and applied to the New York Central Labor Union for a charter. Sadie Seigrist was temporary chairman, Sarina Schwartz secretary, and Nana Deasy treasurer.

1894 — Kate Richards (later Kate Richards O'Hare) learned the machinists' trade and forced the Kansas City local of the International Association of Machinists to accept her "as a union man," thus becoming the first woman member of the union.

April 1897 — The first national union of servant girls, the American Servant Girls' Association, was formed in Kansas City, Missouri. Thirty lodges were said to have been formed, and Mary Hartopp was appointed national organizer. The objectives of the association, as set forth in its organizing pamphlet, were:

> To advance the social standing of the laboring girl; to secure for the servant girl a better appreciation of her services on the part of the employer; to protect the servant girl against the infamous blacklisting system adopted by mistresses generally; to secure for the servant girl a revised system of household duties and the payment of a fair remuneration for her services; to secure for servant girls the consent of all employers for a general half-holiday each week, and for the privilege of enjoying freedom from bondage on the Sabbath; to provide a means of concerted action, whenever occasion requires for such action; to furnish employment for the unemployed members, and to care for them when disabled.

August 1897 — Florence Fairview, organizer of women's trade unions, was the first woman trade unionist to charge that she was being persecuted by male labor leaders "because she is a woman." She brought her grievance before the New York City Central Labor Union, which voted to investigate the charge. However, nothing was done.

December 13, 1899 — The first organization of unmarried working women to prevent the employment of married women was founded. Women workers in Boston restaurants, department stores, and factories secured the promise of employers that they would employ only unmarried women, "with such exceptions as may be offered in favor of women who have lost their husbands or are otherwise needy."

July 28, 1901 — For the first time, a servant girls' union adopted a wage scale. The Workingwomen of America, a new servants' girls union based in Chicago, adopted the following scale of union wages for servants: cooks and housekeepers, $5 to $7 a week; general and second girls, $4 to $5 a week; young and inexperienced girls, $3 to $4 a week. Three hundred servants belonged to the organization, whose president was May Murphy.

October 20, 1903 — The first woman union bartender was Mary Hylick, eighteen years old. She enjoyed "the distinction of being the only female member of the Bartenders' Union. She was initiated at Wednesday's meeting of the Portchester, N.Y. local, and when her name was presented and accepted it was heartily cheered" *(The New York Times,* October 21, 1903).

November 14, 1903 — The meeting that led to the formation of the National Women's Trade Union League was held in Boston. The league's constitution stated that its objective "shall be to assist in the organization of women wage workers into trade unions." Any person who declared himself or herself willing to assist trade unions that admitted women members, and to aid in the formation of new unions, was eligible for admission. Mary Morton Kehew of Boston was elected president; Jane Addams of Chicago, vice president; and Mary Donovan, secretary of the Lynn (Massachusetts) Central Labor Union, treasurer. During the next year, the league formed branches in Chicago, New York, and Boston.

March 26, 1905 — The first national convention called to discuss the organization of working women into trade unions was held in New York City's Berkeley Lyceum under the sponsorship of the Women's Trade Union League. It was addressed by Samuel Gompers, Jane Addams, Mary K. Sullivan of New York City, and Mary McDowell of Chicago, and adopted a resolution that read: "Resolved, That it is the sense of this meeting that public opinion should support the efforts of the American Federation of Labor and the Women's Trade Union League to organize the women wage earners of the country into

trade unions for industrial and social improvement."

March 1907 — The first public exhibition to "reveal that hard and material side of life which goes on in factories and workshops, to epitomize the labor which clothes and feeds the modern world" was the Chicago Industrial Exhibit, sponsored by Jane Addams of Hull House and the Women's Trade Union League of Chicago. Statistics presented at the exhibit showed that female workers were earning an average of $7.25 a week, with many earning as little as $3.00.

November 1907 — The first woman to preside at an AFL convention was Agnes Nestor, secretary-treasurer of the International Glove Workers' Union and fraternal delegate from the Women's Trade Union League. Samuel Gompers permitted her to preside at one session of the AFL convention.

1908 — Annie Fitzgerald became the first woman organizer appointed by the AFL in the twentieth century. She held the position for only a short time.

November 22, 1909 — In the first mass strike by women workers, twenty thousand workers in the shirtwaist industry, members of the ILGWU, four-fifths of them Jewish and Italian women, began a general strike in New York City. They won their strike after enduring months of police brutality and arrests.

January 1911—The first issue of *Life and Labor,* the official organ of the Women's Trade Union League, was published. For two and one-half years, the league had run a "Women's Department" in the *Union Labor Advocate* of Chicago, but the need for a larger publication led to the launching of *Life and Labor,* with Alice Henry as editor-in-chief. The monthly magazine had eight departments dealing with women workers, suffrage, law, and so on.

1913—Agnes Nestor was elected president of the International Glove Workers' Union. She was the first woman president of an international trade union.

1913—For the first time, women constituted over 50 percent of the membership of a union that included both men and women. Women made up more than half the ninety thousand members of the International Ladies' Garment Workers' Union. Even so, ILGWU locals sent only eighteen women delegates to the biennial convention.

November 2, 1914—The first strike by hospital nurses occurred when twenty-seven nurses at Flushing Hospital in New York City struck for better working conditions.

December 2, 1914—The first committee formed to open up a wider field of employment for women was the Committee of 100, organized in New York City with Mary Beard as its head.

1915—The first full-time woman organizer appointed by the ILGWU was Rose Schneiderman. By 1916, the union had eight women organizers in the field.

July 1916—The first strike in which wives and children did the picketing for their husbands and fathers was led by the IWW at the Mesabi Range in Minnesota. While the strikers worked in harvest fields, their wives and children picketed. The strike was eventually lost.

1919—Michigan and Montana became the first states to enact equal pay legislation for women.

1920—The first Women's Bureau was created, under the Department of Labor.

October 1933—Elizabeth Christman of the Women's Trade Union League was the first woman to introduce a resolution in favor of industrial unionism at an AFL convention. Her resolution was not voted on.

1933—The first public-supported nursery school program was launched by the Works Progress Administration (WPA) as part of its "family life" project. It lasted until 1943.

September 1, 1940—The National Defense Advisory Commission first announced that "workers should not be discriminated against because of age, sex, race or color."

June 1941 — Texas Congressman Fritz Lanham added federal financing of child-care centers for working women to the act setting up the Federal Works Agency. The first day-care project was not approved until August 31, 1942.

January 27, 1942 — The War, Navy, and Labor departments agreed for the first time that "wage rates for women should be the same as for men, including the entrance rate."

February 10, 1942 — The War Production Board ended its policy of restricting job training to men. It announced the "immediate extension of defense training to women on a basis of equality with the training of men." However, the federal agencies involved continued to recommend that conversion-unemployed males receive top priority. These men had lost their jobs because of the change to war work.

September 26, 1942 — The National War Labor Board took its first decision involving discrimination against women workers. The UAW and UE charged General Motors with paying its new women employees less than men on comparable jobs and argued that such differentials would promote "tremendous resistance toward that influx of women on the part of the male workers in the plants." The board ruled that where women did work of "the same quality and quantity" as male workers, differentials were discriminatory. Furthermore, the board warned that "using

slight or inconsequential changes in a job as a reason for setting up a wage differential against women employees" would not be tolerated.

In November 1942, the National War Labor Board went a step further in promoting equal pay by issuing General Order 16, a ruling that allowed voluntary equalization of female wage rates for "comparable quality of work on the same or similar operations" without prior approval by the board.

Despite the board ruling against General Motors, equal pay was still not in effect in the plant in question by May 1943.

December 1942 — The first "Women to Win the War" Conference was held by the Columbus, Ohio, District Council of the United Electrical, Radio, and Machine Workers of America (UE), CIO, to urge locals to maintain union gains while the men were away, and to "educate and activize its women to take full responsibility for the well-being of the Local Union."

1942 — The International Association of Machinists, the Moulders, and Foundry Workers, the Iron Shipbuilders and Helpers, the Iron Workers, and the Carpenters and Joiners allowed women to become members for the first time. The International Brotherhood of Boilermakers was the last to give in to government pressure, ceasing its opposition to women members in September 1942. All of these unions were AFL affiliates. The Carpenters and Joiners granted full status only to those women who directly replaced men, forcing all other women in the industry to accept nonvoting auxiliary status.

1943 — The first woman added to a union educational staff to deal with women's problems was the writer Elizabeth Hawes. She was appointed by the United Automobile Workers (UAW).

1944 — This was the first year in which women's membership in unions exceeded a million. It increased from approximately 800,000 before the war to over three million in 1944. In this year, eleven national unions reported more than forty thousand women in their ranks. The UAW and the UE (CIO) had the largest number of women members. The UE reported eighteen female local presidents and forty-seven women on the international staff.

1944 — The UAW became the first union to press for measures for women workers not directly related to job conditions, such as improved child care and shopping and laundry facilities in war communities.

1945 — For the first time, unions called upon the federal government to outlaw wage discrimination against women. The AFL, the CIO, and a number of individual unions urged Congress to end wage discrimination at hearings on the Federal Equal Pay Bill.

June 20, 1973 — At a Midwest Conference of Union Women in Chicago, some two hundred women from eighteen states and twenty national and international unions recommended the convening of a national conference of union women and the establishment of an interunion framework for cooperative action in a common cause.

March 22–24, 1974 — The first National Conference in Chicago, attended by over thirty-two hundred women trade unionists, formed the Coalition of Labor Union Women (CLUW). The call to the conference included the following statement adopted by the National Planning Conference Committee: "To bring together women union members and retirees of bona fide collective bargaining organizations to deal with our special concerns as unionists and women in the labor force . . . in an inter-union framework, the Conference will consider positive action in the areas of equal pay, equal rights and equal opportunity . . . more specifically . . . education about women's legal rights, adequate maternity benefits and child-care, equitable hiring and promotion practices, adequate minimum wage, up-grading and affirmative action, organizing the unorganized women workers, and equitable representation of women in union structures and policy-making decisions." Olga Madar of the UAW was elected president; Addie Wyatt of the Amalgamated Meat Cutters and Butcher Workmen was elected vice president; Gloria Johnson of the International Union of Electrical, Radio, and Machine Workers (IUE) was elected treasurer; and Joyce Miller of the Amalgamated Clothing Workers was elected secretary of the CLUW.

August 1, 1974 — The first American women miners began work. Three women went to work at the Bethlehem Mine Corporation's Mine No. 51 in Ellsworth, Pennsylvania. One of the women was black — the first black woman miner in Pennsylvania history. A century-old state law had prohibited women from working in the mines, but it was superseded by federal laws against discrimination in employment. Bethlehem was the first major concern to send women underground. In June 1980, there were 3,061 women miners working in mines in Kentucky, Pennsylvania, and West Virginia.

November 1976 — The UAW installed a bronze medallion honoring its women members in its headquarters building in Detroit. The medallion was intended to balance the statue of a male worker that has long stood outside the building.

February 1979 — The first long-shorewomen began work in New York City after the New York Waterfront Commission granted fifty women permits to work on the docks. The women won their jobs through the efforts of the National Organization of Women's (NOW's) Urban Woman Project.

August 22, 1980 — The AFL-CIO Executive Council filled one of its vacancies by electing Joyce Miller. Miller is the vice president of the Amalgamated Clothing and Textile Workers and president of the Coalition of Labor Union Women (CLUW). Her election marked the first time a woman held such an office in the twenty-five-year history of the AFL-CIO.

1980 — The first program drawn up on behalf of working women, the Working Women's 1980 Platform, was presented to presidential candidates. The platform was put together by the Coalition of Labor Union Women, the Displaced Homemakers Network, Wider Opportunities for Women, and the National Commission on Working Women. In a joint statement issued on Labor Day 1980, these organizations said the platform's objectives were to send "an urgent message to the presidential candidates" and to "focus public attention on the concerns of working women."

The Working Women's 1980 Platform contained fifteen proposals for recognizing the importance of women workers in all aspects of social, political, and economic life in America: the special needs, concerns, and problems of minority women workers "who face both sexism and racism"; elimination of job segregation by sex, of wage discrimination by sex, of sex stereotyping, and other barriers to equity in all publicly funded education, employment, and training programs; expansion and creation of special programs to improve employment opportunities for all women; enforcement of laws and regulations mandating equal employment opportunities for women; maintaining a work environment free of sexual harassment and intimidation; providing accessible quality care for children and other dependents; recognizing homemakers as an important segment of the country's labor force; promoting the participation of women in the formulation and evaluation of public policy affecting employment.

May 30, 1982 —Actress Ellen Burstyn was elected the first woman president of the Actors' Equity Association. Ms. Burstyn, who starred in such movies as *The Exorcist* and *Alice Doesn't Live Here Anymore,* succeeded actor Theodore Bikel, who had served for nine years as top elected officer of the sixty-nine-year-old, thirty thousand-member union. She defeated another actress, Lynn Oliver, by a vote of 6,112 to 2,131 in a mail referendum.

Work Councils

1898 —The first work councils in the United States were established at the Filene store in Boston and the Nernst Lamp Company in Pittsburgh.

Workers' Compensation (Formerly called Workmen's Compensation)

1902 —Montana enacted the first state workmen's compensation law. It was declared unconstitutional by the state Supreme Court.

1908 —The Republican party of Wisconsin's election platform of 1908 was the first major party platform to endorse workmen's compensation legislation.

1908 —The first federal employees' compensation law was passed. President Theodore Roosevelt advocated the proposal, saying: "It is a matter of humiliation to the nation that there should not be in our statutes provisions to meet and partially to atone for such misfortune when it comes upon a man through no fault of his own while faithfully serving the public."

1909 —The first states to appoint legislative commissions to formulate workmen's compensation legislation were Wisconsin, Minnesota, New York, and Illinois.

1911 —The first book by employers advocating workmen's compensation legislation was *Accident Prevention and Relief,* a publication financed by the National Association of Manufacturers.

The book argued that European workmen's compensation systems reduced accidents and virtually eliminated court suits against employers by injured workers.

1917 — The U.S. Supreme Court, in a series of rulings, upheld for the first time several types of workmen's compensation laws, ratifying virtually all such laws then in existence. By 1920, every state but six — all in the South — had enacted workmen's compensation laws.

Work-or-Fight Laws

May 20, 1917 — The first "work-or-fight" law was passed by West Virginia. It compelled every able-bodied man who had not joined the armed forces to work at least thirty-six hours a week.

World War I

March 9, 1917 — For the first time, the AFL and Railroad Brotherhoods announced their readiness to support America's entrance into World War I. "American Labor's Position in Peace or in War," a declaration drawn up by the AFL Executive Council and signed by

148 officers representing 79 international unions, the AFL Departments, and the Railroad Brotherhoods, stated that if, "despite all our endeavors and hopes, . . . our country should be drawn into the maelstrom of the European conflict, we . . . offer our services to our country in every field of activity to defend, safeguard, and preserve the Republic of the United States of America against its enemies whomsoever they may be, and call upon our fellow workers and fellow citizens in the holy name of labor, justice, freedom, and humanity devotedly and patriotically to give like service." The only important international unions not represented in the declaration were the International Ladies' Garment Workers' Union, the International Union of Mine, Mill and Smelter Workers, the Journeymen Barbers' Union, and the International Typographical Union.

August 16, 1917 — The American Alliance for Labor and Democracy, the first organization launched to support World War I and oppose antiwar elements in the ranks of labor, was founded with the help of Samuel Gompers.

Y

Yellow-Dog Contracts

1834 —Factory girls in New England textile mills were forced to sign the following statement as a condition of obtaining employment: "We also agree not to be engaged in any combination whereby the work may be impeded or the company's interest in any way injured; if we do, we agree to forfeit to the use of the company the amount due us at the time." This was the first "yellow-dog" contract.

1908 —The U.S. Supreme Court sanctioned the "yellow-dog" contract and the blacklist when it declared Section 10 of the Erdman Act of 1898 unconstitutional. This law, which applied solely to railroad workers, had made it illegal for any employer to discriminate against or discharge a worker because of the latter's membership in a union.

December 10, 1917 —For the first time, the U.S. Supreme Court upheld the constitutionality of a specific "yellow-dog" contract.

March 23, 1932 —The Norris-LaGuardia Act was the first law outlawing "yellow-dog" contracts in general and limiting injunctions against strikes.

Index

Abel, I. W., 176
Abernathy, Reverand Ralph, 175–76
Ablowitz, Rebecca, 31
Academy Award winners, 3, 119
Accident Prevention and Relief, 214–215
Accidents, 3–4
"Act in Relation to the Employment of Labor by Corporations, An," 147
Actors, 4, 142, 166, 170–71, 192, 214
Actors Equity Association, 4, 127, 170–71, 192, 214
Adamson Act, 77
Addams, Jane, 209
Address, Delivered before the Mechanics . . . , 103, 112
Address to the Members of Trade Societies . . . , 103
"Address to the People of Philadelphia," 202
"Address to the Workingmen of Massachusetts," 61
Address to the Workingmen of New England, 103
Address to the Workingmen of the United States, 21
Adkins v. Children's Hospital, 118
Adler, Felix, 36
Administration on Aging, 130
Advertising, 4
AFL. *See* American Federation of Labor
AFL–CIO. *See* American Federation–Congress of Industrial Organizations
AFL Rank and File Federationist, 144–45
Age Discrimination in Employment Act, 132
Agricultural Workers' Industrial League, 6
Agricultural Workers' Organization, 6
Agricultural Workers' Organizing Committee, AFL-CIO, 8
Air Line Pilots' Association, AFL, 8, 84
Air Traffic Controllers, 9
Airline Flight Attendants, 8
Akron (Ohio) 112, 172
Alabama, 6, 104, 157
Alabama Sharecroppers Union, 6
Alaska, 77
Albany (N.Y.), 104, 124
Alliance for Labor Action, 123
Allied Printing Trades' Council, 195

Alschaler, Judge Samuel, 78
Altgeld, John Peter, 62–63, 92
Amalgamated Association of Iron and Steel Workers, 9, 14, 21, 134, 166
Amalgamated Association of Street Car Employees, 127
Amalgamated Association of Street Railway Employees, 67, 191
Amalgamated Clothing and Textile Workers Unions, 158, 194
Amalgamated Clothing Workers of America, 10, 11, 29, 39, 40, 78, 80, 85, 89, 108, 117, 127, 128, 133, 187, 213
Amalgamated Meat Cutters and Butcher Workmen of North America, 10, 11, 110, 127, 167
Amalgamated Society of Engineers, 136–37
Amalgamated Textile Workers, 40
Amalgamations and mergers, 9–11
American Academy of Political and Social Sciences, 36
American Alliance for Labor and Democracy, 43
American Anti-Imperialist League, 13
American Association for Labor Legislation, 131, 186
American Communication Association, 12, 60
American District Telegraph Messenger Boys, 164
American Emigrant Company, 46
American Express Company, 137
American Federation of Hosiery Workers, 201
American Federation of Labor (AFL), 26, 33, 52, 53, 55, 56, 59, 66, 77, 86, 88, 90, 92, 93, 96, 99, 105, 107, 108–9, 110, 117, 118, 121, 130, 137, 140, 141, 144, 158, 178, 179, 181, 184, 185, 192, 194, 195, 198, 201, 206, 207, 212, 213, 215; Executive Council, 60, 62, 78, 84–85, 108, 189, 215; Housing Committee, 80; Railway Employees' Department, 68, 196. *See also* American Federation of Labor–Congress of Industrial Organizations (AFL–CIO)
American Federation of Labor–Congress of Industrial Organizations (AFL–CIO), 10–11, 32, 39, 71, 99, 110, 122–23, 145; Department of Ur-

ban Affairs, 80–81; Executive Council, 213; Industrial Union Department, 194–95; Mortgage Investment Trust, 80
American Federation of State, County, and Municipal Employees (AFSCME), 134, 175
American Federation of Teachers (AFT), 128, 139
American Federation of Television and Radio Artists (AFTRA), 175
American Federationist, 48, 85, 105
American flag, 159–60
American Institute of Social Sciences, 3
American Labor Party, 107
American Labor Union, 182, 201
"American Labor's Position in Peace or in War," 215
American League of Colored Laborers, 20
American Legionnaires, 94
American Lumber Company, 108
American Medical Association, 131
American Miners' Association, 125
American Museum of Safety, 3
American Negro Labor Congress, 25
American Newspaper Guild, 128
"American Plan," 132
"American Plan for an Unemployment Reserve Fund, An," 187–88
American Railroad Employees and Investors Association, 196
American Railway Union, 31, 83–84, 85, 165–66
American Revolution, 11–12, 103, 136
American Seamen's Protective Association, 21, 152, 182
American Servant Girls' Association, 208
American Society of Arbitration, Inc., 17
American Society of Mechanical Engineers, 152
American Workers Party, 139, 190–91
Amter, Israel, 187
Anaconda Copper Company, 150
Anarchists, 57
Anthony, Susan B., 204, 205
Anthracite Coal Strike Commission, 16
Anti-Chinese, 12
Anti-communism, 12, 180
Anti-imperialism, 12–13
Anti-Imperialist League, 12
Anti-labor banks, 67
Anti-Negro riots, 24–25
Antipicketing law, 86
Antistrike laws, 13
Antitrust act, 13
Antiwar, 13–15
Apartheid, 32
Apex Hosiery Co. v. Leader, 173
Appalachian agreement, 192–93
Appeal to Reason, 156
Apprentices, 15

Arbeiter Secretariat, 200
Arbitration Act of 1888, 16
Arbitration and mediation, 15–18
Arkansas, 7, 150, 158, 195
Armies of the Commonweal, 186
Arthur, Chester A., 33
Arthur, Peter M., 144
Assassinations, 175, 176
Assembly of Associated Mechanics and Workingmen of Philadelphia, 73
Associated Brotherhood of Iron and Steel Heaters, 9
Association of Black Caulkers of Baltimore, 21
Association of Vaudeville Managers of the United States, 166
Association of Western Pulp and Paper Workers, 145
Atlanta, 158
Atlanta University, 24
Atlantic Coast Steamship Owners, 200
Attucks, Crispus, 11
Australia, 122
Austria, 63–64
Austro-Hungarians, 63–64
Auto workers, 154, 170. *See also* United Automobile Workers of America.
Auto Workers' Union, 128
Automation, 18, 69, 175
Avery, Sewell, 63
Aviators' and Pilots' Union, AFL, 8

Baer, George F., 166–67
Bagley, Sarah G., 104, 203
Baker, Newton D., 198
Bakers, 160, 179
Ballet dancers, 162–63, 207
Baltimore, 21, 74, 95, 96, 121, 124, 161, 182, 198
Baltimore and Ohio Plan of Welfare Capitalism, 196
Baltimore Typographical Society, 15
Banda Rosa band, 166
Banks, 91
Barrett, Judge George C., 31
Barry, Leonora M., 207
Bartenders, 127
Bartenders' International League, 127
Bartenders' Union, 208–9
Baseball players, 18, 19, 114, 128, 131, 146, 170, 183–84
Baseball Players' Fraternity, 128
Bates, John, 102, 182
Bates' Union, 182
Baths, 132
Battle of Anacostia Heights, 189–90
Battle of Buena Vista, 19
Battle of the Overpass, 134

Bayonne, 44
Beard, Mary, 210
Belgium, 122
Bell, Sherman, 63
Bendix Products Corporation, 154
Bennett, Harry, 134, 194
Berger, Victor L., 45, 137, 156, 157
Berry, George, 85
Bethlehem Mine Corporation, 41
Bethlehem Steel Corporation, 152, 171, 194
Beveridge, Albert, 36
Beyer, Otto S., 196
Biberman, Herbert, 119
"Big Steel," 193
Bikel, Theodore, 214
Bill of Grievances, 108–9
Bill of Rights, 20
Billings, Warren K., 93
Bindery workers, 207
Birmingham, 56
Black bill, 78–79
Black caucuses, 29, 30
Black firemen, 26, 28
Black labor leaders, 95–96
Black lung, 71
Black Lung Benefit Act, 71
Black sanitation workers, 175
Black seamen, 152, 182
Black Socialists, 25
Black strikebreakers, 158
Black union officers, 129
Black-white unity, 22–23, 66, 106, 109–10, 158, 162, 175–176
Black women, 21, 158, 213
Black workers, 20–30, 170
Blacklists, 20
Blanchard, I. G., 110–11
Blind workers, 134–35
"Bloody Thursday," 67
Blue Cross Leagues, 39
Bogolusa (La.) Press, 110
Bonus, 188
Bonus Army, 189–190
Bookbinders' Union, 141
Bookkeepers', Stenographers' and Accountants' Union, 59
Bordoise, Nick, 67
Boring-from-within, 30, 97
Boston, 21, 36, 46, 47, 55, 58, 69, 70, 72, 74, 100, 103, 104, 124, 127, 129, 153, 161, 162, 165, 198, 200, 206, 209, 214
Boston Central Labor Union, 178
Boston Daily Evening Voice, 178
Boston Economic Club, 151
Boston Eight-Hour League, 34
Boston Journeymen Bootmakers' Society, 46

Boston Labor Council, 55
"Boston Massacre," 111
Boston Social Club, 184
Boston Trades' Assembly, 74
Bouchillon, A., 110
Boulware, Lemuel, 176
"Boulwarism," 176
Boyce, Ed, 181
Boycotter, The, 105
Boycotts, 30–33, 86, 99, 105, 165, 194, 195
Boyle, W. A. ("Tony"), 145
Boys choir, 165
Braceros, 117, 174. See also Chicanos, Mexican-Americans
Brain Workers' Union, 183
Bread and Roses, 50
Bricklayers, 124, 125
Bricklayers' International Union of the United States of North America, 125
Bridgeport (Conn.), 138, 191
Bridges, Harry, 18, 67, 129
Brindell, Robert, 33
Brisbane, Albert, 155
British Columbia, 133
British Trades' Union Congress, 88
Brooklyn, 41, 100, 126, 132, 164–65
Brooklyn Labor Lyceum, 41
Brookside Mine, 3
Brookwood Labor College, 55–56
Brookwood League, 19
Brophy, John, 133
Brotherhood of Interborough Rapid Transit Employees, 44
Brotherhood of Iron and Steel Heaters, Rollers and Roughers of the United States, 126
Brotherhood of Locomotive Engineers, 86, 125, 144
Brotherhood of Locomotive Firemen, 9, 26, 106
Brotherhood of Locomotive Firemen and Enginemen, 28
Brotherhood of Railway Clerks, 56
Brotherhood of Railway Conductors, 126
Brotherhood of Railway Trainmen, 52
Brotherhood of Sleeping Car Porters, 21, 29, 76
Brotherhod of Timber Workers, 24, 108, 109–10
Brotherhood of the Footboard, 125
Brotherhood Welfare Association, 186
Broun, Heywood, 128
Brown, Ada, J., 8
Brown, Thomas H., 133
Brown, Viola, 172
Bryant, William Cullen, 46
Bucharest, 151
Bucks' Stove and Range Company, 48, 86
Budapest, 88
Buffalo (N.Y.), 100, 104, 124, 132

Building trades, 73, 100
Building Trades Department, 33
Building Trades' Employers' Association, 33
"Bull pen," 62
Bureau of Engravers, 28
Bureau of Immigration, 58
Bureau of Labor Statistics, 17, 33, 34, 132
Burritt, Elihu, 13
Burstyn, Ellen, 214
Burt, Sam, 66
Butchers, 127
Butte Miners' Union, 192
Butte (Montana), 114
Buzzard, William, 49

Cab drivers, 166
Cabinetmakers, 109
Caldwell, Clifton, 14
Caldwell, James, 11
California, 5–7, 74, 93, 99, 117, 131, 132, 150, 160, 174, 178
California Citizens' Alliance, 40
California Federation of Labor, 56, 188
Cameron, Andrew C., 21, 87, 104, 121
Canada, 44, 64–65, 122, 133, 136–37, 138
Canadian Northern Railway, 133, 138
Cannery and Agricultural Workers' Industrial Union, 6, 178, 193
Cantonment Adjustment Commission, 198
Captive coal mines, 193
Carey, James B., 122, 128, 144
Carl Sahm Club, 31
Carnegie Steel Company, 48, 159
Carpenters, 72, 124, 161
Carpenters' and Joiners' International Union, 125, 211–12
Carpenters' Company of the City and County of Philadelphia, 69, 100–101
Carpenters' Hall, 69, 100–101
Carr, Patrick, 11
Carriage, Wagon and Automobile Workers, 127
Carter, Jimmy, 4, 174
"Casey Jones—the Union Scab," 111
Catholic Church, 39–40
Caulkers, 21, 74, 96, 200
Central Building Trades' Council, 33
Central Committee of United Trades of New York City, 41
Central competitive field, 192
Central Federated Union of New York City, 49, 113
Central Freight Handlers' Union, 151
Central Labor and Building Trades Council, 9
Central Labor Council of Rochester, 67–68
Central Labor Federation of New York City, 183

Central Labor Union of New York City and Vicinity, 41, 91, 156
Central Labor Union of Philadelphia, 67
Central Workingmen's Committee of Philadelphia, 185
Centralia, 94
Century Air Lines, 8
Chaplin, Ralph, 111–12
Charleston, (S.C.), 20, 22, 104, 139, 160, 175–76
Chavez, Cesar, 7, 18, 32, 99
Chesapeake and Ohio Canal, 62, 162
Chesapeake Marine Railway and Dry Dock Company, 21, 96
Chicago, 25, 32, 38, 44, 45, 55, 57, 67, 75–76, 84, 104, 107, 116, 122, 125, 131, 133, 134–35, 153, 167, 183, 187, 197, 200, 206, 207, 208, 209, 212
Chicago Federation of Labor, 77, 84, 108
Chicago Industrial Exhibit, 209
Chicago Packing Trades' Council, 10
Chicanos, 99, 117
Child day-care centers, 35, 211, 212, 214
Child labor, 35–37, 107
Child Labor Day, 37
Child labor laws, 35–36, 37, 38, 79
Children and strikes, 37–39; and unions, 39
Chinese, 83, 192
Chinese exclusion, 108
Christensen, Parley, 62
Christman, Elizabeth, 210
Church and labor, 39–40, 186
Church Association for the Advancement of the Interests of Labor, 40
Cigar makers, 49, 163
Cigar Makers' International Union, 31, 52, 96, 163, 176, 181, 204
Cigar Makers' National Union, 124
Cigar packers, 206
Cincinnati (Ohio), 22, 47, 118, 123, 124
CIO. See Congress of Industrial Organizations
Citizens' Alliances, 40
Citizens' Industrial Association, 132
"City Beautiful," 156
City Central Labor Unions, 40–41
City Front Federation of San Francisco, 10
Civil Rights Act of 1964, 30, 41–42
Civil Rights Department, 42
Civil War, 95, 104, 109, 120, 171
Clark, Peter H., 22
Class struggle, 122
Clayton Anti-Trust Act, 147
Cleveland, Grover, 16, 62–63, 92
Cleveland (Ohio), 78, 112, 193
Cloakmakers, 9, 143, 168
Closed shop, 42, 161, 180, 197
Cluer, John C., 66

Coach Makers' International Union, 125
Coal Mine Health and Safety Act, 71
Coalition of Black Trade Unionists, 30
Coalition of Labor Union Women, 212–13
Cobb, Ty, 168–69
Coeur d'Alene, 150, 159
Collar Laundry Workingwomen's Association of Troy, 205
Collective bargaining, 42–43, 154
Colorado, 44, 52, 63, 92, 116, 164, 183, 192
Colorado Fuel and Iron Company, 44, 120
Colorado Industrial Plan, 44
Colored Caulkers' Trade Union Society of Baltimore, 72, 96
Colored Employees of America, 25
Colored National Labor Union, 22, 95–96, 101
Colored Seamen's Home, 182
Colored Teachers Cooperative Association of Cincinnati, 22
Colored Waiters' Protective Union, 22
Columbia Exposition, 88
Columbus (Ohio), 106–7, 211
Columnists, 91
Commission on Workers' Education, 56
Committee for Industrial Organization, 26, 27, 52, 60, 85, 97, 98, 128, 129, 130, 133–34, 142, 144, 172–73, 193, 196, 211, 212
Committee of Interns and Residents, 176–77
Committee on Social Betterment of the President's Home Commission, 70
Committee on Women's Work, 207
Commonwealth College, 56
Commonwealth v. Carlisle, 46
Commonwealth v. Hunt, 46
Communism, 180
Communist Club of New York City, 43, 156
Communist Party, 25, 60, 67, 97, 180, 187, 188, 190
Communists, 29, 43, 59–60, 67, 145, 156
Community Service Organization, 99
Company stores, 43, 193
Company unionism, 192
Company unions, 43–44
Compensation laws, 214–15
Compulsory arbitration, 17
Compulsory education, 54, 107
Concerned Transit Workers, 30
Condon-Wadlin law, 175
Conductors, 182
Confederation of Mexican Labor Unions, 6, 117
Conference of Labor for Peace, 14–15
Conference on Progressive Labor Action, 190
Congress, 44–45, 57
Congress of Industrial Organizations (CIO), 85, 97, 122; Committee on Housing, 80; Industrial

Union Council, 63. See also American Federation of Labor–Congress of Industrial Organizations.
Connecticut, 35, 138, 140, 150
Conner, Bishop James A., 158
Conspiracy cases, 45–46, 94
Conspiracy trials, 31
Continental Congress, 69, 101, 122
Continental Congress of Workers and Farmers, 157
Contract labor, 46
Contract labor law, 107
Convict labor, 46–47, 199
Convict lease system, 158
Cooks' Union, 67
Coolidge, Calvin, 171
Cooperative Welfare Association, 44
Cooperatives, 21, 47, 95, 96
Coopers' International Union, 45, 50
Cordwainers, 31, 42, 101, 134, 161, 177, 181
Cordwainers' National Union, 125
Corruption, 33, 47–48
Cost-of-living, 48, 194
Cotton pickers, 23, 178
Council of London, 160
Council of National Defense, 130, 198
Counterfeit union label, 195
Cowdrey, Robert, H., 107
Cox, George, 23
Cox, Henry, 23
Cox, James R., 188
Coxes, Eckley B., 15
Coxey, Jacob Sechler, 186
Coxey's Army, 186
Craft unionism, 122
Cranberry Pickers' Union, 6
Criminal prosecutions, 48–49
Criminal Syndicalist laws, 49, 198
Crosswaith, Frank, 26
Croton Dam, 166
Cruising Picket squad, 138–39
Culture, 49–50
Curran, Joseph, 128–29

Dacus, Sol, 110
Dailey Committee, 33
Daily Sentinel, 104
Damrosch, Walter, 165
Danbury Hatters' Case, 31
Darrow, Clarence, 48, 93, 94
Daughters of Liberty, 31, 202
Daughters of St. Crispin, 101, 204
Davis, David, 107
Davis, Richard L., 23
Davis-Bacon Act, 199
Davis Machine and Computer Scale Company, 132
Dayton (Ohio), 58, 132

De Leon, Daniel, 52, 156
Deasy, Nana, 207
Debs, Eugene V., 83, 85, 141, 156
Decertification, 109
Declaration of Independence, 103, 109
Delano (Calif.), 32, 99
Delaware, 104, 178
Delaware Free Press, 104
Democratic Party, 44, 45, 124, 181, 190
Dennison Manufacturing Company, 187
Denver, 66
Department of Commerce and Labor, 37
Department of Justice, 197
Department of Labor, 51–52, 58, 210
Department of Women's Work, 207
Department store workers, 205
Department Store Workers Union (CIO), 113
Deportation, 63
Detective agency, 112
Detroit, 200, 213
Detroit Tigers, 168–69
Detroit Trades' Assembly, 102
Dewey, Thomas E., 181
Diamond Match Company, 70
Die Reform, 43
Die Revolution, 43, 156
Disabled American Veterans, 113
Disabled Miners and Widows of Southern West
    Virginia, 145
Discrimination, 52, 210
Displaced Homemakers' Network, 213
District of Columbia. See Washington, D.C.
District 1199, 50, 176
District 65, 29
Doak, William Nuckles, 51
Doctors, 176–77
Dodge, Grace, 206–7
Dodge Revolutionary Union Movement, 175
Doehring, C.F.W., 70, 132
Dole, 189
Donovan, Mary, 209
Douglass, Frederick, 20
Dover Manufacturing Company, 202
Dreiser, Theodore, 171–72
Dress and Cloak Makers' Union, 82, 164
Dress and Waistmakers' Union, 55
Dressmakers, 9, 55, 167–68
Drug and Hospital Workers' Union, 14
Du Bois, W.E.B., 24
Dual Union, 52
Dubinsky, David, 85, 133
Duke Power Company, 3, 134, 176
Duncan, James, 197

Early Closing Association of Sales Clerks and De-
    partment Store Workers, 75

Easley, Ralph M., 195
East St. Louis riot, 24–25
Eastman, Crystal, 4
"Economic Bill of Rights," 141–42
Education, 54, 56
Eight-hour day, 10, 73, 74, 75, 76, 77, 78, 82,
    91, 107, 116–17, 158, 165, 167, 170, 179,
    192, 193, 199, 200–201
Eight-hour laws, 74–75, 76, 108, 179
Eight-hour leagues, 74
Eight-hour song, 110–11
Eight-hour strikes, 75–76, 77, 78
Ekrengen, W.A.F., 93
Elections, 57; of 1860, 113–14; of 1872, 107; of
    1940, 98; of 1948, 179
Electric Autolite Company, 139
Electrical workers, 28, 79
Eliot, Charles W., 151
Emergency Relief and Construction Act, 189
Empire Protective Association, 165
Employer-financed unemployment benefit plan,
    187–88
Employers' associations, 181
Employers' liability, 57
Employers' offensive, 57–58
Employment offices, 58
Emspak, Julius, 128
Engel, George, 88
Engineers, 124
England, 88, 99, 100, 122
English, William, 57
Epstein, Abraham, 132
Equal employment legislation, 205
Equal pay for comparable work, 57
Equal pay for equal work, 58–59, 197, 204, 207,
    210, 211, 212
Equal Rights Act, 58
Equal Rights Amendment, 59
Equal Rights Party, 140
"Equalization of funds," 183
ERA. See Equal Rights Amendment.
ERAmerica, 59
Erdman Act of 1898, 16, 216
Erwin, Charles W., 25
Espionage Act, 25, 49, 105, 141, 171, 198
Ethridge, Mark, 27
Ettor, Joseph, 32, 93, 169
Evans, George Henry, 104, 113
Evictions, 188
Ewell, Judge William, 15
Excessive heat, 71–72
Excessive noise, 71
Exclusion of blacks, 23–24
Executive Order 10988, 68
Experimental Negotiating Agreement, 177
Expulsions, 12, 59–60, 97

Facing Old Age, 132
Factory girls, 162
Factory Girls, The, 103
Factory inspection, 61
Factory inspection laws, 131
Factory Sanitation and Labor Protection, 70, 132
Factory Tracts, 103
Factory workers, 61, 161, 202
"Factory Workers in General Throughout the United States," 61
Fair Employment Practices Committee (FEPC), 27, 28, 61
Fair Labor Standards Act, 79, 112–13, 118, 200
Fair Practices Clause, 61
Fairmount Coal Company, 4
Fairview, Florence, 208
Fall River (Mass.), 58, 163, 192, 202
"Family life" project, 210
Farah Manufacturing Company, 117
Farmer and Mechanics' Party of Albany, N.Y., 61; of Salina, N.Y., 61
Farmer-Labor Party, 61–62, 107
Farmers' and Mechanics' Advocate, 104
"Father of Labor Day," 92
"Father of the Eight-Hour Day," 74
Federal aid to education, 56
Federal Children's Bureau, 37
Federal Conference on Unemployment, 187
Federal employees, 180, 214
Federal Equal Pay Bill, 212
Federal Housing Act, 81
Federal Labor Unions, 209
Federal Society of Journeymen Cordwainers of Philadelphia, 42, 105, 110, 161
Federal Society of Philadelphia Cabinet Makers, 109, 120
Federal troops and labor disputes, 62–63
Federal Works Agency, 35, 211
Federation of Mexican Workers' Unions, 117
Federation of Organized Trades and Labor Unions of the United States and Canada, 75, 91–92, 96, 102, 116–17, 121. *See also* American Federation of Labor
Federation of railroad crafts, 10
"Female Department," 104, 203–4
Female Industrial Association of New York City, 20
Female Labor Reform Associations, 180
Ferguson, Reverend H., 146
Ferrell, Frank J., 23
Field, Sally, 3
Fielden, Samuel, 92
"52-40 or Fight," 79
"Fight—Don't Starve," 187
Fincher, Jonathan C., 104, 125
Fincher's Trades' Review, 104

Firemen, 175
Firestone Tire and Rubber Company, 169, 172–73
First International. *See* International Working-men's Association.
Fischer, Adolph, 88
Fishermen, 160
Fitzgerald, Annie, 209
Fitzpatrick, John, 77
Fletcher, Benjamin Harrison, 25, 170
Flint Glass Workers' Union, 188
Florida, 150
Folks, Homer, 36
Foner, Henry, 113
Foner, Moe, 50
Food bank, 197
Food, Tobacco, Agricultural, and Allied Workers Union (CIO), 27–28, 174
Food, Tobacco and Agricultural Workers, 12, 60
Foran, Martin A., 45, 50
Ford, Ebenezer, 57
Ford, Henry, 77
Ford Company "service men," 134
Ford Local 600, 128
Ford Motor Company, 79–80, 98, 117–18, 154, 187, 194
Ford Service Company, 189, 194
Fort Wayne (Ind.), 201
Fort-Whitman, Lovett, 25
Fortie, Reverend John, 95
Forty-four-hour week, 78, 171
Forty-hour week, 78, 192, 193, 199
Foster, William Z., 30, 77, 97, 144, 171
Four-day week, 79–80
Fourier, Charles, 95, 155
Fourth of July, 64
France, 122
Frank, Waldo, 176
Frankensteen, Richard, 134
Franklin, Norman, 113
Franklin Typographical Society of Cincinnati, 123; of New York, 200
Fraser, Douglas A., 52
Free Enquirer, 164
Free speech fights, 64–65, 97
French-Canadians, 182
French Revolution, 86, 117
Frick, Henry C., 48, 114
Fuller, Ida, 138
Fultz, David L., 183–84
Fur workers, 59–60, 66, 78, 79, 127, 169, 188, 190, 193
Fur Workers' Union, 59–60
Furniture workers, 126
Furniture Workers' National Union, 126

Gaines, Thomas, 110

Galaxy, 50
Gallatin, Albert, 142
Gangsters, 66
Garment workers, 14, 126, 127, 164, 167–68, 206
General Council, International Workingmen's Association, 87
General Electric Corporation, 61, 136, 174, 193, 201
General Electric Industrial Workers Union, 84, 154
General Motors Corporation, 48, 98, 134, 154, 172, 194, 211
General strike, 23, 66, 73, 162, 163
General Trades Union of New York City, 57
George, Henry, 40
Georgia, 57, 72, 158, 176
German-Americans, 41, 86, 104, 155–56, 182, 183, 185, 200
Germany, 89, 130
Germer, Adolph, 151, 173
Gibbons, Harold, 14
Giovannitti, Arturo, 32, 93, 169
Glass workers, 160
Gold, Ben, 32, 43, 59–60
Golden, John, 41
Gompers, Samuel, 12, 13, 48, 77, 96, 104, 105, 109, 121, 128, 130, 147, 167, 183, 187, 189, 195–96, 198, 209, 215
Gould, Jay, 87–88, 164
Government employees, 42, 76, 126, 127
Government ownership, 68
Government Printing Office, 141
Gowen, Franklin B., 92
Grainmen's Protective Union of New York City, 114
Grand Eight-Hour League, 74
Grand Labor Parade, 105, 106
Grandeson, Peter, 22
Grant, Ulysses S., 75
Grape boycott, 99
Gray, Samuel, 11
Great Depression, 136, 137, 187
"Great Migration," 24
Great Northern Railroad, 165
"Great Revolt, The," 43
"Great Vacation," 163
Greater New York Negro Labor Council, 28
Greeks, 86
Green, William, 86, 96–97, 99
Greenback Labor Party, 96, 107
Grievance procedure, 68
Guaranteed annual wage, 68–69
Guild Reporter, 105
Guilds, 69, 100
Guinier, Ewart, 28

Gutstadt, Herman, 12

"Hallelujah on the Bum," 111
Hanna, Mark, 193
Harlan County (Ky.), 31, 69–70, 134, 171–72, 176, 178
Harlan County, USA, 3
Harlan Miners Speak, 172
Harriman System Federation, 168
Harrisburg (Pa.), 124
Hart, Schaffner and Marx, 17, 133, 197
Hartopp, Mary, 208
Harvard University, 159
Hat finishers, 124
Hat Finishers' National Association, 124
"Hate strikes," 27, 28, 63
Hawes, Elizabeth, 212
Hawkins, Octavia, 29
Hayes, Rutherford B., 62, 140
Haymarket Affair, 57, 67, 88, 92, 117, 179
Haywood, William D. ("Big Bill"), 72, 109–10, 122, 141, 156, 198
Health and safety, 70–72
Health inspectors, 70
Heat strike, 177
Hebrew Actors' Union, 166
Hegner, Anton, 165
Heighton, William, 94, 102–3
Henderson, Donald, 7
Henry, Alice, 210
Hewitt, Abram S., 44
Hewitt, S. C., 102
High cost of living, 72
Highlander Folk School, 56
Hill, Joe, 93, 111, 141
Hillman, Sidney, 122, 127, 133, 140
Hillquit, Morris, 25
Hillstrom, Joseph. *See* Hill, Joe.
Hiring hall, 72
Hod Carriers' and Laborers' Association of Phildelphia, 22
Hodgson, James D., 30
Hoe and Company, 15
Hoffman, Frederick, 21, 70
"Hold the Fort," 111
Holden v. Hardy, 177
Holidays, 91–92, 94
Homestead, 114, 197
Homestead Mining Company, 70, 131
Homestead strike, 48, 159, 165
Hood, William R., 28
Hoover, Herbert, 52, 58
Hop Pickers General Strike Committee, 5–6
Hopkins, Velma, 172
Horton, Myles, 56
Hosiery workers, 80

Hospital workers, 134, 174, 175–76, 210
Hotel workers, 127
Hours of work, 72–80
House, Jonathan, 177
House carpenters, 100–101, 161
House painters, 124
House Un-American Activities Committee, 118–19
Housesmiths' Union, 47–48, 90
Housing, 70, 80–81
Houston, Charles, 28
Howard, Charles P., 133
Howard, Earl Dean, 17
Hull House, 209
"Hunger Demonstration," 111
Hylick, Mary, 208–9

Idaho, 49, 150, 186
Illinois, 62–63, 83, 131, 135, 140, 162, 195, 205, 214
Illinois Central Railroad, 168
Illinois Commission on Occupational Diseases, 131
Illinois Supreme Court, 42
Immigration and Labor, 82
Immigrants, 82–83; strikes by, 82
Imperial Valley Workers' Union, 6
Imprisonment, for debt, 188; of labor leaders, 5–6, 204
Incorporation of trade unions, 83
Indentured servants, 20
Independent labor party of Chicago, 107
Independent Order of Pickets, 139
Independent political action, 30, 95
Indiana, 44, 135, 151–52, 154, 155, 156, 201
Indianapolis, 156
Industrial accidents, 131
Industrial Brotherhood, 75
Industrial Congress of the United States, 13, 75, 83
Industrial hygiene, 70, 132
Industrial Relations Counsellors, Inc., 132
Industrial statistics, 83
Industrial Union Bulletin, 111
Industrial Union Councils, 60
Industrial Union Department, AFL-CIO, 134
Industrial Union Manifesto, 122
Industrial unionism, 30, 83–85, 122, 209, 210
Industrial Worker, 64, 105
Industrial Workers Club of Chicago, 67
Industrial Workers of the World (IWW), 5, 6, 24, 32, 38, 49, 52, 63, 64, 65, 77, 83, 88, 93, 94, 97, 105, 108, 109–10, 111, 112, 113, 114, 118, 122, 132, 133, 138, 146, 150, 151–52, 154, 167, 168, 170–71, 186, 192, 197, 198, 210; General Executive Board, 189, 198
Injunctions, 85–86, 183, 216
Insurance, 86

Insurance Workers of America, 18
International alliance of labor, 86–87
International Association of Bridge and Structural Iron Workers, 48, 49, 118, 127, 196
International Association of Fur Workers, 127
International Association of Machinists, 23, 42, 211; bank of, 91
International Association of Unemployed, 184
International Brotherhood of Bookbinders, 181–82
International Brotherhood of Teamsters, 127, 138–39
International Brotherhood of Teamsters, Chauffeurs, Warehousemen, and Helpers, 123
International Confederation of Free Trade Unions, 12, 99
International Federation of Trade Unions, 88
International Fishermen and Allied Workers, 12, 60
International Fur and Leather Workers' Union, 10, 12, 27, 68
International Fur Workers, 32, 43
International Glove Workers' Union, 209, 210
International Labor Bureau, 89
International Labor Day, 76
International Labor Organization, 89
International labor solidarity, 86–89, 151
International Ladies' Garment Workers' Union (ILGWU), 55, 66, 85, 86, 113, 127, 133, 167–68, 170, 208, 213
International Longshoreman's Association, 197
International Longshoreman's and Warehousemen's Union, 14, 32, 60, 112, 129
International Machinists' Association, 178
International Molders' Union of North America, 16, 137
International Pressmen and Assistants' Union, 181–82
International Seamen's Union, 169, 171, 200
International Secretariat, 88
International Trade Union Educational League, 97
International Timber Workers, 110
International Typographical Union, 32, 101, 114, 124, 137, 167, 181–82, 183
International Union of Coopers, 126
International Union of Electrical, Radio, and Machine Workers (IUE), 144, 212–13
International Union of Machinists, 67
International Union of Mine, Mill, and Smelter Workers, 11, 60, 128, 133, 215
International Workingmen's Association, 87
Interstate Commerce Commission, 16
Iowa, 84
Ireland, 122
Irish-Americans, 162, 182
"Iron Batallions," 138
Iron Molders' International Union, 42, 47

Iron workers, 9, 125, 162, 182, 211
Italians, 166, 209
Italy, 166
IWW. *See* Industrial Workers of the World

J. P. Stevens and Company, 3, 32–33, 134, 158, 194
Jackson, Andrew, 40, 62, 140
Japan, 32, 130
Japanese, 5, 83
Jersey Standard Oil Company, 190
Jewish workers, 31, 32, 41, 82, 92, 105, 127, 151, 164, 209
Jewish Workingmen's Union, 82
Jim Crow unionism, 23–24, 29
"Joan of Arc" Assembly, 207
Job control, 90
"Job Delegate" system, 6, 132
Job training, 211
John Swinton's Paper, 105
Johnson, Andrew, 74
Johnson, Ban, 168–69
Johnson, Gloria, 212–13
Johnson, Hiram, 6
Johnson, Lyndon B., 14
Joint Board Fur Workers' Union, 59–60
Joint Board of Cloak, Skirt, and Reefers Makers' Union, 86
Jones, Mother Mary Harris, 36, 38, 89, 100, 102, 116, 191, 207
Jones, Reverend Jesse H., 110–11
Jones Speedometer v. International Machinists' Association, 195
Jordan, Crystal Lee, 3
Journeymen Barbers' Union, 215
Journeymen Cordwainers' Society, 45–46; of Baltimore, 161; of New York City, 42, 202; of Philadelphia, 151
Journeymen Cutters' Association of the United States and Canada, 14
Journeymen Mechanics' Advocate, 103
Journeymen Molders' Union Foundry, 47
Journeymen printers, 5
Journeymen Printers of Great Britain, 151
Journeymen Tailors' National Union, 126
Judges, 90
Junior Sons of '76, 146
Jurisdiction, 90
Jurisdictional disputes, 90

Kansas, 156, 199
Kansas City, 173, 208
Kearney, Denis, 12
Keating-Owen Law, 37
Kehew, Mary Morton, 209
Kelley, Florence, 76

Kennedy, Robert F., 14
Kenney, Mary E., 207
Kentucky, 107, 120, 134, 171–72, 176, 192–93, 213
Kidnapping, 92–93
Killings, of strikers, 6–7, 23, 62, 67, 115–16, 120, 150, 163, 169, 173; of unemployed, 187; of union members, 110
King, Coretta Scott, 134
King, Mackenzie, 44
King, Martin Luther, Jr., 29, 172, 173, 174
Knapp, Judge Dennis R., 90
Knights of Labor, 9, 22–23, 31, 38, 39, 46, 47, 52, 55, 57, 83, 87–88, 96, 106, 107, 111, 121, 122, 140, 164, 205–6, 207
Knights of St. Crispin, 189
Kober, Dr. George M., 70
Kopple, Barbara, 3
Korean War, 122
Kuhn, Bowie, 144

La Unión de Trabajadores del Valle Imperial, 6
Labor: conditions in, 91; emancipation day for, 178; frame-ups in, 92–93; jury for, 94; martyrs for, 67; memorial day for, 100; novels about, 40, 45, 50; organizations for, 100–102; organizers for, 102; parades for, 105–6; solidarity in, 109–110; speeches on, 112; spies for, 112; standards in, 112–13; unity in, 21
Labor, 105
Labor Committee for ERA, 59
Labor Correspondence Bureau, 200
Labor Leadership Assembly for Peace, 14
Labor-Management Relations Act. *See* Taft-Hartley Act
Labor-Populists, 62
Labor Reform Party, 106–7
Labor Standard, 110–11
"Labor Temple," 11
Labour for Labour Association of Philadelphia, 47
Lackawanna, (N.Y.) 173
"Ladies' Anti-Beef Trust Association," 31
Ladies' Shoe Binders of Lynn, 202
LaFollette, Philip, 45
LaFollette, Robert M., 62, 107
LaFollette Committee, 45
LaFollette Seamen's Act, 152–53
LaGuardia, Fiorello H., 173
Land reform, 113
Landrum-Griffin Act, 20, 32
Lanham, Fritz, 211
Lanham Act, 35
Laski, Harold J., 55
Lassalle, Ferdinand, 156
Lathrop, Julia Clifford, 37
"Lattimer Massacre," 43, 63–64, 115–16

Laundresses, 154
Laundry workers, 47, 154
Lawrence (Mass.), 3, 40, 41, 138
Lawrence strike, 38, 50, 93, 138, 154, 168
Lawyers, 94
League for Political Action, 99
League of Universal Brotherhood, 13
Leather workers, 126
Legalization, of trade unions, 183
Legislation, 99–100
Lehr and Wehr Verein, 153
Leiserson, William, 18
Lemlich, Clara, 167–68
Lenin, V. I., 89
Lepke-Gurrah mob, 66
Letter carriers, 182
Lewis, Gussie, 205
Lewis, John L., 85, 97–98, 122, 133, 193, 194
Libel, 139
Liberalist, 104
Life and Labor, 210
Lincoln, Abraham, 113–14, 196
Lingg, Louis, 88
Literacy tests, 82
Lithographers' National Union, 124
Little, Frank H., 114
Little Red Song Book, The, 111
"Little Steel Formula," 201
Littlefield, Charles E., 109
Living wage, 201
Livingston, David, 14
Lloyd-LaFollette Act, 42, 147
Lobby, 100
Local 1199, Drug and Hospital Employees' Union, 134, 141, 174
Lochner v. New York, 76
Lockout, 114
"Loco-Foco" ticket, 139
Locomotive Engineers' Advocate, 144
Locomotive firemen, 126
Locomotive Firemen's Magazine, 9
Locomotive Mutual Life Insurance Association, 86
Lodge, John Davis, 4
London, Meyer, 187
London Company, 199
Longshoremen, 67
Longshoremen's Protective Union of Charleston, 22
Los Angeles, 6, 198
Los Angeles Dodgers, 18, 146
Louisiana, 22, 24, 104, 108, 109–10, 134
Louisville (Ky.), 107, 120
Louisville Courier, 27
Louisville and Nashville Railroad, 28
Lowell Factory Girls' Association, 202, 203
Lowell Female Labor Reform Association, 103, 203–4

Lowell (Mass.), 95
Lowell Union of Associationists, 95
Lowe v. Lawler, 195
Lucretia Mott Amendment. *See* Equal Rights Amendment
"Ludlow Massacre," 16, 100, 120
Lumber workers, 108
Lundeen Unemployment Insurance Bill, 191
Luther, Seth, 102, 103
Lynching, 114
Lynn (Mass.), 38, 105, 162, 192, 193
Lynn Central Labor Union, 209
Lynn Cordwainers' Union, 202

MacArthur, Douglas, 190
McBride, James, 96
McDonald, Mary 102
McDonnell, J. P., 105
McDowell, Mary, 209
McGlynn, Father Edward, 40
McGuire, Peter J., 92
Machinists' and Blacksmiths' Review, 125
Machinists' and Blacksmiths' Union, 104
McKees Rocks (Penn.), 167
McIlvaine, John, 110
McMahon, Thomas, 133
McManigal, Ortie, 48
McNally, David, 18, 46
McNamara, J. B., 48
McNamara, J. M., 48
McNamara case, 48, 94, 118
McNeill, George E., 12, 34
McParlan, James, 92, 112
M'Cready, B.W., 70, 131
McCusker, Marilyn, J., 4
Macy, V. Everitt, 36
Madar, Olga, 210
Madden, Joseph Warren, 147
Madden, Martin B., 197
Magazines, 116
"Magna Charta of the U. S. Labor Movement," 43, 147
Maguire, Matthew, 92
Maguire law, 152
Maine, 104, 149, 160
Male auxiliary, 203
Male-female unity, 202
Man, The, 104
Manford Act, 197
Manhattan Elevated Company, 192
March, Thomas, 44–45
"March of the Mill Children," 36, 38
March on Washington for Jobs and an End to Discrimination against Negroes (1941), 26–27, 61; for Jobs and Freedom (1963), 29
Marine Firemen's Union, 23

Marine Transport Workers, 24
Marine Workers' Industrial Union, 133
Maritime Federation of the Pacific, 10
Martyr to His Cause, A, 118
Marx, Karl, 41, 43, 156
Marxism, 155–56
Marxists, 182
Maryland, 16, 62, 124
Masons, 124
Mass parades, 8
Massachusetts, 16, 35–36, 37, 54, 58, 69, 70, 73, 74, 75, 91, 95, 100, 106, 117, 129, 131, 137, 138, 140, 162, 163, 185, 187, 199, 201, 202, 204
Massachusetts Bay Colony, 199
Massachusetts Bureau of Labor, 34
Massachusetts House Document No. 153, 70
Massachusetts Labor Reform party, 106
Massachusetts State Board of Health, 70
Massacres, 115–16
Matles, James J., 128
Maurer, James H., 13
Maverick, Sam, 11
May Day, 116–17, 165
Mazey, Emil, 14
Meany, George, 11, 29, 98–99
Meat cutters, 127
Mechanic, The, 107
Mechanics Education Society, 172
Mechanics' Free Press, 10, 54, 94, 104, 114
Mechanics' lien laws, 106
Mechanics' Press, 104
Mechanics' Union, 139
Mechanics' Union of Trade Associations, 10, 41, 94, 103, 106, 119
Medical Society of New York, 70
Medicare, 132
Membership, 121, 123, 124, 127, 128, 129, 166, 196
Memorial Day Massacre, 116
Memphis, 175
Men's clothing workers, 127, 133, 167, 168, 169
Merchants' and Manufacturers' Association of Los Angeles, 11
Merganthaler linotype machine, 115
Messenger, The, 25
Messenger boys, 164
Messersmith, Andy, 18, 146
Metal Trades Department, 52
Mexican-Americans, 5, 6, 99, 117, 119, 174, 178
Mexican war, 13
Mexico, 117
Michigan, 140, 149, 154, 176, 199, 210
Midwest Conference of Union Women, 212
Militia, 23, 38, 106, 115–16, 117, 159

Miller, Arnold R., 145, 176
Miller, Joyce, 213
Miller, Reverend George Frazier, 25
Miller, William A., 141
Milwaukee, 15, 26, 116, 183, 198
Mine inspection law, 99
Mine, Mill and Smelter Workers' Union, 112, 119
Miners (coal), 19, 43, 62, 63, 64, 71, 102, 111–14, 115–16, 125, 126, 128, 135, 162, 163, 171, 181, 182, 192; (copper), 128, 166, 183
Miners' and Laborers' Benevolent Association, 179
"Miners Day," 94
Miners for Democracy, 145
Miners' National Association, 126
Minimum wage, 117–18
Minimum Wage Commission, 117
Minimum wage law, 199
Mining Department, 52
Minneapolis, 64, 80, 138–39, 198
Minneapolis Central Labor Union, 80
Minnesota, 154, 162, 176, 210, 214
Missouri, 140
Missouri State Federation of Labor, 140
Mitchell, John, 48, 140
Mitten Plan, 44
Model unemployment insurance plan, 187–88
Mohawk Valley Formula, 132–33
Molders' Union, 41
Molly Maguires, 92, 112
Montana, 37, 64, 137, 192, 199, 214
Montgomery Ward, 63
Montreal, 39–40
Montreal Expos, 18, 146
Mooney, Thomas J., 88–89, 93
Mooney-Billings case, 93
Moore, Ely, 40, 44, 57, 107, 112
Morgan, J. P., 167
Morris, William, 88
Morrison, Frank, 48
"Mortality from Consumption in Dusty Trades," 70
Mother Jones, 116
Motion pictures, 118–19
"Moving picket line," 138
Moyer, Charles H., 92–93, 114
Mullaney, Kate, 47, 205
Murphy, May, 208
Murray, Philip, 68–69, 98, 122, 129, 134
Musical Mutual Protective Union, 165
Musicians, 165, 166
Musicians' Union, 108
Muste, Reverend A. J., 40, 55–56, 88
Myers, Isaac, 21, 22, 95

Nailers' Union, 180
Nashville, 124

National Agricultural Workers' Union, 99
National Association for the Promotion of Labor Unionism among Negroes, 25
National Association of Letter Carriers, 126
National Association of Machinists, 23
National Association of Manufacturers, 132, 214
National Association of Post Office Clerks, 126
National Bituminous Coal Wage Agreement, 194
National Brotherhood of America, 25
National Building Trades Council of America, 133
National Child Labor Committee, 36
National Civic Federation, 195–96
National Commission on Working Women, 213
National Committee of Correspondence and Action, 156
National Committee for the Defense of Political Prisoners, 171–72
National Committee for the Organizing of the Iron and Steel Industry, 77, 171
National Conference on Industrial Diseases, 131
National Consumers' League, 31
National Cooperative Association of Journeymen Cordwainers, 101, 123–24
National Cotton Mule Spinners' Association, 124–25
National Defense Advisory Commission, 210
National employment bureau, 186
National Endowment for the Humanities, 50
National Farm Workers' Association, 7, 8, 99
National Federation of Post Office Clerks, 127
National Federation of the Blind, 134–35
National Forge of the Sons of Vulcan, 125
National Guard, 120, 139, 159, 176
National Hunger March, 188, 190
National Industrial Recovery Act, 17, 118, 149
National Labor Board, 17
National Labor Federations, 120–23
National Labor organizations, 101
National Labor Relations Act, 149
National Labor Relations Board, 12, 149, 180
National Labor Union, 21, 22, 34, 51, 58, 74, 83, 87, 95, 100, 102, 106–7, 121, 202, 204, 205
National Laborer, 54, 104
National Maritime Union, 128–29
National Mediation Board, 17–18, 26
National Mediation Defense Board, 99
National Miners' Union, 53, 97, 169
National Molders' Union, 95
National Negro Congress, 26
National Negro Labor Council, 28–29
National Organization of Women (NOW), 33, 213
National Organization of Women's Urban Woman Project, 213
National Organizing Committee of Hospital and Nursing Home Employees, 134
National Political Action Committee, 142

National Press Club, 128
National Progressive Union, 23
National Protective Association, 124
National Reform Association, 113
National Textile Workers' Union, 97, 137, 156
National Trade Unions, 123–29
National Trades' Union, 44, 86–87, 101, 107, 120
National Typographical Society, 124
National Unemployed Leagues, 190
National Union of Brewers of the United States, 126
National Union of Building Trades, 124
National Union of Horseshoers, 126
National Union of Hospital and Health Care Employees, 50
National Union of Hospital and Nursing Home Employees, 175–76
National Union of Iron Molders, 102, 125
National Union of Machinists and Blacksmiths, 74, 114, 125
National Union of Marine Cooks and Stewards, 12, 60
National Union of Morocco Dressers, 126
National Union of Painters, 126
National Union of Ship Carpenters and Caulkers, 125
National Union of Silver Platers, 124
National Union of Telegraphers, 126
National Union of United Brewery Workmen of the United States, 126
National Urban League, 28
National War Labor Board, 99, 211
National Woman's Party, 59
National Women's Trade Union League, 209
National Workers' Educational Conference, 56
Navy Department, 79
Navy Yard, 73
Nazi Germany, 32, 130, 194
Needle, Oscar, 92
Needle Trades Workers' Industrial Union, 79, 97, 190
Negro American Labor Alliance, 29
Negro American Labor Council, 14, 29
Negro Labor Committee, 26
Negro slavery, 129
Negro suffrage, 178
Nestor, Agnes, 209, 210
Nevada, 63, 137
New England, 138
New England Artisan, 102, 104
New England Association of Farmers, Mechanics and Other Workingmen, 61, 91, 103, 146
New England Farmer and Mechanic, 104
New England Workingmen's Association, 95, 129, 182, 203
New Hampshire, 73

New Harmony, 155
New Haven, 113–14
New Jersey, 70, 73, 92, 124, 147, 161, 169, 183, 193
New Mexico, 119
New Orleans, 23, 24, 66, 74, 104, 106, 124, 157, 162, 182
New Orleans Central Labor Union, 24
New Orleans Central Trades and Labor Assembly, 106
New Republic, The, 89
Newark Ledger, 170
New York Call, 25
New York Central Labor Council, 174
New York Central Labor Union, 207, 208
New York City, 19, 21, 31, 33, 40–43, 44–49, 55, 57, 58–59, 70, 73, 78, 80, 82–83, 86–87, 90–93, 98–101, 104–5, 107, 113, 114, 120, 124, 126–28, 139–40, 142, 143, 151, 154–55, 160–63, 173, 174–75, 176, 177, 179, 182, 183, 184, 185, 187, 192, 195, 198, 200, 202, 204, 208, 209, 211
New York City Central Federated Union, 67
New York City Central Trades and Labor Assembly, 99
New York Clothing Manufacturers' Association, 167
New York Compositors' Union, 87
New York *Evening Post,* 44
New York *Evening World,* 164
New York General Trades' Union, 41, 87, 90
New York Guild of Newspapermen and Women, 184
New York Hat Finishers' Protective Society, 15
New York Journeymen Tailors, 46
New York, New Haven and Hartford Railway, 17
New York Operative Bakers' Union, 72
New York Society of Printers, 200
New York (State), 16, 51, 52, 61, 71, 74, 75, 86, 92, 104, 139, 149, 173, 174, 186, 214
New York State Assembly, 139
New York State Charity Aid Association, 36
New York State Commission Against Discrimination, 52
New York State Federation of Labor, 99
New York *Sun,* 105, 164
New York Symphony Orchestra, 165
New York Times, 38, 39, 71, 72, 89, 163, 164, 189
New York Tribune, 31, 105, 155
New York Typographical Society, 83, 196
New York Waterfront Commission, 213
New York Weavers' Society, 90
New York *Weekly Journal,* 202
New York Working Men's Party, 57
New York Working Women's Protective Association, 204

New York Working Women's Society, 207
New York Yankees, 168–69
New York Yiddish Volkszeitung, 105
New Zealand, 122
Newsboys, 164
Newspaper Guild, 105, 172, 193
Newspaper workers, 169
Newspapers, 21, 54, 95, 103–5
Night work, 129
Nixon, Richard M., 14, 71, 176
"No raiding" agreement, 144
Nockels, Edward N., 108
Noise at work, 129–30
Non-Partisan League, 107, 140
Norma Rae, 3
Norris-LaGuardia Act, 86, 114
North Carolina, 32–33, 97, 158, 174
North Carolina Federation of Labor, 158
North Dakota, 70, 131
Northrup, Herbert, 27
Norton, George L., 23
No-strike agreement, 176
No-strike pledge, 129–30

Occupational diseases, 131
Occupational health hazards, 70
Occupational Safety and Health Administration (OSHA), 4, 71
Office of Defense Mobilization, 122
Ohio, 76, 96–97, 104, 106–7, 112, 190, 192–93, 204
Oil, Chemical and Atomic Workers' International Union, 71, 72
Oil Workers, 170
Oil Workers' Industrial Union, 79, 133
Oklahoma, 7
Older Americans Act, 132
Older workers, 52, 132
Oliver, Henry Kemble, 34
Oliver, Lynn, 214
Omaha, 198
"On the Influence of Trades, Professions and Occupations . . . ," 131, 158
"On the job strike," 77, 78
"Open mouth" sabotage, 132
Open shop, 132, 172
Open-shop drive, 11
Operation Dixie, 158
Oppenheim, James, 50, 155
Order of Railroad Telegraphers, 23
Order of Sovereigns of Industry, 47
Oregon, 92, 117, 118, 167
Organized Labor and the Negro, 27
Organizing, 132–35
Other Side, The, 45, 50
Otis, Harrison Gray, 48

Our Own Club, 153
Outlaw strikes, 135
Owen, Chandler, 25
Owen, Robert, 155

Packinghouse workers, 167
Pageant of the Paterson Strike, 113
Paid holidays, 136
Paid vacations, 136
Painters, 126
Painters' National Union, 125
Pan-American Federation of Labor, 89
Pan-American Labor Conference, 89
Para-professional Teacher Education Program, 139
Paris, 86, 117
Paris Conference on Unemployment, 186
Parker, Judge John, J., 179
Parks, Sam, 47
Parry, David M., 132
Parsons, Albert R., 67, 88
Parsons, Lucy, 66–67
Parties, 106–7
Passaic (N.J.), 39, 118, 169
Passaic Textile Strike, The, 118
PATCO. *See* Professional Air Traffic Controllers Organization.
Patents, 70
Paterson *Labor Standard*, 105
Paterson (N.J.), 37–38, 113, 159–60, 161
Paterson strike, 113, 159–60
Patriotic Society, 11–12
Pawtucket (R.I.), 161, 202
Pemberton Mill, 3
Pennsylvania, 16, 35–36, 43, 54, 57, 62, 90, 95, 98, 105, 106, 115–16, 121, 124, 137, 142, 155, 159, 165, 167, 178, 192–93, 194, 197, 199, 213
Pennsylvania Mercury and Universal Advertiser, 4
Pennsylvania Railroad, 144
Pennsylvania State Federation of Labor, 13, 67
Pensions, 136–38
"People's Institute of Civics, The," 55
Perkins, Frances, 52, 202
Petitions, 72, 107–8, 73
Petrograd, 88–89
Pettibone, George, 92
Philadelphia, 4, 13, 21, 24, 28, 40, 42, 44, 45, 47, 54, 61, 62, 66, 67, 69, 72, 73, 74, 80, 94, 96, 100–103, 109–10, 120–21, 124–27, 133–34, 147, 149, 151, 156, 159, 160–61, 162, 168, 181, 185, 197, 202, 206
Philadelphia and Reading Railway, 166
Philadelphia Area Project on Occupational Safety and Health (PHILAPOSH), 150
Philadelphia Athletics, 168–69
Philadelphia Aurora, 151

Philadelphia Cordwainers' Society, 94, 147
Philadelphia *Public Record*, 91
Philadelphia Rapid Transit Company, 44
Philadelphia *Record*, 193
Philadelphia Social Science Association, 15
Philadelphia Transit Company, 67
Philadelphia Transport Company Employees' Union, 28
Philadelphia Typographical Society, 83, 185, 200
Philco of Philadelphia, 133, 197
Phillips, Thomas, 91
Philrod Fishing Club, 133
Picketing, 138–39
Pinchot, Mrs. Gifford, 39
Pinkertons, 114, 153, 159, 165
Pittsburgh, 15, 44, 73, 90, 106, 121, 122, 144, 154, 162, 183, 198, 203, 204, 214
Pittsburgh Survey, 4
"Plank 10," 68
Plasterers, 124
Plasterers' National Union, 125
Players' Association, 114, 138
Players' Fraternity, 181–82
Plumb Plan, 68
Plumbers, 124
Plymouth Colony, 136
Poetry, 93
Poets, 46
Police, 171, 184, 189, 190
Polish workers, 60
Political Action, 139–40
Political Action Committee (PAC), 140
Political Action News, 140
Political League, 102
Political prisoners, strikes for release of, 169, 171
Pope Motor Company, 167
Popular Party, 139
Populists, 159
Portland (Oregon), 167, 198
Postal workers, 75, 176
Potash, Irving, 66
Pound, Roscoe, 55
Powderly, Terence V., 23, 96
Powell, William P., 21, 182
Practical Program for the Prevention of Unemployment in America, A, 186
Preferential union shop, 197
Preparedness Day parade, 93
Preparedness rally, 88–89
Presidents, 74, 113–14
Press, 21, 54, 95, 102–4
Pressed Steel Car Company, 64, 167
Pressmen, 171
Prevailing wage, 199
Printers, 42, 76–77, 114, 160–61, 171, 177, 184
Printing industry, 76–77

Printing pressmen, 85
Prison, formation of union in, 183
Prison labor, 107
Procter and Gamble, 68
Professional Air Traffic Controllers Organization, 9, 142
Profit-sharing, 142
Progressive Cigar Makers' Union, 52
Progressive Farmer-Labor Party, 62
Proletarierbund, 155
Protective Association, 86
Protocol of Peace, 143
Public Contracts Act, 112
Public employees, 60, 67–68, 73, 134, 141, 147, 162, 175
Public labor exchange, 185
Public works, 185, 186, 188
Pullman Company, 26, 31
Pullman strike, 16, 52, 62–63, 93, 141, 166
Punch, John, 20
Putnam, Mary Kellogg, 204

Quill, Michael, 175
Quota law, 83

R. J. Reynolds Tobacco Company, 174
Race riots, 27
Racism, 32, 158, 179
Radio and Allied Trades National Labor Council, 128
Radio and Television Workers' Federal Labor Union, 190
Radio Corporation of America, 17
Radio industry, 197
Radio stations, 108
Radio workers, 128
Rag pickers, 184
Raiding, 144
Raids, 198
Railroad Brotherhoods, 62, 68, 86, 125, 126, 144, 196, 200–201, 215
Railroad Labor Act, 18
Railroad Labor Board, 144
Railroad strike of 1877, 107, 163
Railroad workers, 76, 77, 125, 126, 135, 162, 164–66, 170, 182, 196, 201–2
Railway Clerks, 17
Railway Men's Benevolent Association, 24
Ralph Nader's Study Group on Disease and Injury on the Job, 71
Randolph, A. Philip, 14, 25–26, 27, 29, 61, 174
Rank and file, 144–45, 177
Reade, Charles, 50
Reading Convention, 121
Reading Railroad Company, 92
Reagan, Ronald, 4, 91, 110, 142

"Reaganomics," 110
Recall, 146
Red Cross, 189
Reed, John, 113
Regional organizations, 146
"Remember Ludlow," 116
Remington Rand Company, 132–33
Reparations for discrimination, 146
Republic Steel Company, 116
Republican Party, 24, 45, 113–14, 181, 214
Republik der Arbeiter, 104
"Reserve Clause," 18, 146
Restaurant workers, 127
Restriction of production, 146
Restriction on immigration, 82–83
Retail Kosher Butchers' Union, 32
Retired Members Homes, 147
Reuther, Walter, 14, 29, 98, 134
Revenue Act of 1919, 37
Rhode Island, 161
Richards, Kate, 208
Richmond Soap Factory, 47
Richmond (Va.), 22–23, 124, 162
Rickert, T. A., 169
Right to belong to a union, 147–49
"Right to Know" laws, 149–50
"Right-to-work" laws, 150, 181
Robinson, Cleveland, 29
Roche, Josephine A., 192
Rochester (N.Y.), 41, 67
Rockefeller, John D., Jr., 120, 132, 192
Rockefeller Employee Representation Plan, 44
Rodney, Caesar A., 94
Rogers, Elizabeth, 206
Rogers, Peet and Company, 142
"Rolling strike," 163
Rolph, James, 178
Rome, Harold, 113
Roosevelt, Franklin D., 27, 28, 45, 52, 61, 63, 79, 98, 141–42, 149, 174, 190, 201, 202
Roosevelt, Theodore, 36, 37, 63, 109, 140, 214
Root, Elihu, 167, 198
Rosecrans, William, 62
Rubber workers, 169, 172–73
Rumania, 151
Rumanian Syndicalist General Commission, 151
Rund, Neil D., 191
Rushton Mining Company, 14
Russia. See also Soviet Union, 88, 197
Russian-American Industrial Corporation, 89
Russian-Jewish Workers' Farein, 82
"Rustling Card," 150
Ryan, Frank, 49
Ryan, Joseph P., 197

Sacco, Nicola, 93

Sacco-Vanzetti case, 93
Sacramento, 49
Sadlowski, Edward, 177
Sailors, 163
Sailors' Union of the Pacific, 152
St. Louis, 14, 23, 65, 163, 167, 205
St. Petersburg, 88
Salesmen, 165
Salt of the Earth, 18
San Francisco, 10, 67, 74, 84–85, 88–89, 93, 138, 185, 195, 198
San Francisco Trades' Assembly, 41
San Jose, 59
Sargent, Frank P., 9
Sawmill workers, 167
Scabs, 151–52
Schenectady (N.Y.), 84, 193
Schlossberg, Joseph, 25, 127
Schneiderman, Rose, 210
Schoen, Jacob, 82
School children, 164–65
Schouler, William, 204
Schuylkill County Anthracite Board of Trade, 191
Schwab, Justus, 92
Schwartz, Sarina, 207
"Scientific management," 152
Scranton, 96
Scranton Declaration, 84
Screen Actors' Guild, 4, 128, 142
Screwmen's Benevolent Association of New Orleans, 182
Seamen, 11, 21, 149, 152–53, 160, 182
Seattle, 55, 58, 67, 160, 198
Seattle Central Labor Council, 100, 188
Seattle Daily Times, 100
Seattle Metal Trades, 94
Seattle Newsboys Union, 39
Second Independence Day, 66
Second International, 76, 117
Secrecy, 121
Section 7(a), 149
Segregation, 28
Seigrist, Sadie, 207
Self-defense, 153
Seniority, 30
Servants, 101, 208
Seven-hour day, 188
Sewing Girls' Union of Chicago, 205
Sexual harassment, 214
Share-the-work Committee, 190
Shaw, George Bernard, 88
Shaw, Judge Lemuel, 46
Sherman Anti-Trust Act, 13, 42–43, 85, 173, 195
Ship carpenters, 73, 74, 162
Ship Carpenters' and Caulkers' International Union, 102

Ship caulkers, 47, 73
Shoe workers, 106, 125, 162, 192, 197
"Shop Management," 152
"Silent Defense," 49
"Silent demonstration," 138
Simpson, Stephen, 57
Siney, John, 126
"Singing strike," 168
"Sit Down," 112
Sit-down strikes, 7, 112, 153–54, 162, 172–73
Six-hour day, 78, 188, 189
Skeffington, Harry J., 206
Skidmore, Thomas, 114
Slave labor, 162
Slave revolts, 20
Slavery, 162
Slaves, 20
Sliding wage scale, 200
Sloan, Janet, 4
Slogans, 154–55, 175, 176, 181, 187
Smith, Ferdinand, 129
Smith Act, 155
Smith-Connolly Act, 45
Social Democracy, 156
Social Security Act, 138
Socialism, 155–57
Socialist Labor Party, 52, 82, 156
Socialist Party of America, 45, 88, 97, 100, 156
Socialist Trades and Labor Alliance, 52
Socialist Workers' Party, 155
Socialists, 25, 32, 86, 94, 153, 188
Society for the Diffusion of Knowledge Among the Working Classes, 54
Sojourner Truth Houses, 27
Solidarity, 105
"Solidarity Day," 110
"Solidarity Forever," 111–12
Songs, 7–8
Song writers, 158
Sons of Liberty, 11, 30–31, 202
Sons of Vulcan, 15, 182, 200
Sorge, Friedrich A., 87
South, 112, 134, 157–58, 162, 175–76, 182
South Carolina, 104, 160
Southern Christian Leadership Conference, 175–76
Southern Confederacy of Labor, 157
Southern Free Press, 104
Southern Industrial Conference, 158
Southern Labor Conference, 158–59
Southern Negro Youth Congress, 26
Southern organizing campaign, 158
Southern Summer School for Women Workers, 158
Southern Tenant Farmers' Union, 7, 158
Soviet Union, 30, 89
Sperry, Howard, 67
Spies, August, 88

Spies et al. v. The People, 179
Spirit of the Age, 104
Spokane (Wash.), 64–65, 105, 198
Springfield (Mass.), 58
Spry, William, 93, 141
Standard Oil Company, 44, 170
Standard Steel Works, 151–52
State Factory Investigation Commissions, 71
State Labor Bureaus, 70
Steamfitters' Helpers' Union of Chicago, 197
Steel industry, 78
Steel workers, 9, 126, 166, 169, 171, 173, 174
Steel Workers' Organizing Committee, 98, 134, 159, 193
Steele, Bester Williams, 28
Steffens, Lincoln, 48
Stephens, Uriah S., 83, 96, 121
Stepp, Marc, 71–72
Sterling, Mary, 206
Steward, Ira, 74
Stonecutters, 124, 200
"Storm the Fort ye Knights," 111
Stove Molders' Union, 181
Strasser, Adolph, 96, 183
Street car workers, 67, 127, 163, 169
Streeter, A. J., 107
Strike ban, 177
Strike benefits, 4, 159, 177
Strike fund, 177
Strike relief, 178
Strikebreakers, 142, 158, 205
Strikebreaking, 140, 159–60
Strikers, killing of, 6–7
Strikes. *See* pp. 160–77
Strong, Sidney, 55
Structural Building Trades' Alliance, 33
Structural iron workers, 127
Suffrage, 178
Sugar, Maurice, 112, 154
Sugar Beet and Farm Laborers' Union, 5
Sugar workers, 22, 134
Suhr, Herman D., 5–6
Sun Shipbuilding and Dry Dock Company, 4
Sunday work, 179
Supreme Court of the United States, 28, 30, 37, 42–43, 48, 76–77, 86, 118, 146, 149, 152, 173, 174, 179, 195, 199, 215, 216
Swank, Lizzie, 206
"Sweating system," 179
Sweden, 32, 88, 93
Swinton, John, 105
Sylvania (Penn.), 155
Sylvis, William H., 51, 95, 100, 102, 125, 205
Sympathy strike, 161
Syndicalist League of North America, 97

Syndicalist Militant Minority League, 30
"Syracuse Agreement," 179

Taft, William Howard, 51, 70, 131, 141, 148
Taft-Hartley Act, 12, 13, 42, 180–81
Tailors, 126, 163
Tampa, 49
Tannenbaum, Frank, 186
Taylor, Frederick W., 152
Taylor, Myron C., 193
Teachers, 128, 139, 174–75
Teachers' Union, 188
Teagle, Walter C., 190
Team Drivers' International Union, 127
Teamsters, 32, 95, 108, 127
Telegraph operators, 95, 164
Telegraphers, 126
Telephone operators, 170
Tenement house system, 163
Ten-Hour Circular, 72
Ten-hour day, 66, 72, 73, 74, 102, 161, 202, 204
Ten-hour laws, 73, 74, 75
Tennessee, 72, 158, 192–93
Tent colonies, 120
Texas, 197, 211
Texas State Federation of Labor, 158
Textile workers, 118, 123–24, 138, 162, 163, 192, 194–95, 203, 216
Textile Workers' Organizing Committee, 134
Textile Workers' Union of America, 11, 134, 158
Theater, 113
Theiss, George, 31
Third Avenue Railroad Company, 165
Thirty-hour week, 78–80
Thomason, Raymond E., 56
Thompson, Ernest, 29
"Thousand mile picket line," 138
Thursdays Till Nine, 113
Tikas, Louis, 116
Title VII of the Civil Rights Act of 1964, 41–42
"To the Journeymen Curriers of All Parts of the Union," 151
Tobacco workers, 26, 27–28
Toledo, 139, 167
Tompkins Square riot, 185
Toronto, 64, 127
Townsend, Dr. Francis, 137
Townsend Plan, 137
Trade agreements, 181–82
Trade Union College, 55
Trade Union Conference for the Relief of the Unemployed, 185
Trade Union Educational League, 30, 53, 59, 97, 144, 171
Trade Union Leadership Council, 29

Trade Union Unity League, 97, 133, 188, 189, 190
Trade unions, 112, 182–84
Trades and Central Labor Union of New York City, 41
Trades' Assembly of Rochester, New York, 41
Trainmen, 182
Transit workers, 67
Transport Workers' Union, 175
Transportation Act of 1920, 68
Traveling cards, 184
Treason, prosecution of strikers for, 48, 149
Tredegar Iron Works, 162
Trenton, 124
Trevellick, Richard F., 87, 102
Triangle Fire, 4, 71
Triangle Waist Company, 4, 71
Troy Collar Laundry Union, 47
Troy Cooperative Collar Company, 147
Troy Cooperative Iron-Founders' Association, 47
Troy (N.Y.), 47, 165, 207
Troy Trades' Assembly, 47
Truman, Harry S, 79, 174, 180, 181, 201
Turner, Henry C., 52
Twenty-five-hour week, 79
Twenty-four-hour shift, 171
Two-tiered dues policy, 4
Typographical Association of New York, 151
Typographical Society of Philadelphia, 159
Typographical Union, 31, 105, 133, 175, 185, 205

"Undesirable Citizens," 141
Unemployed, 111, 139, 155, 185–91
Unemployed Council of Greater New York, 187
Unemployed Councils, 188, 189
Unemployed meetings, 185
Unemployment Compensation plan, 184
Unemployment Conference, 186
Unemployment Insurance, 145, 185–91
Uniform wage scale, 200
Union Advocate, The, 105
Union Building and Loan Association of Minneapolis, 80
Union cemetery, 191
Union contracts, 191
Union label, 195
Union Label Department, 195
Union Labor Advocate, 210
Union Labor party, 107
Union liability, 195
Union membership, 196, 210, 212
Union Miners Cemetery, 191
Union officers, 196–97
Union Printer, 105
Union Printers' Home, 147

Union shop, 197
Union Soup Line, 197
Union-sponsored housing projects, 80
Union Trade Society of Journeymen Tailors of New York City, 20
United Airlines, 8
United Association of Plumbers and Steam Fitters of the United States and Canada, 99
United Association of Railway Employees, 135
United Automobile Workers of America (UAW), 14, 29, 48, 71, 79–80, 89, 98, 112, 123, 128, 134, 154, 173, 177, 194, 211, 212, 213
United Brotherhood of Railway Employees, 84
United Cannery, Agricultural Packing and Allied Workers, CIO, 7
United Electrical and Radio Workers of America, 10, 128
United Electrical, Radio and Machine Workers of America (UE), 10, 12, 29, 60, 61, 128, 136, 193, 211, 212
United Farm Equipment Workers, 12, 60
United Farm Workers' Organizing Committee, AFL-CIO, 89
United Federation of Teachers, 174–75
United Garment Workers, 9, 17, 82, 126, 128, 168, 169
United German Trades, 183
United Hatters, Cap and Millinery Workers, 133, 195
United Hatters of North America, 31
United Hebrew Trades, 41, 82, 88, 166
United Labor party, 40, 107
United Men and Women's Trading Society of Baltimore, 182
United Mine Workers of America (UMW), 3, 16, 23, 40, 44, 51, 52, 53, 62, 64, 83, 84, 90, 96–97, 115–16, 120, 128, 133, 134, 135, 145, 166, 171, 173–74, 176, 179, 189, 191, 192, 195
United Office and Professional Workers, 12, 60
United Order of Railway Employees, 19
United Packinghouse Workers of America, 11
United Public Workers of America, 12, 28, 60
United Rubber Workers, 89, 172–73
United Society of Cordwainers of New York City, 42
United Sons of Vulcan, 9
United States Army, 62–63, 140, 162, 163, 176, 183
United States Board of Mediation, 18
United States Bureau of Labor, 70
United States Bureau of Labor Statistics, 48, 194
United States Civil Service Retirement Act, 137
United States Commission on Industrial Relations, 148
United States Court of Appeals, 4

United States Department of Labor, 17, 71
United States Employment Service, 58
United States Employment Stabilization Board, 188
United States government and labor, 197–98
United States Housing Act, 80
United States Postal Service, 176
United States Shipping Board, 200
United States Steel Corporation, 160, 174, 193, 197
United Steel Workers of America, 11, 30, 68, 69, 129, 174, 177, 197, 201
United Tailoresses Society of New York, 101, 158, 161
United Textile Workers, 41, 153, 158, 172, 192
United Transportation Union, 11
United Typothae, 181–82
Unity Centers, 55
Unity Committee, AFL and CIO, 122–23
University of California, 56
"Unknown Committee," 167
Unmarried vs. married women, 208
Upholsterers' Union of New York City, 182
Uranium contamination, 72
Usery, William J., 9
Utah, 62, 93, 94, 141, 179
Utopian Socialists, 95, 155

V-J Day, 201
"Vacationist movement," 171
Valesh, Eva McDonald, 207
Van Arsdale, Harry, Jr., 79
Van Buren, Martin, 73
Van Etten, Ida, 207
Vancouver, 65, 138
Vanzetti, Bartolomeo, 93
Vaudeville, 166
Vermont, 178
Vietnam War, 14
Vigilantes, 110
Vindication of the Rights of Woman, 203
Virginia, 46, 140, 156, 160, 162, 199
Voice of Industry, 55, 104, 203–4
Vorse, Mary Heaton, 178
"Vote Yourself a Farm," 113

Wage controls, 201
"Wage freeze," 201
Wage, Labor and Capital, 156
Wage Labor Board, 201
Wage legislation, 199–200
Wage scales, 200
Wage Stabilization Board, 122
Wages, 200–201
Wagner Act, 43, 149–50, 201
Wagner-Peyser Act, 58

Waistmakers, 167–68, 209
Wait, William E., 83
Waiters, 21
Waiters' Industrial Union, 186
Waiters' Protective Union, 21
Waitresses, 132
"Walker, The," 11, 93
Wall Street Journal, 4
Walsh, Frank P., 148
Walsh-Healy Act, 37, 79, 132, 199
War Department, 198
War Labor Board, 58, 63, 78, 148–49
War Production Board, 211
Washerwomen, 21
Washington Agreement, 26, 28
Washington, D.C., 55, 64–65, 124, 127, 128, 146, 162, 186
Wayland, J. A., 156
"We Don't Patronize," 8, 48
"We Want Bread and Roses, Too," 155
Weaver, James B., 107
Weavers, 202
Weavers' Union, 182
Weinstock, Louis, 145
Weitling, Wilhelm, 41, 104
Welfare Department, 175
West, Don, 56
West Virginia, 4, 11, 49, 62, 90, 98, 120, 166, 179, 192–93, 213
Western Association, 201–2
Western Electric Company, 43–44, 63
Western Federation of Miners, 38, 63, 120, 122, 128, 130–31, 183, 192
Western Labor Union. *See* American Labor Union
Western Union, 164
Westinghouse, 119, 136
Weydemeyer, Joseph, 43, 155, 156, 182
Wheatland riot, 5
Wheeling Mold and Foundry Company, 78
Wheeling (W.V.), 98
White-black unity, 21
White House, 109
White Rats' Association, 166
"Whites only" clause, 42
Whitfield, Reverend Owen H., 7
Whittier, John Greenleaf, 46
Wider Opportunities for Women, 213
Wiggins, Ella May, 158
"Wildcat strikes," 28, 30, 71–72, 90, 175
Wilkie, Wendell, 98
Williams, L. E., 110
Wilmington (Delaware), 104, 190
Wilson, Charles, 144
Wilson, Edmund, 178
Wilson, Michael, 119
Wilson, William B., 45, 89, 137, 151

Wilson, Woodrow, 37, 51, 55, 63, 77, 89, 141, 147, 198
Wing, Simon, 156
Winston-Salem (N.C.), 27–28, 174
Wisconsin, 113, 189, 191, 214
Wives, as pickets, 210
Wobblies. *See* Industrial Workers of the World
Woll, Matthew, 86
Wollstonecraft, Mary, 203
Woman State Industrial Commissioner, 202
Women, allowed to join Knights of Labor, 206; antiscab battalion of, 151–52; auxiliaries of, 38, 202; coal miners, 213; first cabinet member, 52; killed in industrial accidents, 4; labor editors, 94–98, 104, 203; longshoremen, 213; honored by United Auto Workers, 213; most significant struggles by for unionism, 167–68; organizers, 210; organizations for, 101; prohibited from employment in coal mines, 205; rights of, 95, 203; suffrage for, 176; unemployed movement among, 191; union membership for, 40; unions drop exclusion of, 211–212; workers, 202–14
"Women to Win the War" Conference, 211
Women's Bureau, 51, 210
"Women's Department" in *Union Labor Advocate*, 210
Women's Protective Labor Union of Mount Vernon, New York, 204
Women's Trade Union League, 210
Women's Typographical Union, No. 1, 205
Wood, Fernando, 185
World Auto Workers Conference, 89
World Federation of Trade Unions, 89, 99
"World Peace Resolution," 14
World War I, 24, 25, 129–30, 198, 215
World War II, 99, 130
World-wide boycott, 32
Work Councils, 214
"Work or fight" laws, 213
Workers' compensation, 214–15
Workers' Education Bureau, 56
Workers' International Industrial Union, 52

Workers Unemployment Insurance Bill, 144–45
Workers University, 55
Working Girls' Club, 206–7
Working Girls of Boston, The, 206
Working Men's Advocate, 21, 45, 104
"Working Men's Measures," 106
Working Men's Party of Philadelphia, 57, 94, 103, 106
Working Men's Protective Union, 47
Working People of New Castle, Delaware, 178
Working Women's 1980 Platform, 213–14
Working Women's Protective Union, 204
Workingmen of the World, 87–88
Workingmen's Benevolent Association, 15, 146
Workingmen's Bulletin, 104
Workingmen's Convention of Boston, 74
Workingmen's Emporium, 47
Workingmen's library, 103
Workingmen's Party of California, 12
Workingmen's Party of Louisville, 107
Workingmen's Party of the United States, 156
Workingmen's Trade and Labor Union of San Francisco, 12
Workingwomen of America, 208
Workmen's Compensation. *See* Workers' Compensation
Workmen's Sick and Death Benefit Fund of the United States, 86
Works Progress Administration (WPA), 35, 210
Wright, Carroll D., 16, 33, 206
Wright, Judge Daniel T., 48
Writers, 178
Wyatt, Addie, 212

Yablonski, Joseph, 145
"Yellow dog" contract, 8, 216
Yiddish, 82, 156
Young, Coleman, 28–29

Zaritsky, Max, 133
Zenger, John Peter, 139